# George Orwell Studies

Volume One

No. 1

# George Orwell Studies

**Publishing Office**
Abramis Academic
ASK House
Northgate Avenue
Bury St. Edmunds
Suffolk
IP32 6BB
UK

Tel: +44 (0)1284 700321
Fax: +44 (0)1284 717889
Email: info@abramis.co.uk
Web: www.abramis.co.uk

**Copyright**
All rights reserved. No part of this publication may be reproduced in any material form (including photocopying or storing it in any medium by electronic means, and whether or not transiently or incidentally to some other use of this publication) without the written permission of the copyright owner, except in accordance with the provisions of the Copyright, Designs and Patents Act 1988, or under terms of a licence issued by the Copyright Licensing Agency Ltd, 33-34, Alfred Place, London WC1E 7DP, UK. Applications for the copyright owner's permission to reproduce part of this publication should be addressed to the Publishers.

© 2016 George Orwell Studies & Abramis Academic

ISSN 2399-1267
ISBN 978-1-84549-693-7

# George Orwell

# Contents

### Editorial
Orwell: Why Research into his Life and Works Continues – by Richard Lance Keeble and John Newsinger — Page 3

### Papers
Orwell, Poland and Polish Exiles in Paris and London – by Krystyna Wieszczek — Page 5
George Orwell's Conrad – by Douglas Kerr — Page 21
Orwell and the Anarchists – by David Goodway — Page 37
Only Donkeys Survive Tyranny and Dictatorship: Was Benjamin George Orwell's Alter Ego in *Animal Farm*? – by Tim Crook — Page 56
'The End was Contained in the Beginning': Orwell's Kyauktada and Oceania – by Firas A. J. Al-Jubouri — Page 73
'The Lesser Evil': Orwell and America – by John Newsinger — Page 89

### Articles
The Edges of the Empire: The Symbolism of Bladed Weapons in Orwell's *Burmese Days* – by Don Arp, Jr. — Page 107
The Poet Who Wanted to Shoot an Elephant – by Gerry Abbott — Page 116

### Reviews
Peter Stansky on *Forgotten Places: Barcelona and the Spanish Civil War*, by Nick Lloyd; Nick Hubble on *Worktown: The Astonishing Story of the Birth of Mass-Observation*, by David Hall; Simon Hammond on *The Prose Factory: Literary Life in England Since 1918*, by D. J. Taylor; Luke Davies on *George Orwell: English Rebel*, by Robert Colls; Philip Bounds on *David Astor: A Life in Print*, by Jeremy Lewis; Richard Lance Keeble on *Or Orwell: Writing and Democratic Socialism*, by Alex Woloch, Richard Young on *George Orwell Now!*, edited by Richard Lance Keeble — Page 124

### Soundings
The Mysteries Surrounding Andrew Gow; Film of 'Shooting an Elephant'; Orwell Statue Finally Gets the Go-Ahead — Page 151

**Editors**
John Newsinger — Bath Spa University
Richard Lance Keeble — University of Lincoln

**Reviews Editor**
Luke Seaber — University College London

**Editorial Board**
Paul Anderson — University Campus Suffolk
Kristin Bluemel — Monmouth University, New Jersey
Tim Crook — Goldsmiths, University of London
Peter Marks — University of Sydney
Marina Remy — Paris Sorbonne
Jean Seaton — University of Westminster
Peter Stansky — Stanford University, US
D. J. Taylor — Author, journalist, biographer of Orwell
Florian Zollmann — Newcastle University

EDITORIAL

# Orwell:
## Why Research into his Life and Works Continues

**RICHARD LANCE KEEBLE AND JOHN NEWSINGER**

Welcome to the first, bumper issue of the biannual, academic journal *George Orwell Studies*. George Orwell (1903-1950) is one of the most celebrated writers in the history of English literature. Perhaps most famous for his novels *Animal Farm* (1945) and *Nineteen Eighty-Four* (1949), Orwell was also the author of political polemics, literary essays and a great deal of journalism. In his writings on everyday things such the common toad, boys' weeklies, cups of tea and sexy seaside postcards he virtually invented the discipline of cultural studies.

Indeed, the persistence of George Orwell and 'Orwellian' as reference points in the mass media, in the broader culture and in current political debates is remarkable. After the NSA contractor and whistleblower Edward Snowden in June 2013 revealed through the London-based *Guardian* and other international news media details of the massive global surveillance systems operated by intelligence agencies in the United States and United Kingdom, Orwell's *Nineteen Eighty-Four* – and its description of a Big Brother society in which the state intrudes into the inner-most parts of everyday life – was a constant reference point, globally.

Orwell must be one of the most commented upon writers today. Yet still remarkable new insights into his life and writings continue to appear.

*George Orwell Studies* aims to explore and debate major issues relating to Orwell's life and works through a range of genres: academic papers, shorter articles, polemical pieces, reviews and news items. In particular, it will aim to promote international perspectives – and from a range of different disciplines: feminist studies, gender studies, international relations, politics, literature, cultural studies, journalism, communication ethics, intelligence studies and so on. Its work is supported by a distinguished editorial board of Orwell scholars and experts.

This first issue reflects the extraordinary range of contemporary Orwellian research. The subjects covered in the papers are diverse: Orwell's relationships with Poland, America, and the anarchists, his views on Conrad, his attitudes to animals and his representation of Benjamin, the donkey, in *Animal Farm*; and the links between his first novel, *Burmese Days*, and his last, the dystopian *Nineteen Eighty-Four*. Two shorter articles look at the symbolism of bladed weapons in Orwell's *Burmese Days* and at his essay, 'Shooting an Elephant'. Did Orwell really shoot the elephant? Read on!

Next comes a book reviews section which again shows the wealth of materials still appearing which Orwell scholars are likely to find fascinating. And we end with three short news stories in a 'Soundings' section.

We are keen to hear your thoughts on the journal – and ideas for improving it. So please contact us at rkeeble@lincoln.ac.uk and j.newsinger@virginmedia.com.

PAPER

# Orwell, Poland and Polish Exiles in Paris and London

### KRYSTYNA WIESZCZEK

*While the official publishing market in communist Poland would condemn Orwell to being an 'unperson' for almost forty years after his death, Orwell's outspoken political views, in particular his fierce opposition towards Stalin's politics and sympathy for Poland, turned him into one of the most appreciated representatives of the British left within Polish communities scattered around the globe by the Second World War and their country's subsequent Soviet occupation. Polish exiles would not only mention him frequently in the Polish press and collaborate internationally on translating and publishing his works abroad, but would also be his friends and first-hand sources of information. Drawing on primary material, including Orwell's letters to Teresa Jeleńska deemed lost by Orwell scholars, the paper discusses Orwell's attitude to Polish problems as well as aspects of Orwell's early Polish reception and relationships with Poles in Paris and London. In doing so, it attempts to bring new insights not only to Orwell studies, but also to how we think about the reception of writers generally in times of censorship.*

Keywords: Orwell, Poland, Polish exiles, Polish reception, British censorship

POLAND LOSES INDEPENDENCE IN THE CAMP OF VICTORY

The outcome of the Second World War for Poland, despite having been Britain's longest fighting ally and in the winning camp, was a loss of independence, since its Western allies decided that Poland and other countries in the region should be sacrificed to appease Stalin. Significantly, Poles comprised around 70 per cent of all war refugees in Europe when the conflict ended (Habielski 1999: 7). Whether voluntarily or not, many returned to their country with much-changed borders and an uncertain political future, but around 500,000 remained in the West. Britain allowed Polish veterans fighting under its command to settle in the country with their families, and by the end of the 1940s around 157,000 Poles had taken the invitation (Machcewicz 1999: 38). With many settling in London and with the Polish government-in-exile established there, the capital became one of the main centres of an

**KRYSTYNA WIESZCZEK**

alternative 'Poland outside Poland' during the Cold War, hosting a myriad of Polish associations and publishing undertakings. Paris, the capital of a country of rich cultural, political and economic connections historically, once a seat of an informal government of 19th-century Polish political exiles and the city attracting such Polish immigrants as the composer Frederic Chopin and celebrated physicist and chemist Marie Skłodowska-Curie, soon became another important centre for Polish 20th-century exiles too.

This was particularly the case after the political and literary journal *Kultura* (*Culture*) and its publishing house Literary Institute, founded by Jerzy Giedroyc, moved there from Rome in 1947 (today its archive is on UNESCO's Memory of the World Register). While London, generally speaking, represented an uncompromising, 'indomitable', stance towards the decisions of the Yalta conference (February 1945), demanding the return to Poland of Lviv and Vilnus, cities of important heritage symbolising the half of the Polish territory annexed to the USSR, and prescribing Polish exiles to forsake publishing in communist Poland, *Kultura* followed a more 'pragmatic' path, accepting the new Polish borders as *fait accompli* and seeking to reach not only the exile audience, but also intellectuals behind the Iron Curtain and thus exert some political influence there. Polish exiles around the world, but particularly those connected with the two capitals, showed an eager and early interest in Orwell and his works, sometimes collaborating across borders on related journalism and translation and publication projects.

Unsurprisingly, Orwell and other rebellious foreign and Polish authors remained largely 'unpersons' in the state-controlled publishing market under the communist regime until the late 1980s. Yet – curiously – Orwell's name did feature sporadically in the press or encyclopaedias, albeit typically in a carefully crafted context with negative or dismissive comments (e.g. Budrecki 1954 or *Wielka encyklopedia powszechna PWN* 1966: 318-319). Soon after the war, Orwell was known only to the elite in Poland, and it was not until the clandestine publishing market gained strength in the late 1970s that his name became more widely known. In fact, Poles abroad were able to embrace Orwell more fully much sooner than their compatriots behind the Iron Curtain. Accordingly, the post-war Soviet occupation caused the national literature to be divided into 'home' (i.e. state-approved 'official'), 'émigré' and 'underground', and this inevitably influenced the nature of cultural and literary reception, including the reception of Orwell's works.

There has been a certain amount of research on the reception of Orwell in Spain, Russia or Germany (see Lázaro, for example 2001, 2002 or 2005; Blyum 2003 or Rodden 1987) but only a limited amount on the Polish reception, and still less on its 'émigré' aspect.

*The Complete Works of George Orwell*, edited by Peter Davison, made a considerable contribution also to the knowledge about Polish 'émigré' reception and Orwell's relationships with the Poles after it was published in 1998. Polish studies relating to Orwell very often focus on *Nineteen Eighty-Four* and its language, ideology and translations (see, e.g. Rokoszowa and Twardzik 1985 or Tambor 1999; Cichoń 1990 or Czapliński 1996; Dąmbska-Prokop 2007 or Sidorowicz 1996), although Andrzej Stoff's article (2008), for instance, comments briefly on its first official edition as well as on Orwell's clandestine reception. Sometimes Polish scholars focus on Orwell's activities fighting on the Republican side during the Spanish civil war 1936-1937 (see e.g. Kędzierska 2005). Orwell appears also in the context of other studies on communist censorship and clandestine or émigré publishing activities (see, for instance Dorosz 1992 or Ptasińska-Wójcik 2006). A notable early attempt to discuss Orwell's Polish reception in the 'official' context was undertaken by Jadwiga Piątkowska (1987), while later Paweł Kłoczowski (2000) looked at traces of Orwell's presence in Poland. Nevertheless, Orwell's Polish reception as a whole has still been understudied. As part of a larger research project, this paper attempts to contribute to the knowledge about selected aspects of Orwell's relationships with Poland and Polish exiles in Paris and London as well as his early Polish 'émigré' reception, presenting at the same time certain ideas that may be useful in the study of the reception of other authors subject to censorship.

**PAPER**

ORWELL – A FRIEND AND AN ANTI-COMMUNIST ALLY

One of the characteristics of Orwell's writing which attracted his Polish audience the most was his outspokenness against Stalin's politics. This, coming from his stance as a British left-wing intellectual, was seen as very rare and, therefore, particularly appreciated. Seen as just as rare and equally, if not more, appreciated was his sympathetic interest in Polish matters. Orwell many times tried to defend Polish interests against pro-Soviet censorship and propaganda in his journalism. For instance, he criticised the left-wing press's attempts to justify the Russo-German pact and their joint invasion of Poland in September 1939 (see e.g. Orwell 1941: 344). In this context, he once used the pretext of a book review to point out bluntly that 'it had been argued that the speed with which Poland collapsed proved its inner rottenness. But actually the Polish army fought as long as the French, against far heavier odds, nor did the Poles suddenly change sides in the middle of the war'. And he emotively concluded: 'This nation of thirty million souls, with its long tradition of struggle against the Emperor and the Tsar, deserves its independence in any world where national sovereignty is possible' (Orwell 1940a: 217).

He also spoke up, for example, during the doomed Warsaw rising in 1944, demanding greater Allied support for it and accusing British

**KRYSTYNA WIESZCZEK**

left-wing intellectuals of dishonesty and blind support for Stalin in dismissing the Polish legal government in favour of a body appointed entirely by the Soviet ruler (Orwell 1944). This publication would cost him a polemic in *Tribune* lasting a few weeks and probably also irrevocably falling into disgrace with another important left-wing paper, *New Statesman and Nation* (Davison 1998a: 362-376, Orwell 1946a: 450, Davison 2001b: 450, 451, n. 3).

Orwell protested over the biased coverage in *Tribune* of the trial of 16 Polish leaders invited to Moscow for political negotiations only to be abducted by the NKVD (the predecessor of the KGB) just in the wake of the Yalta conference which was supposed to guarantee free and unfettered elections in Poland. In a letter to *Tribune* (where Orwell was a regular columnist and literary editor), he admitted to having been initially swayed by partial press reports into believing that 'the accused were technically guilty', a reflection having come later: 'just what were they guilty of? Apparently … of trying to preserve the independence of their country against an unelected puppet government, and of remaining obedient to a government which at that time was recognised by the whole world except the USR'. He highlighted the 'double standard of morality' in the British press, which tended to condemn crimes by others, but overlook the Soviet ones, noting likewise that after the politicians' arrest 'all mention of their status as political delegates was dropped' (Orwell 1945a: 193-194). Orwell's letter was, however, not to be published (Davison 1998b: 193).

Sometimes – in some cases possibly not being able to write in detail due to censorship – Orwell hinted at certain questions concerning Poland while commenting on news events (see e.g. 1941b: 42, 1945b: 162-163 or 1947b: 24). Interestingly, Radio Free Europe presenter Tadeusz Nowakowski reported that Bolesław Wierzbiański (from the World League of Poles Abroad 'Światpol', which would ultimately publish *Animal Farm* in Polish in 1946/1947) remembered how Orwell once proposed to have his books translated and published first in Polish and only then in English, as 'a demonstration of his dissatisfaction with the publishing practice on the British Isles and, secondly, a demonstration of sympathies for Poland'[1] (Nowakowski 1984).

It is not surprising, then, that Poles were extremely appreciative of Orwell's interventions. For example, *Wiadomości (The News)*, the London successor of one of the most influential Polish inter-war literary and social weeklies *Wiadomości Literackie* and one of the most important newspapers of Polish exiles, would mention him regularly after its post-war rebirth following its closure in 1944 by the British authorities on Stalin's orders (Świderska 1992). Significantly, mention was made already in its first post-war issue (Theates 1946), and the newspaper would go on to describe Orwell as 'one of the most tried and tested friends of Poland among British writers' (*Wiadomości* 1947: 3). Similarly, the then-London-based literary scholar and future Harvard professor, Wiktor Weintraub, wrote at Orwell's death in the Parisian *Kultura*:

> It is pleasant to remember that it was this particular writer who in his war-time articles turned out to be a reliable and dedicated friend of Poland and the Poles. One read his articles convinced that his voice would never sound false or jarring, and his argumentation get entangled in sophisms (1950: 91).

Many years later, Nowakowski (1984) would call him on Radio Free Europe a 'Polonophile'.

Over time, Orwell's circle of Polish contacts, and thus informers, grew, particularly owing to the gravitation towards London of many anti-communist intellectuals. Orwell got to know such Polish Londoners as, for instance, the *Animal Farm* and essays translator Teresa Jeleńska. Aside from professional contacts, their preserved correspondence indicates they had various meals out together, while her son affirmed that 'Orwell used to come to hers for tea ... indeed, my mother had a very close and warm relationship with Orwell' (Jeleński 1984). Wiktor Weintraub also met Orwell at her place, in the company of the poet Stanisław Baliński (1950: 87). Tadeusz Nowakowski claimed (1984) that Orwell frequented the house of the author and journalist Stefania Zahorska and the socialist politician Adam Pragier (where Nowakowski himself met Orwell during his London years), knew the artist Feliks Topolski (whose one illustration appeared in *The English People* (1947: 7)) and had 'very good contacts' with Maria Gryziewicz and Munro Czarski and Bolesław Wierzbiański (from the World League of Poles Abroad).

It is impossible to identify precisely the extent to which Orwell benefited from his Polish sources of information. He mentioned some important meetings in his diaries. For example, in December 1940, Orwell noted down what 'a Pole who has only recently escaped from Poland by some underground route he would not disclose' told him about the desperate situation of Warsaw residents during the German siege and how, though waiting in vain, 'the people were upheld by the belief that the English were coming to help them, rumours all the while of an English army in Danzig...' (Orwell 1940b: 305). Some of the Polish influences are explicit in Orwell's published journalism, such as in one 'As I Please' column (1947c: 43) that anonymously cites excerpts from Scottish nationalist John Sutherland's letter to Zygmunt Nagórski or in his 1945 article reporting: 'I am told' – presumably by his Polish friends – 'that the last speech made to his ministers by Mr. Arciszewsky [sic], the premier of the outgoing London Polish Government, began:

"In the words of a man whom we once trusted, I have nothing to offer you except blood, toil, tears and sweat…"[2] but I believe none of the papers had the guts to mention it' (1945c: 223). Orwell's preserved correspondence, too, reveals drawing information from various Polish sources and – not always being determined to share it with his readers, although it could still prompt him to action. Such was, for instance, the case of Orwell's involvement in the fate of Polish veteran Franciszek Kiliański and a related report on the US practice of deporting Polish refugees to the Soviet occupational zone in Germany (Davison 1998c: 54).

SUPPORT FOR POLISH EXILES BEYOND THE WRITTEN WORD

Indeed, Orwell showed concern for the fate of Poland and Poles not only with his pen. For instance, Orwell called for a greater involvement by the Allies in the Warsaw uprising (1 August to 2 October 1944) not only through his journalism. Nowakowski indicated that he had also participated in a quite remarkable type of protest:

> … as we remember, on the news of the Warsaw uprising having broken out and the minimal airborne help provided by the Allies [Orwell] took a blanket and lied down in the evening at the door to the Prime Minister's residence at Number 10 Downing Street in order to alarm the public opinion about the lack of sufficient help for the Warsaw rising (Nowakowski 1984).

Arguably one of the most interesting pro-Polish actions outside his own writing occurred in 1945 and 1946. During his time as a war correspondent for the *Observer* in Paris, probably in mid-March 1945, Orwell met the Polish painter, author and army officer Józef (Joseph) Czapski, later a pivotal figure in the formation of the Literary Institute and its periodical *Kultura*. Besides Czapski's well-known gentle personal charm, he impressed Orwell also for other reasons. Czapski was one of around 400 survivors of the 'Katyń massacre', in which nearly 22,000 Poles captured in the Soviet-occupied part of Poland, mostly members of the elite, were shot in the spring of 1940, their mass graves being discovered by the Germans in 1943. Following the German invasion of Russia in June 1941 and the Sikorski-Maisky agreement between Poland and the USSR the following month, Stalin 'amnestied' camp survivors of Polish nationality so that they could form an army and fight alongside the Soviet troops for the Allied cause. Czapski was then tasked by the Polish side with tracing the thousands of missing officers needed for the so-called General Anders's Army, later reorganised as the 2nd Polish Corps. Despite all this, he would still assert to Orwell that it was Stalin's 'greatness' and 'courage' that saved Russia during the German siege of Leningrad. As Orwell stated, considering what he had been through, this seemed sufficient proof to him of Czapski's 'reliability' (Orwell 1946b: 136).

Therefore, even though Orwell had only just concluded his lengthy search for a publisher independent enough to take on his own *Animal Farm*, which carried an implicit critique of the Soviet Union's betrayal of communist ideals, he undertook to embark on a similar project on Czapski's behalf. Keen to expose the issue of Katyn to the British public, he attempted to find a British publisher for the translation of Czapski's book *Wspomnienia starobielskie* (*Starobielsk Memoirs*) (1944), which placed the blame for the massacre on the Soviets and not the Germans, contrary to the official propaganda also in the UK.

Yet Czapski's pre-Christmas optimism upon learning 'through my friend Poznanski that you told him to have found an English publisher' and his expectation that the book 'may have some relevance in the weeks to come owing to the Nuremberg trials, which will put the issue on the table' (Czapski 1945) were short-lived. A few months later, Orwell would still write to Arthur Koestler, his new ally in the publishing mission, that 'Warburg wouldn't do it b[ecause] he said it was an awkward length, and latterly I gave it t[o the] Anarchist (Freedom Press) group. ... If the Freedom Press people fall thro[ugh, what about] Arthur Ballard, who is now beginning to publish pamp[hlets]?'[3] (1946b: 136-137). Moreover, there was to be no in-depth examination of the Katyn atrocity at the Nuremberg trials (Cienciala, Lebedeva and Materski 2007: 238-239).

Though Orwell finally found a publisher (Secker and Warburg) for *Animal Farm* in 1945, his efforts proved unsuccessful this time, as *Starobielsk Memoirs* was being increasingly frowned upon by the Allies. When Orwell was meeting its author in Paris, hundreds of miles away to the south-east, the future Polish translator of *Nineteen Eighty-Four*, Juliusz Mieroszewski, then editor of a Polish war-time paper *Parada*, was complaining: 'We've now got ever greater problems over censorship ... it's better to break rocks these days than be a Polish journalist. ... I couldn't publish even a five-line note about Czapski's book' (Mieroszewski 1945). Little could Orwell and Czapski imagine that it was not until 1990 that the USSR would take the blame for Katyn massacre and the British and US governments stop largely suppressing its public discussion in their countries.

Despite the obvious failure of their publishing venture, meeting and corresponding with Czapski, whom Orwell described as a 'not only authentic but a rather exce[ptional] person' (Orwell 1946b: 136), yielded some benefits for Orwell too. It is thought that it was the conversation with Czapski that made Orwell reconsider a detail. In the plot of *Animal Farm*: the phrase '...all the animals, Napoleon

PAPER

*included*, flung themselves flat on their bellies and hid their faces' at the Battle of the Windmill was amended to '...all the animals, *except* Napoleon ...' (author's emphasis), since Orwell thought that 'the alteration would be fair to J. S. [Joseph Stalin], as he did stay in Moscow during the German advance' (Orwell 1987: 69 and 202, n. 69/22; 1945d: 90). Peter Davison also suggests that Czapski's experiences had 'an indirect influence on *Nineteen Eighty-Four*' as well (2001a: 439). Moreover, Orwell considered Czapski's memoirs 'a rather treasured item of my collection' and even asked to retain Koestler's copy whilst his was being sent off to prospective publishers (Orwell 1946b: 137). Both Davison (2001b: 215) and Bartłomiej Zborski (2015), Polish translator of many Orwell's works, also suggest that Orwell considered tackling the subject of Katyn in a larger work himself. Orwell was becoming more aware of not only the Polish political situation, but also cultural initiatives abroad. For example, from Czapski's letter to Koestler (1946) that made it to Orwell's hands, he could learn about the setting up of Jerzy Giedroyc's Literary Institute and his interest in publishing a Polish translation of Koestler.

POLISH FRIENDS TRY TO PAY BACK

Naturally, Orwell's sympathetic interest in Poland generated responses in kind in the Polish publishing world outside occupied Poland. Orwell's Polish audience was willing to pay Orwell back. Very shortly after contacting Koestler, the Literary Institute would communicate to Orwell a similar interest in relation to his own works (see e.g. Orwell 1946c and 1946d). Still well before that – within only two weeks of its publication (Orwell 1945e: 275; Jeleńska 1968: 3) – Orwell received an authorisation request for the translation of *Animal Farm* into Polish from an 'electrified' Teresa Jeleńska (1968: 3). A member of European high society before the war, Jeleńska found herself, like many others, living in relatively modest circumstances in Britain. She not only instantly undertook to translate *Animal Farm*, she soon acted as an intermediary between the Literary Institute and the author and for them translated also Orwell's essays. At discovering *Animal Farm*, she immediately encouraged Orwell to have it turned into a Disney production film (Orwell 1945f). Later, she would be instrumental in putting its Ukrainian translator (Szewczenko 1946) in touch with Orwell and urged Orwell to send a copy of *Animal Farm* to her friend Count Carlo Sforza with a view to it being published in Italian – but primarily for it to serve him and his circle as a warning against falling into Communists' hands (Jeleńska 1946). Most of all, however, with Orwell both 'extremely anxious that the book should be translated into one Slav language at least' (Orwell 1945g: 286) but not knowing how to go about it and not being confident about its publishing prospects in the USA, Jeleńska quickly took it on herself to explore options for both a Polish and an English edition there. Orwell's oldest identified letter to her, dated 7 September 1945, indicates that she put him into contact with Marian Kister from one of Warsaw's largest pre-war publishing houses who resumed his business in New York and was at the time visiting London:

> Following your telephone call last night, I rang up Mr Kister and then went and saw him this afternoon. I gave him a copy of the book, which he will airmail to the USA. He said – what I know to be true – that there are great difficulties in the USA about very short books such as this one. … However, his firm will consider it, also the Polish translation (Orwell 1945f).

Alerted that the project might not go ahead, yet so keen on it, Orwell still advised his literary agent: 'I would much rather they had it than some other firm which might give better terms but would not translate' (Orwell 1945g: 286). Indeed, the project with Kister's Roy Publishers did not materialise. Incidentally, Fredric Warburg's rationale for rejecting Czapski's book, 'awkward length', was the reason for Orwell's rejection too. The celebrated writer Gustaw Herling-Grudziński, like Czapski a lucky survivor of the Siberian exile, liked to recount the story of Kister's missed opportunity with amusement:

> It was actually Mr Marian Kister's life's tragedy. … Kister generally had this habit of smelling manuscripts, nobody knows why. At any rate, he smelled this manuscript also, thought it was too short, and over a coffee, or a tea … said to Orwell that 'This is too short, how am I to publish it? Neither a hundred pages, nor two hundred. It doesn't work. The best are two hundred-page books.' And gave Orwell a lecture on the subject (Herling-Grudziński 1984).

Jeleńska continued to explore her contacts in search of a Polish publisher and in November 1945 Orwell was sending her 'about half a dozen of the better cuttings', explaining apologetically that 'Of course no reviews are very good these days, as there is not enough space, but the book did get good notices' (Orwell 1945h). In January 1946, he was 'so glad to hear that the translation is going well' and assured her that 'If you should feel in doubt about the meaning of any word or phrase, perhaps you will ring me up. I do not, of course, know a word of Polish, but as we both speak French and English I expect we can explain ourselves' (Orwell 1946e). Shortly afterwards, he updated his agent that the Polish translation might be taken by the Anders's Army (2nd Polish Corps) in Italy, adding: 'This is still all somewhat in the air, but I have definitely told her, and told her to tell them, that I do not want any money out of it myself' (Orwell 1946f: 24).

In the end, however, the World League of Poles Abroad (Światpol), a pre-war governmental organisation set up to reinforce ties between Polish expatriates and their homeland, then operating in London exile, published *Animal Farm – Zwierzęcy folwark* – just at the end of 1946. Though busy and overworked, in the course of the process Orwell attended various appointments with Poles, meeting, for example, Bolesław Wierzbiański, of Światpol, and the war-time Deputy Minister of Information, Juliusz Sakowski (Wierzbiański 1984). Wierzbiański remembered how 'Wacław Czarski, a book publisher in Warsaw before the war, in London heading the publishing department in our Światpol, was full of enthusiasm' (ibid.). Jeleńska, too, expected that *Animal Farm* 'would be a huge success in our 2nd Army Corps in Italy – around 180,000 men – where English is not spoken', she only worried about the future of that readership by the time the book came out: 'God knows what can happen – the Russians want Anders's head and without a doubt it will be offered on a silver platter' (Jeleńska 1946).

With enthusiasm about Orwell's book spreading in this tragic period of occupation by the country targeted by it, Wierzbiański commissioned Wojciech Jastrzębowski, a former vice-chancellor of the Academy of Fine Arts in Warsaw and a prize-winning designer exiled in London during the war, to illustrate its Polish edition (Wierzbiański 1984). The cover featured an emblem-like bust of a rather disagreeable-looking pig wearing a decorated uniform with the insignia of the Republic of the Animals (resembling those of the Soviet Union) on the epaulettes, topped by an overarching ribbon with the telling inscription: 'All animals are equal but some animals are more equal than others'. But of the six illustrations, Orwell seemed particularly fond of a small one at the text's end. As he wrote to Jeleńska from Jura on 7 August 1946: 'I was sent copies of the illustrations to *Animal Farm* and thought that they were suitable and some of them very nice, especially the one of Churchill shaking hands with Stalin' (Orwell 1946g). Interestingly, unlike some Polish repatriates from the West who upon their returning to Poland in the Stalinist period faced persecution, Jastrzębowski was able to resume his career, despite having lent his talent to such a subversive book (Sejm Library n.d.).

Another sign of this enthusiasm was definitely the book's print run. While just 4,500 copies of the first English edition were printed due to paper shortages, followed by an impression of 10,000 (Davison 2001a: 228, 231), Wierzbiański recalled that *Zwierzęcy folwark* was issued 'possibly in 5,000 copies, which was a very large number in those days and exile conditions' (Wierzbiański 1984). Światpol had by then a well-developed global network of contacts and, although prices of books by UK-based publishers were generally higher than those by, for instance, Giedoryc's Literary Institute then still based in Rome, Wierzbiański maintained that the book 'sold out quickly' (ibid).

The Polish edition received 'good notices' in the Polish press too. *Wiadomości* described it as 'a superb satire on the Soviet system' (*Wiadomości* 1947: 2). Weintraub's review (1947: 2) paid much attention to the reasons a book of this kind came into being, seeing it as Orwell's reaction to the period of the most intense glorification of the USSR in Britain. And as a philologist, he discussed the book's form, language and message: 'The form of an animal fable allows the author to concentrate on what is most significant, simplify and condense paradoxes, and bring out the whole grotesqueness and moral falsehood of the Soviets.' He noticed also the author's sympathies and similarities with Jonathan Swift and applauded both the author and the translator. The former government's publication, *The Polish Daily*, now merged with *The Soldiers' Daily*, also reviewed it positively, noting that 'Orwell is a well-known and esteemed socialist writer and a regular contributor to *Tribune*, whose opinions on the Poles are exceptionally friendly' (*Polish Daily and Soldiers' Daily* 1947: 2-3).

Wierzbiański recalled many years later on Radio Free Europe how Orwell's friend, the journalist and former intelligence officer, Malcolm Muggeridge, asserted that Orwell was 'very content' with the Polish edition and was particularly interested in whether some of it reached his ideal target audience: the one behind the Iron Curtain, emphatically declaring 'it did!' (Wierzbiański 1984). Thus, the collaborative project undertaken by the English author and a group of Polish exiles brought together by common political interests, fears and the desire to spread an anti-totalitarian message seems to have yielded excellent results. Other Polish initiatives would follow soon afterwards, bringing together in the name of Orwell Poles scattered around the world.

CONCLUSION

The Polish reception of George Orwell is a complex one. The paper has proposed to interpret and localise not only the literary production and publishing under the three categories of 'official', 'underground' and 'émigré', each defined by specific political circumstances and also by each other, but to look through these lenses at literary reception as well. The particularity of Orwell's 'émigré' reception, however, the aspect focused on here, seems to be that it drew richly on multifaceted relationships between the author and his Polish readers, some of whom became his acquaintances and friends and then informed and to a certain extent influenced his own output.

This was enabled by Orwell's own particularities: that of a left-wing intellectual from early on aware of the dangerous nature of Soviet communism in practice on the one hand and that of a solidary journalist and author dedicated to fighting for political honesty and freedom on the other. While many intellectuals jumped on the pro-Soviet bandwagon, Orwell tried to promote a more objective view of Stalin's politics, highlighting the 'doublespeak' of the British government and left-wing press towards what mattered the most to the Poles: the freedom of their country for which they had been fighting during the lengthy war years. Both as an author and a sympathetic friend, Orwell seems to have given Poles hope and moral support like few other British men of letters.

The story of this reception can also bring hope in our times. Despite the censorship and propaganda, both in Britain and Poland, his voice could be heard by those longing to hear it.

## NOTES

[1] Quotes from other languages in author's translation

[2] Winston Churchill's words in an address to the House of Commons upon assuming his office as Prime Minister in 1940. They were quoted by Tomasz Arciszewski's government in an address to the nation in the wake of the Western allies' decision to withdraw recognition to the Polish government and recognise as Polish authorities the Provisional Government of National Unity appointed by Stalin (effective in July 1945)

[3] Letter quoted after Peter Davison with his reconstruction of fragments torn off the surviving letter given in square brackets

## REFERENCES

Blyum, Arlen (2003) George Orwell in the Soviet Union: A documentary chronicle on the centenary of his birth, *Library*, Vol. 4, No. 4 pp 402-416

Budrecki, Lech (1954) Milczenie i 'ucho igielne' [Silence and 'the eye of a needle'], *Nowa Kultura* [*New Culture*], No. 34 p. 4

Cichoń, Anna (1990) Two blueprints of society, *Anglica Wratislaviensia*, No. 18 pp 35-49

Cienciala, Anna M., Lebedeva, Natalia S. and Materski, Wojciech (2007) *Katyn: A Crime Without Punishment*, New Haven, CT, USA: Yale University Press

Czapliński, Przemysław (1996) Wątpliwe rozstanie z utopią [A dubious parting with Utopia], *Teksty Drugie*, No. 40 pp 92-105

Czapski, Józef (1944) *Wspomnienia starobielskie* [*Starobielsk Memoirs*], Culture and Press Department of the Polish 2nd Corps; published also in French: (1945) *Souvenirs de Starobielsk*, Rome: Collection 'Temoignages' and Italian: (1945) *Ricordi di Starobielsk*, Rome: Collezione 'Testimonianze'

Czapski, Józef (1945) Letter to Orwell, 11 December, George Orwell Archive, UCL, London, Letters to Orwell: A-L, ORWELL/H/1

Czapski, Józef (1946) Letter to Arthur Koestler, 26 March, George Orwell Papers, ADD MS 73083, British Library, London, f 135 r+v

Davison, Peter (ed.) (1998a) *Complete Works of George Orwell* (hereafter: *CWGO*), Vol. 16, London: Secker & Warburg

Davison, Peter (ed.) (1998b) *CWGO*, Vol. 17, London: Secker & Warburg

Davison, Peter (ed.) (1998c) Note on Orwell's letter to the Secretary, Freedom Defence Committee (George Woodcock), 28 February, *CWGO* Vol. 19, London: Secker & Warburg p. 54

Davidson, Peter (ed.) (2001a) *Orwell and Politics*, London: Penguin

Davison, Peter (ed.) (2001b) *CWGO* Vol. 18, London: Secker & Warburg

Dąmbska-Prokop, Urszula (2007) *Stylistyka i przekłady: Conrad, Orwell, Beckett* [*Stylistics and Translations: Conrad, Orwell, Beckett*], Kielce: Stanisław Staszic Higher School of Skills

Dorosz, Beata (1992) Literatura i krytyka literacka w drugim obiegu (1977-1989). Rekonesans bibliograficzny w zakresie druków zwartych [Literature and literary criticism in clandestine circulation (1977-1989). A bibliographic exploration of books], Kostecki, Janusz and Brodzka, Alina (eds) *Piśmiennictwo – systemy kontroli – obiegi alternatywne* [*Literature – Control Systems – Alternative Circulations*], Warsaw: National Library pp 335-355

Giedroyc, Jerzy (1950a) Letter to Zofia Hertz, 27 June, Chruślińska, Iza (2003) *Była raz Kultura ... rozmowy z Zofią Hertz* [*There was once Kultura ... Conversations with Zofia Hertz*], Lublin: Marie Curie-Skłodowska University, second edition pp 157-159

Giedroyc, Jerzy (1950b) Letter to Zofia Hertz, 24 June, Chruślińska, Iza (2003) *Była raz Kultura ... rozmowy z Zofią Hertz* [*There was once Kultura ... Conversations with Zofia Hertz*], Lublin: Marie Curie-Skłodowska University, second edition pp 149-150

Habielski, Rafal (1999) *Życie społeczne i kulturalne emigracji* [*Social and Cultural Life of Polish Exiles*] 1945-1990, Warsaw: Więź

Herling-Grudziński, Gustaw (1984) Nowakowski, Tadeusz, *Na progu roku orwellowskiego* [*On the Threshold of the Orwellian Year*] on Radio Free Europe. Available online at http://www.polskieradio.pl/68/2461/Audio/325265,Program-specjalny, accessed on 19 October 2015

Jeleńska, Teresa (1946) Letter to Orwell, 9 November, British Library, London, George Orwell Papers, ADD MS 73083, ff 105-108

Jeleńska, Teresa (1968) Wspomnienie o Orwellu [A memoir of Orwell], *Wiadomości* [*The News*], No. 18, 4 May p. 3

Jeleński, Konstanty (1984) Nowakowski, Tadeusz, [*On the Threshold of the Orwellian Year*] on Radio Free Europe. Available online at http://www.polskieradio.pl/68/2461/Audio/325265,Program-specjalny, accessed on 19 October 2015

Kędzierska, Aleksandra (2005) Orwell i John Cornford: angielscy kombatanci o wojnie domowej w Hiszpanii 1936-1939 [Orwell and John Cornford: English combatants about the Civil War in Spain 1936-1939], Łoch, Eugenia (ed.) *Człowiek wobec rewolucji i terroru* [*The Man in the Face of Revolution and Terror*], Lublin: Lubelskie Towarzystwo Naukowe pp 157-165

Kłoczowski, Paweł (2000) Tropy obecności [Traces of presence], interview by Wojciech Duda, *Przegląd Polityczny* [*Political Review*], No. 43 pp 126-129

Kłoczowski, Piotr (2009) Neapol, 26 września 1950 roku [Naples, 26 September 1950], *Jerzy Giedroyc: Kultura, polityka, wiek XX* [*Jerzy Giedroyc: Culture, Politics, 20th Century*]. Mencwel, Andrzej et al (eds), Warsaw: University of Warsaw pp 203-207

Koestler, Arthur (1946) Letter to George Orwell, 3 April, Davison, Peter (ed.) (2001) *CWGO*, Vol. 18, London: Secker & Warburg p. 215

Lázaro, Alberto (2001) George Orwell's *Homage to Catalonia*: A politically incorrect story, Lázaro, Alberto (ed.) *The Road from George Orwell: His Achievement and Legacy*, Bern: Peter Lang pp 71-91

Lázaro, Alberto (2002) La sátira de George Orwell ante la censura española [George Orwell's satire in the face of Spanish censorship], Falces Sierra, Marta, Díaz Dueñas, Mercedes and Pérez Fernández, José María (eds) *Proceedings of the XXVth AEDEAN Conference*, Granada: Universidad de Granada pp 1-15

Lázaro, Alberto (2005) The censorship of Orwell's essays in Spain, Gomis van Heteren, Annette and Onega Jaén, Susana (eds) *George Orwell: A Centenary Celebration*, Heidelberg: Universitätsverlag Winter pp 121-141

Machcewicz, Paweł (1999) *Emigracja w polityce międzynarodowej* [Polish Exiles in International Politics] 1945-1990, Warsaw: Więź

Mieroszewski, Juliusz (1945) Letter to Jerzy Giedroyc, 11 March, Archive of the *Kultura* Literary Institute in Maisons-Laffitte (hereafter: *Kultura* Archive), Listy do Jerzego Giedroycia jako redaktora *Kultury* [Letters to Jerzy Giedroyc as the Editor of *Kultura*], KOR RED, Mieroszewski, file 1

Nowakowski, Tadeusz (1984) *Na progu roku orwellowskiego* [On the Threshold of the Orwellian Year] on Radio Free Europe. Available online at http://www.polskieradio.pl/68/2461/Audio/325265,Program-specjalny, accessed on 19 October 2015

Orwell, George (1940a) Review of *Polish Profile* by Princess Paul Sapieha, *New Statesman and Nation*, 13 July, Davison, Peter (ed.) (2000) *CWGO*, Vol. 12, London: Secker and Warburg pp 216-217

Orwell, George (1940b) War-time Diary, 8.12.40, Davison, Peter (ed.) (2000) *CWGO*, Vol. 12, London: Secker and Warburg p. 305

Orwell, George (1941a) Our opportunity, *The Left News*, No. 55, January, Davison, Peter (ed.) (2000) *CWGO*, Vol. 12, London: Secker and Warburg pp 343-350

Orwell, George (1941b) No, not one, *The Adelphi*, October, Davison, Peter (ed.) (2000) *CWGO*, Vol. 12, London: Secker and Warburg pp 39-44

Orwell, George (1944) As I Please, *Tribune*, 1 September, Davison, Peter (ed.) (1998) *CWGO*, Vol.16, London: Secker & Warburg pp 363-366

Orwell, George (1945a) Unpublished letter to *Tribune*, 26[?] June, Davison, Peter (ed.) (1998) *CWGO*, Vol. 17, London: Secker & Warburg pp 193-195

Orwell, George (1945b) London Letter, *Partisan Review*, Summer, Davison, Peter (ed.) (1998) *CWGO*, Vol. 17, London: Secker and Warburg pp 161-166

Orwell, George (1945c) Personal notes on Scientifiction, *Leader Magazine*, 21 July, Davison, Peter (ed.) (1998) *CWGO*, Vol. 17, London: Secker and Warburg pp 221-224

Orwell, George (1945d) Letter to Roger Senhouse, 17 March, Davison, Peter (ed.) (1998) *CWGO*, Vol. 17, London: Secker and Warburg p. 90

Orwell, George (1945e) Letter to Gleb Struve, 1 September, Davison, Peter (ed.) (1998) *CWGO*, Vol. 17, London: Secker and Warburg p. 275

Orwell, George (1945f) Letter to Teresa Jeleńska, 7 September, *Kultura* Archive, Listy Georga Orwella do Reny Jeleńskiej [George Orwell's letters to Rena Jeleńska], 20 SKAJ

Orwell, George (1945g) Letter to Leonard Moore, 8 September, Davison, Peter (ed.) (1998) *CWGO*, Vol. 17, London: Secker and Warburg p. 286

Orwell, George (1945h) Letter to Teresa Jeleńska, 13 November, *Kultura* Archive, 20 SKAJ

Orwell, George (1946a) Letter to Dwight Macdonald, 15 October, Davison, Peter (2001) *CWGO*, Vol. 18, London: Secker and Warburg pp 449-451

Orwell, George (1946b) Letter to Arthur Koestler, 5 March [sic], Davison, Peter (ed.) (2001) *CWGO*, Vol. 18, London: Secker and Warburg pp 136-138 (The collection dates the letter to 5 March 1946; however, it must have been after April 1946. A discussion on this issue is available in the author's ongoing PhD work.)

Orwell, George (1946c) Letter to Teresa Jeleńska, 4 May, *Kultura* Archive, 20 SKAJ

Orwell, George (1946d) Letter to Teresa Jeleńska, 10 May, *Kultura* Archive, 20 SKAJ

Orwell, George (1946e) Letter to Teresa Jeleńska, 7 January, *Kultura* Archive, 20 SKAJ

Orwell, George (1946f) Letter to Leonard Moore, 9 January, Davison, Peter (ed.) (2001) *CWGO*, Vol. 18, London: Secker and Warburg p. 24

Orwell, George (1946g) Letter to Teresa Jeleńska, 7 August, *Kultura* Archive, 20 SKAJ

Orwell, George (1947a) *The English People*, London: Collins

Orwell, George (1947b) As I Please, *Tribune*, 24 January, Davison, Peter (ed.) (1998) *CWGO*, Vol. 19, London: Secker and Warburg pp 23-27

Orwell, George (1947c) As I Please, *Tribune*, 14 February, Davison, Peter (ed.) (1998) *CWGO*, Vol. 19, London: Secker and Warburg pp 43-46

Orwell, George (1987 [1945]) *Animal Farm: A Fairy Story*, Davison, Peter (ed.) London: Secker & Warburg

Piątkowska, Jadwiga (1987) On the paradoxes of the reception of Orwell's works in Poland, *Lubelskie Materiały Neofilologiczne* [*Lublin Neophilological Materials*] (1990) No. 15 pp 119-128

*Polish Daily & Soldiers' Daily, The* (1947) Nowe książki [New Books], No. 47, 24 February pp 2-3

Ptasińska-Wójcik, Małgorzata (2006) *Z dziejów Biblioteki Kultury: 1946-1966* [*From the History of Kultura's Library*], Warsaw: IPN

Rodden, John (1987) The spectre of Der Große Bruder: George Orwell's reputation in West Germany, *The German Quarterly*, Vol. 60, No. 4, Autumn pp 530-547

Rokoszowa, Jolanta and Twardzik, Wacław (eds) (1985) *Nowo-mowa* [*Newspeak. Materials from an Academic Session on the Problems of Contemporary Polish Language Held at the Jagiellonian University on 16 and 17 January 1981*], London: Polonia Book Fund

Sejm Library (n.d.) Parlamentarzyści [Members of Parliament]: Jastrzębowski Wojciech Tadeusz 1884-1963. Available online at https://bs.sejm.gov.pl/F?func=find-b&request=000002115&find_code=SYS&local_base=ARS10, accessed on 12 October 2015

Sidorowicz, Katarzyna (1996) Porównanie i ocena dwóch wersji tłumaczenia powieści George'a Orwella pt. *Rok 1984* [A comparison and assessment of two translation versions of the novel *Nineteen Eighty-Four* by George Orwell], Snopek, Jerzy (ed.) *Tłumaczenie – rzemiosło i sztuka* [*Translation – A Craft and an Art*], Warsaw: Hungarian Culture Institute pp 143-154

Stoff, Andrzej (2008) Huxley i Orwell jako konkurenci w ostrzeganiu przed niebezpieczeństwami ideologii [Huxley and Orwell as rivals in warning against the dangers of ideologies], Gromadzka, Beata et al (eds) *Kultura – Język – Edukacja: Dialogi współczesności z tradycją* [*Culture – Language – Education: Dialogues of the Present with Tradition*], Poznań: Poznańskie Studia Polonistyczne pp 67-96

Szewczenko, Ihor (1946) Letter to George Orwell, 11 April, Davison, Peter (ed.) (2001) *CWGO*, Vol. 18, London: Secker and Warburg pp 235-238

Świderska, Hanna (1992) Z dziejów polskiej prasy opozycyjnej w Londynie 1941-45 [From the history of the Polish opposition press in London 1941-45], *Zeszyty Historyczne*, No. 101 pp 56-82

**KRYSTYNA WIESZCZEK**

Tambor, Jolanta (1999) Wpływ języka na postrzeganie rzeczywistości w *1984* George'a Orwella [The influence of language on the perception of reality in George Orwell's *1984*], Bartmiński, Jerzy (ed.) *Językowy obraz świata* [*A Language View of the World*], Lublin: Marie Curie-Skłodowska University pp 245-258

Theates [Wiktor Weintraub] (1946) Czasopisma krajowe [Home newspapers], *Wiadomości*, 7 April, No. 1 p. 2

Weintraub, Wiktor (1947) Świnie w polityce [Pigs in politics], *Wiadomości*, No. 2, 12 January p. 2

*Wiadomości* [*The News*] (1947) Miscellanea, No. 39, 28 September p. 3

*Wiadomości* (1947) Nowe książki [*New Books*], No. 2, 12 January, p. 2

*Wielka encyklopedia powszechna PWN* [*PWN's Great Popular Encyclopaedia*] (1966), Warsaw: PWN

Wierzbiański, Bolesław (1984) Nowakowski, Tadeusz, [On the threshold of the Orwellian year], on Radio Free Europe. Available at http://www.polskieradio.pl/68/2461/Audio/325265,Program-specjalny, accessed on 19 October 2015

Zborski, Bartłomiej, and Lisiecka, Anna (2015) Orwell planował powieść o Katyniu [Orwell planned a novel about Katyn], Polish Radio Two. Available online at http://www.polskieradio.pl/8/3669/Artykul/1358405,Orwell-planowal-powiesc-o-Katyniu, accessed on 13 November 2015

## NOTE ON THE CONTRIBUTOR

Krystyna Wieszczek is a PhD candidate in English at the University of Southampton. Her thesis explores George Orwell's Polish reception during the Cold War period, both in Poland (official and underground receptions) and in circles of Polish exiles. Krystyna received her MA in Translation Studies from the Pompeu Fabra University, in Barcelona, and her BA in English Philology in Poland. She has published and presented her work internationally. Her research interests include 20th-century European history, literary reception and censorship. She also works as an English, Polish, Portuguese and Spanish translator.

PAPER

# George Orwell's Conrad

## DOUGLAS KERR

*Joseph Conrad was one of the most important writers to Orwell. His engagement with Conrad was lifelong, and in published articles, essays and letters, he mentions nineteen Conrad works. This paper is not so much a study of 'influence' as an attempt to observe some of the ways his reading of Conrad helped to clarify for Orwell the writer he himself needed to become. His response to Conrad as a writer about Oriental places and people, and as a political novelist, has an important bearing on his own practice, and through his reading of Conrad we can watch him struggling with questions of theme, attitude, and technique he confronted in his own creative work. Finally, this paper looks at the case of the haunting presence of Conrad's* Lord Jim *in the working notes for* A Smoking-Room Story, *the novel Orwell was planning in 1949, the last year of his life.*

Keywords: George Orwell, Joseph Conrad, *A Smoking-Room Story*, *Lord Jim*, political fiction

When Joseph Conrad died in 1924, the man who was not yet George Orwell had not begun his career as a writer. Eric Blair was in the middle of his service of almost five years with the Indian Imperial Police in Burma. He had not been to university, but was intellectually curious and fairly well-read, and no doubt, like John Flory, the anti-hero of his first novel, *Burmese Days* (1934), on trips to Rangoon he rushed to Smart and Mookerdum's bookshop 'for the new novels out from England' (1989 [1934]: 66). Besides keeping up with contemporary fiction, the young policeman not surprisingly was drawn to English literature that engaged with the part of the world where he had decided to make his career, and where his family, on both his father's and his mother's side, had a history of work and residence – the East. It was probably in this context that he first made his acquaintance with three writers who were to remain very important for him – Rudyard Kipling, W. Somerset Maugham and Joseph Conrad.

In tracing the relationship between Orwell and Conrad I am not undertaking to tell a story about textual 'influence', but to observe Orwell thinking about Conrad as a senior member of the writerly

## DOUGLAS KERR

community in which he, in turn, was establishing a place for himself. I will suggest ways in which his reading of the older man helped to clarify for Orwell the writer he needed to become. I will first sketch Orwell's Conrad, which of Conrad's books he knew, and the kind of author Orwell thought Conrad was, and will go on to consider some of the literary problems and issues which Orwell considered in his reading of Conrad, with the older man taken as an example of practice, good or bad. In the second part of this paper, I will focus on the role played by Conrad in Orwell's intellectual life in his final year, 1949, when he had completed the writing of *Nineteen Eighty-Four* and was dying of tuberculosis, but still planning new work.

### CONRAD IN ORWELL

A trawl through the twenty volumes of the *Complete Works of George Orwell* (*CWGO*), edited by Peter Davison (1998), yields evidence that Orwell had read nineteen works by Conrad, as well as some memoirs and criticism about him.[1] The order of this reading cannot be established, but it stretches over his whole career. Asked in a questionnaire to name the three best books of 1947, Orwell rather perversely nominated *Under Western Eyes* (1911), since that was the year in which he first read it (*CWGO* 20: 233).[2] Early in his literary career, when he was struggling to make a name for himself as a writer in London, Orwell named Conrad when compiling a list of the kind of books he would like to be asked to review for the *Adelphi*. 'If you ever get any book (fiction or travel stuff) on India, or on low life in London, or on Villon, Swift, Smollett, Poe, Mark Twain, Zola, Anatole France or Conrad, or anything *by* M. P. Shiel or W. Somerset Maugham, I should enjoy reviewing it' (1998 X:195). This wished-for portfolio reflects the attitudes of a young man who has lived in the East and more recently in bohemian Paris, whose first two books would be *Down and Out in Paris and London* (1933) and *Burmese Days*. The inclusion of M. P. Shiel (a British writer of West Indian descent remembered mostly for his supernatural horror and scientific romances) is a surprise, but apart from him, Conrad takes his place among writers who were to be of abiding importance for Orwell, and his presence on this list is a signal of enthusiasm and a modest claim to expertise. Conrad was a special interest.

As a matter of fact, Orwell (writing as E. A. Blair) had already mentioned Conrad in the pages of the *Adelphi*. In October 1930, he was reviewing J. B. Priestley's *Angel Pavement* (1930) and finding it distinctly inferior, as a London novel, to Dickens's *Bleak House* (1853), Arnold Bennett's *Riceyman Steps* (1923) and Conrad's *The Secret Agent* (1907) (*CWGO* 10: 187). It is, no doubt, just an accident that Orwell's first mention of Conrad in print should refer to a novel whose seedy urban landscape and submerged citizens were to make their way into the London of *Nineteen Eighty-Four*

(1949). Of more significance is the fact that in his review Orwell is already acknowledging Conrad as a modern classic, a cut above the popular but 'merely competent' J. B. Priestley.

In this, Orwell was endorsing the opinion of Conrad held in the more progressive circles of literary London. In essays such as 'Modern Novels' (1919) and 'Mr Bennett and Mrs Brown' (1924), Virginia Woolf had used the word 'Edwardian', as Lytton Strachey had already used 'Victorian' (in his *Eminent Victorians*, of 1918), as a term of disparagement, synonymous with 'superannuated' or 'boring', but she specifically withheld the stigma from Conrad.[3] Leonard Woolf, too, had lectured and written admiringly about him (see Stape 1993). Readers of the iconic poet of Anglo-American modernism, T. S. Eliot, were aware of the impact of Conrad on his *The Waste Land* (of 1922) and 'The Hollow Men' (of 1925). Whatever his fluctuating fortunes in the bookshops, Conrad, after his death in 1924, continued to enjoy a *succès d'estime* among writers of the following generation, and Orwell's use of Conrad as an instrument with which to deflate the reputation of Priestley is entirely in tune with this.[4]

From his earliest days, Conrad had been known, and was advertised, as a writer of the sea. Orwell's enthusasm for *The Secret Agent* (first published in 1907) as a London novel is one hint of his dissent from this characterisation, and in a review written in 1945 he declared that he belonged to 'the minority who prefer Conrad when he sticks to dry land' (*CWGO* 17: 196). Conrad's image in the popular mind as the 'Kipling of the Seas' detracted, Orwell felt, from his more important work, and in 1949, the year his own *Nineteen Eighty-Four* was published, he wrote: 'Conrad had the label "the sea" stuck so firmly upon him that the excellence of his political novels has hardly been noticed even to this day' (*CWGO* 20: 37).

However, there was another orthodoxy about Conrad to which Orwell did assent. This was the critical view that, though his work sold better after the commercial success of *Chance* (1913), in general, the last decade or so of his career saw a falling-off in quality. 'It has been said that a creative writer can only expect to remain at the top of his form for about fifteen years, and the bibliography which is included in the Everyman reprint of Conrad's short stories seems to bear this out. Conrad's great period was from 1902 to 1915' (*CWGO* 17: 190). Very likely, the dates are carefully chosen. Making 1915 the final year allowed *Victory* to be included among Conrad's great works. A starting date of 1902 meant that *Youth*, *Heart of Darkness* and *The End of the Tether* were all included, by virtue of their appearing together in the volume, *Youth: A Narrative and Two Other Stories*, published in 1902. But it also had the effect of excluding a novel many readers would classify as one of Conrad's most important, *Lord Jim*, serialised in *Blackwood's Magazine* in

**DOUGLAS KERR**

1899-1900, after *Youth* and *Heart of Darkness*, but published in book form in 1900, and so denied a place in Orwell's canon of great Conrad books.[5] Meanwhile, bracketing Conrad's period of greatness between 1902 and 1915 reinforced another point, for 'it is only in this period that stories *not* dealing with the sea predominate in his work' (ibid: 190).

So although Orwell may first have been drawn to Conrad as a writer of stirring tales set in Oriental lands and waters, and though he continued to admire stories such as *Youth* and *Typhoon* (also first published in 1902), the Conrad he came to prize most highly was more political than adventurous. 'His most colourful passages may have dealt with the sea, but he is at his most grown-up when he touches dry land' (ibid: 191). The passage from exotic adventurism to political maturity may mirror the way Orwell came to think of his own personal and intellectual development, on what he called 'the road from Mandalay to Wigan Pier' (1986 [1937]: 113).

When it came to politics, Orwell's Conrad knew what he was talking about, and his Polish provenance and particular family history – his father, Orwell believed slightly inaccurately, had been exiled to Siberia by the Czar (*CWGO* 17: 196) – gave him a perspective which no English writer of his generation could command.[6] 'He had a grasp of European history which an English writer of comparable gifts would probably not have had, and he also had a remarkable understanding of the atmosphere of conspiratorial politics' (ibid).[7] In *Homage to Catalonia* (1938), describing his days on the run from the police in Barcelona during the Spanish Civil War in 1937, Orwell had remarked that experience of a long tradition of liberal democracy had left the English dangerously unable to grasp the realities of political life in less comfortable parts of the world.[8] It was an ignorance that would have wider repercussions in the inability of most left intellectuals in Britain – and of the wartime public – to fathom what the Soviet regime was capable of. To Orwell's mind, this naivety was a kind of provincialism.

Orwell was inferring Conrad's politics largely from the evidence of his fiction. Indeed, in his time only a fraction of Conrad's letters had been published, and little was known in England about his Polish background. But works such as *Nostromo* (1904) and *Under Western Eyes* (1911) do convey a strong impression of their author's sense of the dangers of idealism and the futility of political action, while *The Secret Agent* (1907) leaves little doubt about his scorn for revolutionaries. Orwell's socialism found such political pessimism unacceptable: he continued to believe that people's lot could be bettered by the application of compassionate and progressive political principles. But he would also have encountered in Conrad, in *Heart of Darkness* and *Nostromo* for example, powerful stories about the cynicism and greed of imperialism and the material interests it served, stories that find an echo in Orwell's own experience and convictions.

Orwell felt sure that it was Conrad's rueful Polish heritage that delivered the realistic political fiction of *The Secret Agent* and *Under Western Eyes*, and even *Nostromo*. 'Politically he was a reactionary, and never pretended to be anything else, but he was also a member of an oppressed race, and he understood just why people throw bombs, even if he disapproved of such activities' (ibid). Conrad, who came from a country that had been wiped off the map and whose family had suffered under the Romanov autocracy, was not subject to the political naivety of Orwell's contemporaries, of the right or left, who believed that tyranny was something that could only happen to foreigners. It was against this provincialism that Orwell was to set *Nineteen Eighty-Four* in London. For him, the political worldliness that contrasted with this insular English innocence was a function of being 'grown-up', a quality he more than once ascribes to Conrad (ibid: 191; 20: 47). In this respect, Conrad's measuring of the depths of the political cynicism of the absolutely powerful corresponded to the vision of Orwell's own maturity.

Orwell's Conrad is a European, not an English writer. 'Conrad was one of those writers who in the present century civilized English literature and brought it back into contact with Europe, from which it had been almost severed for a hundred years' (*CWGO* 20: 48). The maturity and depth of experience of writers such as the Polish Conrad, the Americans Henry James and Eliot and the Irishman James Joyce, brought into focus Orwell's complaint, in the essay 'Inside the Whale', written in 1939 and published the following year, that even the best of his own English literary contemporaries often sounded like schoolboys.

It is hardly surprising that Orwell was interested in Conrad's class, and class politics. He was fascinated by Conrad's feeling for *noblesse oblige*, as 'a member of a small land-owning aristocracy'; he had 'the outlook of a European aristocrat, and he believed in the existence of the "English gentleman" at a time when this type had been extinct for about two generations' (*CWGO* 17: 190, 191). Orwell felt that this strange class anomaly accounted for both strengths and weaknesses in Conrad. It gave him a quixotic romanticism which was un-English, and a feeling for personal nobility, for example in Captain Whalley's story in *The End of the Tether*, which could produce a truly moving effect, and probably, Orwell thought, could not have been written by an Englishman (ibid: 191). On the other hand, that aristocratic romanticism was probably also responsible for Conrad's florid style, his love of the melodramatic grand gesture which could descend to 'vulgar theatricality', and his taste for exciting exotic tales featuring characters with a capacity for having and appreciating adventures, which Orwell thought would be frankly impossible in real life. '*Lord Jim*, for instance, is an absurdity as a whole' (ibid: 190).

In the last year of his life, 1949, Orwell was doing preparatory reading for a long essay on Conrad. At the same time he had begun to draft an essay on Evelyn Waugh, and it seems the two novelists, very different in most things, came together in Orwell's mind as examples of a literary talent he admired, yoked to political views far removed from his own.[9] This question – of the relation between art and politics – had been the main theme of his important self-reflective essays 'Inside the Whale' (1939) and 'Why I Write' (1946). It had exercised Orwell when he reflected on the unpalatable political views of writers he greatly admired, such as Jonathan Swift (1667-1745) and Charles Dickens (1812-1870), and was a question that, I believe, fascinated him greatly in the months after he completed *Nineteen Eighty-Four*. Evelyn Waugh's main offence in the eyes of his fellow-writers had always been 'his reactionary political tendency', he writes (*CWGO* 20: 75), using an adjective he had also applied to Conrad (*CWGO* 17: 190, 191, 196). Orwell's own political views did not substantially change after about 1942, though they may have clarified. Nonetheless, it is interesting that after writing his great political novel, he was studying and planning to write lengthy essays on two novelists whose politics, as he understood them, might have seemed anathema to him.[10] At the same time his next project in fiction, as he told Fredric Warburg in the month in which *Nineteen Eighty-Four* was published, was for 'a novel of character rather than of ideas' (*CWGO* 20, 132). He did not intend either to be pigeonholed or to repeat himself.

## *LORD JIM* AND *A SMOKING-ROOM STORY*

Although *The Secret Agent* and later *Under Western Eyes* seem to have been his favourites among Conrad's longer fiction, the Conrad novel that bulks most in Orwell's surviving writing is *Lord Jim*, and his quarrel with this book can serve as a focus for the formal and aesthetic issues Conrad's work raised for him. For a start, it seemed to Orwell an egregious example of the exotic, melodramatic adventure story to which Conrad – and his readers – were all too prone. In a review for the *Observer*, he described *Lord Jim* as 'an absurdity as a whole, in spite of the brilliant passages describing the scuttling of the ship' (*CWGO* 17: 191), and was taken to task by a reader, C. E. de Salis, who pointed out that the ship in the novel is abandoned, not scuttled. Orwell apologised for the mistake, then amplified his reasons for disliking the book.

> With regard to the other points in your letter. The rest of *Lord Jim* seems to me absurd, not because a young man who had behaved in that way would not seek redemption, but because the actual incidents of Jim's life among the Malays are of a kind

I find incredible. Conrad could describe life in the Far East from a sailor's angle, with the emphasis on jungle scenery and the life of seaport towns, but if one has actually lived in one of those countries his descriptions of life inland are not convincing. As a whole, *Lord Jim* seems to me to be a very distinguished version of the type of book in which the hero is expelled from his club for cheating at cards and goes off to Central Africa to shoot big game. Even the Dorothy Lamour figure comes in. When I made that remark about people who could have adventures and also appreciate them, I thought of T. E. Lawrence, whom you mention, but after all how common or typical are such people? Marlow himself seems to me quite incredible. A person like that would not be a sea captain. Conrad himself was perhaps rather like that, but then the point is that he left the sea and took to writing. That way of writing a book also seems to me unsatisfactory, because one is so often brought up by the thought, 'No one could possibly talk like this, or at such length' (ibid: 200).[11]

When one writer engages critically with the work of another, the result is always to an extent autobiographical. In the paragraph above we can watch Orwell wrestling, through the medium of Conrad, with some of the issues of his own creative practice. In the rest of this paper, I will isolate some of these issues, and consider them in the light of the tantalisingly little we know of the novel, or novella, *A Smoking-Room Story*, that Orwell was planning in his final year, at the same time as he was pondering the long essays he hoped to write about Conrad and Waugh. *A Smoking-Room Story* has to be surmised from notes Orwell made for the lay-out, a scheme of chapters, a list of images, incidents, and details 'to be brought in', and a handful of pages containing a draft of the novel's beginning (*CWGO* 20: 188-200).

There was, first of all, the question of what to write about. Conrad and Orwell had both worked in the East as young men, and Orwell was frank about the way a writer finds themes for fiction in his or her own experience.[12] To an extent, Orwell was playing the old Burma hand when he complained that Conrad's knowledge of the East was superficial in a way that made Jim's adventures in Patusan implausible. *Lord Jim*, he suggests, at least in its second half, becomes simply generic, inundated with the clichés of the gentlemanly imperial romance, so that Conrad's novel, as Orwell mildly travesties it, sounds like an adventure-story compound of H. Rider Haggard's *Allan Quatermain* (1887), A. E. W. Mason's *The Four Feathers* (1902), and P. C. Wren's *Beau Geste* (1924), a distinctly Hollywood confection topped off with the obligatory dusky maiden in a sarong. Orwell may have felt he had swum more successfully against the generic undertow of the imperial romance in his own *Burmese Days*, though later in 'Why I Write' he confessed that the book was formally and stylistically derivative, and 'full of detailed descriptions and arresting similes, and also full of purple passages in which words were used partly for the sake of their own sound' (*CWGO* 18: 317-318).

Returning now, in 1949, to fiction with an Eastern theme for the first time since completing his first novel, Orwell was going back to a subject matter overgrown, in English fiction, with the luxuriant clichés of romantic exoticism. He seems to court comparison with Conrad by opening the first scene on a ship, and by promising the story of a young Englishman who has suffered some sort of disgrace in the East. In spite of his grumbling about the novel over a number of years, *Lord Jim* haunts Orwell's new project like an unacknowledged ghost. Meanwhile, Conrad is probably also a model for Orwell's determination to write *A Smoking-Room Story* as a 'nouvelle' or long short story – of thirty to forty thousand words, he told Fredric Warburg (*CWGO* 20: 132) – a form he greatly enjoyed and one which Conrad had made his own; Orwell cites *Heart of Darkness* and *The End of the Tether* as distinguished examples (*CWGO* 12: 372; 16: 383).

'The serang, in his white uniform and scarlet sash, swarmed up the lamp-standard like a monkey' (*CWGO* 20: 194). The opening line of the draft of *A Smoking-Room Story* starts with this image that strongly, almost provocatively, places it in the Oriental and maritime world of Conrad's fiction. People who had read Conrad did not need to be told what a serang was.[13] To be sure, if *A Smoking-Room Story* signals a return to Conrad, it is also a return to Orwell's own fictional beginnings, in *Burmese Days*. (It was a return in another sense too. The protagonist of *A Smoking-Room Story* is aged twenty-four and is sailing back from Burma to England in 1927 – at the same age, and in the same year, as Eric Blair made the voyage.)[14]

Though Orwell's chapter scheme promises retrospective revelations about the activities of his hero on dry land, the scene is set not in Burma but on an ocean liner, which has picked up passengers in Burma and Ceylon, and is now steaming towards East Africa with the final destination of England. As if to confirm that this story has *Lord Jim* on its mind, consciously or not, there is even a party of pilgrims on board, a group of Indian Christians travelling as deck passengers from Colombo to Port Said, in the charge of a Catholic priest. Also on board is the central character of the novel, a twenty-four-year-old Englishman, Curly Johnson, who had held a good job with the firm of Peterson's in Burma, but is returning home, it seems, under a cloud. 'That's the boy that's being sent home,' he overhears a fellow-passenger say (*CWGO* 20: 189).

Orwell's own experience of long sea journeys was, no doubt, useful for the setting of the ocean liner, including the voyage out to Burma in 1922, when observing relations between passengers and crew, he remembered, 'taught me more than I could have learned from half a dozen Socialist pamphlets' (*CWGO* 19: 6). As for literary antecedents, Somerset Maugham, and perhaps Kipling, are present in the theme of the boy who has 'gone wrong' in the East, and Orwell's reading of Waugh is certainly behind some of the satirical observation of the behaviour of the younger passengers. But the shadow of Conrad, and particularly *Lord Jim*, looms over the book, too.

Returning to Orwell's objections to *Lord Jim* in the letter to C. E. de Salis quoted above, we can note how they raise an abiding problem for him, one that confronted him at the start of each subsequent novel: the double-headed chimera of subjectivity and narration. He alludes to this when he expresses dissatisfaction with the way Conrad depicts 'people who have adventures and also appreciate them'. How could you plausibly represent a person with a capacity for undergoing exciting action and also reflecting on it? Here, Orwell sounds an authentic note of modernist anti-heroism, the idea that the literary and aesthetic intelligence, which his contemporaries had only quite recently christened 'highbrow', was dangerously far-removed from the world where practical and decisive action was taken.[15] Conrad had solved this problem, in *Lord Jim* and elsewhere, in the participatory-narrating character of the sea captain Marlow, but Orwell clearly feels this was a bit of a cheat, though on this point, as we see from the end of the passage from his letter to de Salis quoted above, he becomes confused. A person like Marlow would not be a sea captain. On the other hand, 'Conrad himself was perhaps rather like that', and he was a sea captain. But he gave up being a sea captain, and became a novelist. And in any case, 'that way of writing a book' is unsatisfactory, because people don't talk like Marlow, and certainly not at such length (*CWGO* 17: 200).

Orwell may have misremembered *Lord Jim* as consisting entirely of Marlow's oral narration, which is not the case. But he was clearly exercised by this question of action and interpretation, and arguably never really resolved it. What was the best angle from which to observe a sequence of actions? In the middle of the early novel *A Clergyman's Daughter* (1935), which is basically a third-person narrative focalised through the central character, Orwell suddenly adopts the form of drama, with dialogue and stage directions, but then sheepishly reverts to a more conventional novelistic narration.[16] *Keep the Aspidistra Flying* (1936) has a highly intelligent protagonist, but he is a failed modernist poet so revolted with his environment that he becomes a sort of comic 'Underground Man', bent on burying himself away from the existential world of decisions and consequences. The later *Coming Up for Air* (1939) is the first-person narrative of one of Orwell's most engaging characters, but has very little plot to speak of. The narratives of both *Homage to Catalonia* (1938), his account of fighting for the Republican side in the Spanish Civil War, and *Nineteen Eighty-Four* are interrupted, and arguably compromised, by long passages explaining the broader political context while the action is put on hold. And *Animal Farm* (1945) deals with characters who, for the most part, are ill-equipped for reflection and unable to appreciate what is going on around them, necessitating some ungainly moves to convey what mental life they have.[17]

It is likely that these questions of narrative modality, of how a story could be best presented, especially preoccupied Orwell when he was contemplating his next fictional project after completing *Nineteen Eighty-Four*, at the same time as planning the essays on Conrad and Evelyn Waugh. He was certainly thinking about the arguments for and against novels written in the first person, for he sets these out in an entry in his last literary notebook (*CWGO* 20: 205).

Interestingly, he describes first-person narration as an indulgence for the novelist, which can develop into an addiction. 'Actually, to write a novel in the first person is like dosing yourself with some stimulating but very deleterious & very habit-forming drug' (ibid). He says it is always easier to finish a novel written in the first person, 'as the use of the "I" seems to do away with the shyness & feeling of helplessness which often prevent one from getting well started' (ibid). Here, too, he may have Conrad in mind, for in an earlier review he had praised Conrad's tale 'The Partner' as 'in essence a very fine story, though it is marred by the queer shyness or clumsiness which made it difficult for Conrad to tell a story straightforwardly in the third person' (*CWGO* 17: 190).

Still, Orwell tells himself, the seductive temptations of first-personal narration are outweighed by disadvantages. Inevitably, the narrator becomes the medium for the novelist's own thoughts and opinions. ('Of course you are perfectly right about my own character constantly intruding on that of the narrator [in *Coming Up for Air*],' he confessed to Julian Symons. 'I am not a real novelist anyway, and that particular vice is inherent in writing a novel in the first person, which one should never do' *CWGO* 19: 336). Furthermore, confined to the consciousness of the narrator, in a first-person narrative other characters have to be made to talk more freely than is credible, or else their thoughts have to be guessed by the first-person narrator. Orwell had an example to hand. His notes for his essay about Evelyn Waugh include the following memorandum: 'Analyse *Brideshead Revisited*. (Note faults due to being written in the first person.)' (*CWGO* 20: 78).

How, then, might the examples of Waugh and Conrad – particularly the Conrad of the Marlow stories – have helped Orwell with decisions about the narrative point of view of his next novel?

MODALITY, NARRATION, GENRE

Before addressing this question, it is instructive to go back to the beginning of Orwell's fictional career. *Burmese Days* is a third-personal narrative, strongly focused on the central character, John Flory, but also visiting the point of view of other characters. But in the nineteen pages of manuscript which appear to be sketch work for *Burmese Days*, written either in Burma or shortly after Orwell's return to Europe in 1927, 'The Tale of John Flory' is a first-person narration. 'What is this tale? It is the tale of the degeneration & ruin, through his native faults, of a gifted man. How was he ruined? That is the story; my degeneration began when I came to Burma, aged eighteen. But a boy of eighteen is not a blank sheet to be written on…' (*CWGO* 10: 96). He promises 'perhaps ten thousand words about my childhood', but in the manuscript there is only a short and general description of Flory's family and upbringing, and there follows an anecdote in which Orwell seems to have already come up against the limitations of a first-personal modality. 'Here for a while I abandon autobiography & commence fiction writer. That is, the main facts of the story here told are known to me, & I have supplied the rest out of my imagination' (ibid: 98). This is confusing, because from Flory's point of view, he is telling a true story, not a fictional one.[18]

The anecdote begins with Flory's first-personal narrative, but then moves to Rangoon to report and comment on events that Flory cannot have witnessed. A partial draft of a later scene, narrated in the first person, is given the title 'A Rebuke to the Author, John Flory' (ibid: 102-104).[19] In other words, the planning of *Burmese Days* shows the young Orwell seriously muddled about the question of narration and modality. He had, however, rejected the *Lord Jim* solution of placing in the story a mediating and commenting character such as Marlow, for two reasons. Firstly, Marlow sounded more like a novelist than a sea captain. And secondly, too much of Marlow's story came in the form of a spoken narration, of literally unbelievable fluency and length.

The draft opening chapter of *A Smoking-Room Story* has a third-personal modality, anchored outside its main character – who 'moved with a grace of which he was not conscious' (*CWGO* 20: 194) – but with access to his point of view – 'Curly watched [the priest] with a faint, fleeting curiosity' (ibid: 194) – while remaining estranged from the interiority of all other characters – 'even Mr Greenfield seemed amused' (ibid: 197). Narrating through a single third-personal character is one of the most common modes of novelistic story-telling; for example, apart from the extracts from

Goldstein's book and the appendix about Newspeak, Orwell narrates *Nineteen Eighty-Four* through Winston Smith in this way. It is not, however, a mode much favoured in Conrad's fiction. *Lord Jim* itself begins in this mode, before evolving into a more complex series of narrations.

Orwell's Curly Johnson, like most of his protagonists, is an unprepossessing figure – 'C's inadequacy' is Orwell's first note about him (*CWGO* 20: 192). He is twenty-four, often 'overwhelmed with gaucherie and shyness' (ibid: 191). His failure to 'get on' has been attributed to 'Lack of "grit", lack of "drive" (& so throughout life)' (ibid: 190). Indeed, he seems a character unlikely either to have adventures or to appreciate them. Even his apparent disgrace fails to arouse much interest in his fellow passengers. 'Yes. He was in Peterson's. Quite a good job, I believe. … Oh, the usual thing, I suppose. Drunkenness, & so on' (ibid: 195). But it appears from the scheme of chapters that the bulk of the book will look back at Curly's own Burmese days, before this journey home. In fact, it looks as if Orwell had in mind a system of time-shifts between the present shipboard life and Curly's past, including his schooldays, but chiefly his time in Burma.

There is not very much to go on. But it seems that his bachelor existence in Burma has led Curly Johnson into a life of *ennui* and demoralisation – 'the dust & squalor of his house, the worn gramophone records, the piled-up whisky bottles, the whores' (ibid: 190). He is rescued by Brother J, a missionary teacher of long standing. Under this man's influence, Curly changes his habits, takes up reading, seems to stop using prostitutes, and embarks on a 'short-lived attempt to live more decently' (ibid: 191). Curly comes to feel that Brother J's mission 'had something that his life lacked', though it is not clear whether this points to a spiritual discovery, such as that of the sunken Sebastian Flyte, in Waugh's *Brideshead Revisited*, or self-respect and the beginnings of an intellectual life ('Reading instead of gramophone') (ibid: 190). Curly's sense that he has made a mess of his life and needs a fresh start may have something in it of Lord Jim's quest for a second chance and, indeed, John Flory's, though degeneration and regeneration were favourite themes in imperial literature.[20] In any case, Orwell's schema for the novel leads to a climax around a word of great importance in *Lord Jim* – 'Uncertainty of C.'s position. The opportunity. Finale' (ibid: 191). Conrad's great novel about 'veiled opportunity' seems often to be glimpsed in these notes and fragments.[21] Other elements of the story, however, have a flavour of Somerset Maugham's tales of expatriate scandal, and Waugh's novel of dissipation and redemption.

On board the liner there are three groups of passengers, and Curly is unable to belong to any of them. First there are the Indian deck passengers, in the charge of a European priest who reminds Curly of Brother J. Then there is the gay and flirtatious younger set in whose games Curly is not included, whom he regards with a sort of envious friendliness. Curly is just as much an outsider to the last group, the older men who frequent the smoking saloon, four American oilmen and four Englishmen – Mr McGillivray who appears to be an old China hand, Mr Greenfield, the supercilious I. C. S. man returning to the home country, a dreary elderly judge and a soldier with sticking-out teeth.

The drafts give no hint of the event at the centre of the story, the scandal – if that is what it was – that has caused Curly to quit his job, leave Burma, and face an uncomfortable reunion with his father. Why is Curly Johnson leaving the East under a cloud? While that question cannot be answered, it is certain the answer was to be revealed by the device of an embedded first-personal spoken narrative – the smoking-room story that gives the novella its title. Orwell's general schema for the book, culminating with 'The opportunity. Finale' was expanded to a more detailed chapter scheme (ibid: 192) which ends like this: '8. The ship; 9. Telling the story; 10 Finale.'

We do not know what the story was, but we know where it is told, and to whom. It is a smoking-room story, as the title indicated. Orwell planned to introduce the geography of the ship's smoking saloon, and to specify the time – around cocktail time, when both the older men and the younger set would be present, and conversation 'just general enough for C. to chip in without being snubbed by the older men' (ibid: 191). Curly's tale is to be told to a mixed audience of the older men and the younger set on board the liner. These are people who have not shown themselves particularly friendly to him. The genre of the spoken 'smoking-room' narrative, practised by Maupassant, Henry James and H. G. Wells and frequently by Conrad, usually involves a male narrator in masculine company, and is furnished with an audience of gentlemen, or professional men.[22] *Heart of Darkness* is the best-known example, though there the story is told not indoors but on the deck of a cruising yawl. Its listeners are a director of companies, a lawyer, an accountant, and a primary narrator of unspecified profession. Leonard Woolf's 'Pearls and Swine' (first published in 1921) is another instance, where a 'story from the East' is told to a retired Colonel, an Archdeacon, and a stock-jobber in the smoking-room of a Torquay hotel (L. Woolf 1963 [1921]: 265-279). A house party after dinner is another favoured way of assembling an audience to listen to the tale. Marlow's spoken narrative in *Lord Jim* is told many times and in many places. 'Perhaps it would be after dinner, on a verandah draped in motionless foliage and crowned with flowers, in the deep dusk speckled by fiery cigar-ends' (Conrad 2012a [1900]: 31). Unlike Curly Johnson's, Marlow's stories are for men only. Unlike Marlow, Curly seems unlikely to get a very sympathetic hearing from his assembled listeners, whatever it is he is about to confess.

Did 'the opportunity' refer to Curly's getting a chance to tell his story, or was it a tale *about* an opportunity? It will never now be known what Orwell had in mind for the climax of his 'novel of character rather than of ideas' (*CWGO* 20: 132). But certainly, for all the dissatisfaction he had expressed about first-person narrative, and in spite of his opinion that Conrad's *Lord Jim* was a flawed book, especially in the matter of its long passages of oral narration which Orwell felt were frankly unbelievable, the book he had started to plan in the last year of his life was to resort at its climax to just this narrative trope, identified above all with Conrad. It was to be a story embedding an oral tale of adventure and suffering told by a man to others as darkness fell. Would he have done it mostly as indirect report, as Marlow recounts Jim's tale of the Patna? Or as a continuous almost uninterrupted spoken discourse, which is the form in which Marlow tells his listeners of his own later interactions, and his last meeting, with Jim? However he would in the end have managed it, the smoking-room story itself is the last and most intriguing clue, and tribute, to George Orwell's Conrad.

- The author gratefully acknowledges a grant, reference No. 743713, from the Hong Kong Research Grants Council.

## NOTES

[1] Orwell referred to the following works by Conrad: *Almayer's Folly, The Arrow of Gold, Chance, The End of the Tether,* 'Falk', *Heart of Darkness, Lord Jim, The Nigger of the Narcissus, Nostromo, Notes on Life and Letters,* 'The Partner', 'The Planter of Malata', *The Secret Agent, The Secret Sharer, The Shadow-Line, Typhoon, Under Western Eyes, Victory, Youth.* He may have known others

[2] His other choices for 1947 were *The Aspern Papers* (1888) and *Framley Parsonage* (1861)

[3] 'Modern Novels' attacks Wells, Bennett and Galsworthy, but claims no quarrel with the 'classics' of the earlier generation. Conrad is mentioned as one for whom 'we reserve our unconditional gratitude' (V. Woolf 1998: 3, 31)

[4] For a summary history of Conrad's posthumous reputation, see the 'Introduction' to Sherry (ed.) (1973: 35-42)

[5] Orwell found these book publication dates in the 'Select Bibliography' on p. xiii of the Everyman edition of *The Nigger of the Narcissus, Typhoon, The Shadow Line*, which he mentions in his review (see above). The bibliography gives the false impression that *Lord Jim* was written before *Youth* and *Heart of Darkness*

[6] In fact, the family was exiled to Vologda, north-east of Moscow, but not in Siberia

[7] Orwell uses a similar locution in a subsequent letter, praising Conrad's 'remarkable understanding of the atmosphere of revolutionary movements' (*CWGO* 17: 200)

[8] 'I had the ineradicable English belief that "they" cannot arrest you unless you have broken the law. It is a most dangerous belief to have during a political pogrom' (1989b: 181)

[9] Orwell's notes for the Waugh essay end: 'Conclude. Waugh is about as good a novelist as one can be (i.e. as novelists go today) while holding untenable opinions' (*CWGO* 20: 79)

[10] His original intention, he told Fredric Warburg, was to write long essays, perhaps 15,000 words the two combined, on Conrad and Gissing (ibid: 132). Later in the year, this had become Conrad and Waugh

[11] Peter Davison explains in a footnote (*CWGO* 17: 201 n.2) that Dorothy Lamour 'was first dressed by Hollywood in a sarong-like garment in *The Jungle Princess* (1936)', and came to typify exotic beauty, and especially 'so dressed in the "Road" films to the point of self-parody'

[12] 'One difficulty I have never solved is that one has masses of experience which one passionately wants to write about, e.g., the part about fishing in that book [*Coming Up for Air*], and no way of using them up except by disguising them as a novel.' Letter to Julian Symons, 10 May 1948 (*CWGO* 19: 336)

[13] However, the serang at the opening of Orwell's story, changing a light-bulb in his smart uniform, belongs to the age of luxury ocean voyages and is different from the scruffy working serangs of Conrad tales such as *The End of the Tether*

[14] In these respects Curly Johnson is closer to Orwell than Flory, the protagonist of *Burmese Days*, who, in 1926, when the action of that novel takes place, is older and has spent more years in Burma than Orwell

[15] A relative of this doubt was the Marxist problem, so often canvassed by writers of Orwell's generation, of how to connect the intellectual, specialist in reflection and theory, to the sphere of events and political action

[16] The model is clearly the 'Nighttown' episode of James Joyce's *Ulysses* (1922), which Orwell greatly admired

[17] With their limited intellectual powers, the mental life of the animal characters sometimes has to be represented with the aid of prosthetic phrases such as 'If she could have spoken her thoughts, it would have been to say...', or 'If she herself had had any picture of the future, it had been...', etc. (1989 [1945]) 58). For a discussion of interiority in this novel, see Kerr 2003: 67

[18] A similar narratorial solecism occurs in Charlotte Brontë's *Jane Eyre* (2006 [1847]): 111), where the narrator, beginning Chapter 11, tells her reader that: 'A new chapter in a novel is something like a new scene in a play', apparently forgetting that she is writing a memoir, not a work of fiction

[19] These notes also include a poem, 'John Flory: My Epitaph', whose inscription moves from the third person – 'Here lies the bones of poor John Flory; / His story was the old, old story' – to the first person – 'But take the single gift I give, / And learn from me how not to live' (*CWGO* 10: 95). However, the genre of the epitaph sanctions this kind of pronominal slippage

[20] For further discussion see for example Spurr 1993: 76-91, Dryden 2000: 137-94, and Kerr 2008: 117-58

[21] 'He was white from head to foot, and remained persistently visible with the stronghold of the night at his back, the sea at his feet, the opportunity by his side – still veiled' (Conrad 2012a [1900]: 253)

[22] Its hyper-masculinity gave the smoking-room story a sometimes *louche* flavour, as suggested by this sentence in Conrad's 'The Planter of Malatta' (2012b [1915]: 69): 'She had already reached the three palms when she heard behind her a loud peal of laughter, cynical and joyless, such as is heard in smoking rooms at the end of a scandalous story.' I am grateful to Andrew Glazzard for drawing my attention to this passage

## DOUGLAS KERR

### REFERENCES

Brontë, Charlotte (2006 [1847]) *Jane Eyre*, London: Penguin

Conrad, Joseph (1945) *The Nigger of the Narcissus, Typhoon, The Shadow Line*, London: J.M. Dent

Conrad, Joseph (2012a [1900]) *Lord Jim*, Stape, J. H. and Sullivan, Ernest W. (eds) Cambridge: Cambridge University Press

Conrad, Joseph (2012b [1915]) *Within the Tides*, Fachard, Alexandre (ed.) Cambridge: Cambridge University Press

Dryden, Linda (2000) *Joseph Conrad and the Imperial Romance*, Basingstoke: Palgrave

Kerr, Douglas (2003) *George Orwell*, Writers and their Work series, Tavistock, Northcote House

Kerr, Douglas (2008) *Eastern Figures: Orient and Empire in British Writing*, Hong Kong: Hong Kong University Press

Orwell, George (1989 [1945]) *Animal Farm*, London, Penguin

Orwell, George (1986 [1937]) *The Road to Wigan Pier*, London: Penguin

Orwell, George (1989 [1934]) *Burmese Days*, London: Penguin

Orwell, George (1998) *The Complete Works of George Orwell* (*CWGO*), 20 Vols., Davison, Peter (ed.) London: Secker & Warburg

Sherry, Norman (ed.) (1973) *Joseph Conrad: The Critical Heritage*, London: Routledge

Spurr, David (1993) *The Rhetoric of Empire: Colonial Discourse in Journalism, Travel Writing and Imperial Administration*, Durham, NC: Duke University Press

Stape, J. H. (1993) The critic as autobiographer: Conrad under Leonard Woolf's eyes, *English Literature in Transition 1880-1920*, Vol. 36, No. 3 pp 277-285

Woolf, Leonard (1963 [1921]) *Diaries in Ceylon and Stories from the East*, London: Hogarth Press

Woolf, Virginia (1988) *The Essays of Virginia Woolf, Vol. 3*, McNeillie, Andrew (ed.) London: Hogarth Press

### NOTE ON THE CONTRIBUTOR

Douglas Kerr is Professor of English at the University of Hong Kong. He is the author of *George Orwell* in the 'Writers and their Work' series (Northcote House, 2003). His other books are *Wilfred Owen's Voices* (Clarendon Press of Oxford University Press, 1993), *A Century of Travels in China* (co-edited, Hong Kong University Press, 2007), *Eastern Figures: Orient and Empire in British Writing* (Hong Kong University Press, 2008) and *Conan Doyle: Writing, Profession and Practice* (Oxford University Press, 2013). His main current research interest is in Orwell and Asia.

# Orwell and Anarchism

## DAVID GOODWAY

*George Orwell can be plausibly claimed for a variety of incompatible ideologies – state socialism, conservatism, nationalism, liberalism, even Trotskyism. But libertarian socialism and especially anarchism have generally been neglected by researchers to date. This paper aims then to examine the evolution of Orwell's politics from his early years – when he actually described himself as a 'Tory anarchist' – and the overall place of anarchism in his thinking. Although Orwell later displayed an empathy with Spanish anarchism, developed warm friendships with most of the prominent British anarchists of the 1940s and participated fully in the work of the Freedom Defence Committee, he was never in his maturity any kind of anarchist. The paper argues that during the final ten years of his life Orwell was a left-wing socialist and supporter of the Labour Party; yet at the same time he exhibited pronounced anarchist tendencies and sympathies, for he was a libertarian socialist.*

Keywords: George Orwell, Spain, anarchism, pacifism, libertarian socialism, revolutionary patriotism

George Orwell can be plausibly claimed for a variety of incompatible ideologies – state socialism, conservatism, nationalism, liberalism, even Trotskyism. But libertarian socialism and especially anarchism have been neglected by the best-known commentators, other than George Woodcock, himself an anarchist, and Bernard Crick. The latter's incisive assessment is excellent: 'He did not accept anarchism in principle, but had, as a socialist who distrusted any kind of state power, a speculative and personal sympathy with anarchists' (Crick 1980: 308).

BLAIR: THE 'TORY ANARCHIST'

In 1927, Eric Blair, aged 24 and after five years' service in Burma, had resigned from the Indian Imperial Police, having come to hate the 'tyranny and exploitation' of imperial rule with, as he was to recall, 'a bitterness which I probably cannot make clear' (Davison 1998 (*CWGO*) 5: 134, 139).[1] During 1928 and 1929, he lived in Paris, working as a *plongeur*, and became a tramp in England, experiences recounted in his striking first book, *Down and Out in Paris and London*, eventually published in 1933 under the pseudonym of

'George Orwell'. From 1930, he became closely associated with the *Adelphi*, founded and owned by John Middleton Murry. Some fifty or so of Blair's articles were to appear there between 1930 and 1936, when it was co-edited by Richard Rees (who was to become his joint literary executor) and Max Plowman. The *Adelphi* was a socialist periodical, increasingly identified with the Independent Labour Party (ILP).

But Blair described himself to those who worked on it as 'a Tory anarchist', while conceding that he 'admitted the *Adelphi*'s socialist case on moral grounds'. Rees remembered him as having 'a kind of Bohemian Anarchist attitude'; and Jon Kimche, with whom he worked in a Hampstead bookshop in the mid-thirties and who was later to become editor of *Tribune*, considered him 'a kind of intellectual anarchist (Coppard and Crick 1984: 124, 142; Heppenstall 1960: 32, 62; Crick 1980: 102, 163).[2] Orwell, in his maturity, was to call Swift 'a Tory anarchist' explaining that this meant 'despising authority while disbelieving in liberty, and preserving the aristocratic outlook while seeing clearly that the existing aristocracy is degenerate and contemptible' (*CWGO* 18: 425).

Yet, during the first half of the 1930s, Orwell's tolerance of any other variety of anarchist would have been very limited, for he complained that for an 'ordinary man, a crank meant a socialist and a socialist meant a crank': 'One sometimes gets the impression that the mere words "socialism" and "communism" draw towards them with magnetic force every fruit-juice drinker, nudist, sandal-wearer, sex-maniac, Quaker, "Nature Cure" quack, pacifist and feminist in England' (*CWGO* 5: 150-151, 161-162, 169, 201). While few anarchists would have been all, still fewer would have satisfied none of these despised categories. He told the working-class Jack Common, co-editor of the *Adelphi* in 1936, that so many of the socialist bourgeoisie 'are the sort of eunuch type with a vegetarian smell who go about spreading sweetness and light and have at the back of their minds a vision of the working class all TT [teetotal], well washed behind the ears, readers of Edward Carpenter or some other pious sodomite and talking with BBC accents' (*CWGO* 10: 471). Orwell's distaste for homosexuals was an abiding characteristic, with him castigating in private 'the pansy left', the 'fashionable pansies', Auden and Spender, being singled out for especial contempt. Yet he insisted, as usual unpredictable and unfailingly contradictory, that he had 'always been very pro-Wilde' (Crick 1980: 171; *CWGO* 11: 67 and 19: 157).[3]

In 1936, Orwell was dispatched to the north of England to collect material on the condition of the unemployed for a book commissioned by Victor Gollancz. The outcome was *The Road to Wigan Pier*, which appeared as a Left Book Club volume in March

1937, while he was fighting in Spain. Direct contact with the lives and attitudes of impoverished industrial workers proved revelatory, and it was now that he first espoused socialism, albeit a distinctively idiosyncratic version, never having any truck with either the Fabianism or the Marxism which so influenced most other middle-class intellectuals on the left. Indeed, he was, as early as 1938, to tell Spender that he had been 'very hostile to the CP since about 1935' (*CWGO* 11: 132). Since he considers in *The Road to Wigan Pier* that 'for the moment the only possible course for any decent person, however much of a Tory or an anarchist by temperament, is to work for the establishment of socialism', he almost certainly still regarded himself a Tory anarchist as late as 1936 (*CWGO* 5: 204).[4]

## ORWELL'S SOCIALISM AND SPAIN

The fundamentals of Orwell's socialism were justice, liberty and decency. For him socialism meant 'justice and common decency', a decency inherent in the culture of the traditional working-class community. He believed that 'the only thing *for* which we can combine is the underlying ideal of socialism; justice and liberty' [sic]; and concluded: 'All that is needed is to hammer two facts home into the public consciousness. One, that the interests of all exploited people are the same; the other, that socialism is compatible with common decency' (*CWGO* 5: 164, 201, 214, Orwell's emphasis).[5]

Bernard Crick argues persuasively that Orwell had attended the ILP summer school in July 1936, and so when at the end of December, having waited to deliver the typescript of *The Road to Wigan Pier* to Gollancz, he left for Spain, principally in search of a new subject, he asked the ILP to furnish him with documentation (Crick 1980: 194, 201; *CWGO* 11: 136). Although he appreciated that the revolution of July and August was probably now starting to recede, he was to write in *Homage to Catalonia*: 'The anarchists were still in virtual control of Catalonia and the revolution was still in full swing.' The experience of Barcelona was

> ...something startling and overwhelming. It was the first time that I had ever been in a town where the working class was in the saddle. Practically every building of any size had been seized by the workers and was draped with red flags or with the red and black flag of the anarchists; every wall was scrawled with the hammer and sickle and with the initials of the revolutionary parties; almost every church had been gutted and its images burnt. ... Every shop and café had an inscription saying that it had been collectivised; even the bootblacks had been collectivised and their boxes painted red and black. Waiters and shop-walkers looked you in the face and treated you as an equal. ... There were no private motor cars, they had all been commandeered, and all the trams and taxis and much of the other transport had been painted red and black. ... In all outward appearance it was

a town in which the wealthy classes had practically ceased to exist. ... Practically everyone wore rough working-class clothes, or blue overalls or some variant of the militia uniform (*CWGO* 6: 2-3).

Although Orwell confesses 'that there was much in it that I did not understand, in some ways I did not even like it', he 'recognised it immediately as a state of affairs worth fighting for' and within a few days had joined the militia of the quasi-Trotskyist POUM since that was the ILP's Spanish affiliate (ibid: 3).[6] He then spent four months on the Aragón front where he:

> ...was among tens of thousands of people, mainly though not entirely of working-class origin, all living at the same level and mingling on terms of equality. In theory it was perfect equality, and even in practice it was not far from it. There is a sense in which it would be true to say that one was experiencing a foretaste of socialism... (ibid: 83).

The positive consequences of his time in Spain were, then, 'to make my desire to see socialism established much more actual than before' and ultimately to escape from the country with 'not less but more belief in the decency of human beings'. He praises the Spaniards for 'their innate decency', which, combined with 'their ever-present anarchist tinge', he considered would enable them to 'make even the opening stages of socialism tolerable if they had the chance' (ibid: 84, 186).

Not only the Spanish people but also the anarchists, therefore, emerge with great credit. Dissatisfied with the inaction and stalemate of the Aragón front Orwell, desperate to engage in the fierce battles around Madrid, was preparing to leave the POUM and transfer to the communist-organised International Brigades, even though 'as far as my purely personal preferences went I would have liked to join the anarchists'. He was even to say that that had he had 'a complete understanding of the situation' when he arrived in Spain he would 'probably have joined the CNT militia' (ibid: 96; *CWGO* 11: 136).[7] *Homage to Catalonia* begins memorably with Orwell's encounter with an Italian militiaman in the POUM's Lenin Barracks:

> Something in his face deeply moved me. It was the face of a man who would commit murder and throw away his life for a friend – the kind of face you would expect in an Anarchist, though as likely as not he was a Communist.... I have seldom seen anyone – any man, I mean – to whom I have taken such an immediate liking (*CWGO* 6: 1).

Some years later, in 'Looking Back on the Spanish War', he more convincingly identified him as 'probably a Trotskyist or an anarchist' and published the moving poem beginning 'The Italian soldier shook my hand / Beside the guard-room table...' and ending:

> But the thing that I saw in your face
> No power can disinherit:
> No bomb that ever burst
> Shatters the crystal spirit (*CWGO* 13: 509-511).

He contrasts the anarchists and the communists, entirely to the former's advantage: 'Philosophically, communism and anarchism are poles apart. ... The communist's emphasis is always on centralism and efficiency, the anarchist's on liberty and equality' (*CWGO* 6: 204).

His brother-in-law considered that 'what changed Eric completely was the Spanish war. ... he came back a different man' (Coppard and Crick: 129-130).[8] Orwell left Spain with his belief in the decency of the common people confirmed, the knowledge that socialism was feasible and an empathy with the anarchists of the CNT-FAI. He wrote to Cyril Connolly: 'I have seen wonderful things & at last really believe in socialism, which I never did before' (*CWGO* 11: 28). But the negative experience of the machinations of international communism was to prove even more decisive. On a fortnight's leave in Barcelona at the end of April, he was astonished by the transformation since January. The revolution was going into reverse: 'Once again it was an ordinary city, a little pinched and chipped by war, but with no outward sign of working-class predominance' (*CWGO* 6: 88). Then came the traumatic events of 3-7 May – the May Days. For Orwell the situation was clear: 'On one side the CNT, on the other side the police ... when I see an actual flesh-and-blood worker in conflict with his natural enemy, the policeman, I do not have to ask myself which side I am on' (ibid: 104).[9]

Back at the front, Orwell was almost immediately badly wounded; and it was from hospital that he wrote so optimistically to Connolly. On his return to Barcelona in June, he found that the POUM, scapegoated for the May Days, had been proscribed and consequently many of his comrades were imprisoned. Of the ILP contingent, Bob Smillie, grandson of the former president of the Miners' Federation of Great Britain, was to die in a Valencia jail (ibid: 39, 134-135, 170).[10] Orwell, Eileen Blair, who had been working for the ILP's Barcelona office, and two ILPers were lucky to escape over the frontier to the safety of France.

Orwell refused to participate in *Authors Take Sides on the Spanish War*. He told its communist instigator, Nancy Cunard, to 'stop sending me this bloody rubbish':

**DAVID GOODWAY**

I was six months in Spain, most of the time fighting, I have a bullet-hole in me at present and I am not going to write blah about defending democracy or gallant little anybody. Moreover, I know what is happening and has been happening on the government side for months past, i.e. that Fascism is being riveted on the Spanish workers under the pretext of resisting Fascism; also that since May a reign of terror has been proceeding and all the jails and any place that will serve as a jail are crammed with prisoners who are not only imprisoned without trial but are half-starved, beaten and insulted (*CWGO* 11: 67).

In contrast, he consented to become a sponsor of the English Section of the SIA (Solidaridad Internacional Antifascista) which the Russo-American anarchist, Emma Goldman, was labouring in London to set up for the CNT-FAI. From March to September 1938, Orwell was in a sanatorium, having fallen ill with a tubercular lesion. There is, therefore, no correspondence between him and Goldman, his wife Eileen acting as intermediary, but he told Stephen Spender: 'I'm all for this SIA business if they are really doing anything to supply food etc., not like that damned rubbish of signing manifestos to say how wicked it all is.'[11]

Orwell had begun to write *Homage to Catalonia* shortly after his return home in July 1937 and completed it early the following year. This was a book turned down (before a word of it was written!) by his publisher, Victor Gollancz, because of Orwell's anti-communism but Secker & Warburg brought it out on 25 April 1938. In a letter of 3 May, Goldman wished that:

> ... the book could circulate in tens of thousands of copies. At least it would show the calibre and the quality of the CNT-FAI and expose the conspiracy against them to the world.

Yet it was to achieve an astonishingly poor sale: gross royalties probably fell short of an advance of £150 by £20, and what was left of the print run of 1,500 was eventually remaindered after Orwell's death in 1950, with the anarchist Freedom Press acquiring the stock. Goldman also hoped that *Homage to Catalonia* would be published in the USA, but that was not to be until as late as 1952 (*CWGO* 11: 53, 81, 135, 260).[12]

In 1947, he opened up to an improbable confidant, Richard Usborne, editor of the *Strand* magazine and shortly to write *Clubland Heroes*, summarising his intense political education of 1935-1937:

> As to politics, I was only intermittently interested in the subject until about 1935, though I think I can say I was always more or less 'left'. In *Wigan Pier*, I first tried to thrash out my ideas. I felt, as I still do, that there are huge deficiencies in the whole

conception of socialism, and I was still wondering whether there was any other way out. After having a fairly good look at British industrialism at its worst, i. e. in the mining areas, I came to the conclusion that it is a duty to work for socialism even if one is not emotionally drawn to it, because the continuance of present conditions is simply not tolerable, and no solution except some kind of collectivism is viable, because that is what the mass of the people want. About the same time I became infected with a horror of totalitarianism, which indeed I already had in the form of hostility towards the Catholic Church. I fought for six months (1936-37) in Spain on the side of [the] government, and had the misfortune to be mixed up in the internal struggle on the government side, which left me with the conviction that there is not much to choose between communism and fascism, though for various reasons I would choose communism if there were no other choice open. I have been vaguely associated with Trotskyists and anarchists, and more closely with the left wing of the Labour Party (the Bevan-Foot end of it). … .But I have never belonged to a political party, and I believe that even politically I am more valuable if I record what I believe to be true and refuse to toe a party line (Davison 2010: xi–xii).

After the publication of *Animal Farm* in 1945, Michael Sayers, who with Rayner Heppenstall had shared a flat in Kentish Town with Orwell ten years before, and now an ardent fellow-traveller, re-established contact. Orwell explained:

I don't think I could fairly be described as Russophobe. I am against all dictatorships and I think the Russian myth has done frightful harm to the leftwing movement in Britain and elsewhere, and that it is above all necessary to make people see the Russian regime for what it is (i. e. what I think it is). But I thought all this as early as 1932 or thereabouts and always said so fairly freely (Davison 2010: 275; Bowker 2003: 338-340).[13]

The origins of his great fable, however, are to be found in counter-revolutionary Barcelona. And not only was there to be the difficulty of the publication and reception of *Homage to Catalonia*; also the *New Statesman* in July rejected a commissioned book review of two books on Spain in which he had stated: 'The most important fact that has emerged from the whole business is that the Communist Party is now … an anti-revolutionary force' (*CWGO* 11: 51). For Orwell the *New Statesman* had thereby exhibited 'the mentality of a whore', a charge to which he was to return in 1944:

Don't imagine that for years on end you can make yourself the boot-licking propagandist of the Soviet regime, or any other regime, and then suddenly return to mental decency. Once a whore, always a whore (Crick 1980: 228, 305; *CWGO* 16: 365).[14]

**DAVID GOODWAY**

After his spell in the sanatorium in 1938, Orwell was sent to recuperate in French Morocco and it was there, brooding on the imminent European war, that he wrote in January and March 1939 to Herbert Read, who had recently declared for anarchism, advocating preparations for 'illegal anti-war activities' by acquiring a printing press and stock of paper. His assumption was that some kind of authoritarian regime, a variety of Austro-Fascism, would come to power, explaining to a sceptical Read:

> So long as the objective, real or pretended, is war against [G]ermany, the greater part of the Left will associate themselves with the fascising process, which will ultimately mean associating themselves with wage-reductions, suppression of free speech, brutalities in the colonies etc. Therefore the revolt against these things will have to be against the Left as well as Right. The revolt will form itself into two sections, that of the dissident lefts like ourselves, and that of the fascists, this time the idealistic Hitler-fascists... (*CWGO* 11: 313-314, 340-341).

He had finally become a member of the ILP in June 1938 (he incorrectly told Usborne that he had never belonged to a political party) and at this time wrote what he called 'my anti-war pamphlet', 'Socialism and the war', which was never published and whose manuscript has not survived (ibid: 151, 169, 223; Crick 1980: 246-247).[15] Fifteen months later, with the Nazi–Soviet Pact and the outbreak of war, although he had just been arguing that 'a left-wing party which, within a capitalist society, becomes a war party, has already thrown up the sponge, because it is demanding a policy which can only be carried out by its opponents', he resigned from the ILP in opposition to its anti-war stance (*CWGO* 11: 406).

### ORWELL AND THE BRITISH ANARCHISTS

Orwell proceeded to advocate the radical, even revolutionary, patriotism of 'My Country Right or Left', an essay of 1940 published in *Folios of New Writing*, and *The Lion and the Unicorn*, the first, small Searchlight Book published in 1941. He contended that 'there is no real alternative between resisting Hitler and surrendering to him', but he believed additionally: 'Only revolution can save England ... but now the revolution has started, and it may proceed quite quickly if only we can keep Hitler out' (*CWGO* 12: 271-272). His onslaughts on the pacifists – he maintained that 'to be effectively anti-war in England now one has to be pro-Hitler' and that 'there is no real answer to the charge that pacifism is objectively pro-Fascist' – led in summer 1942 to a bad-tempered brawl in the columns of *Partisan Review* with three young anarcho-pacifists, D. S. Savage, Alex Comfort and George Woodcock, each laying into him (ibid: 473; *CWGO* 13: 110).

Derek (Stanley) Savage, one of the most highly-regarded literary critics of the 1940s, attacked Orwell, asking:

> What is the actual social system which he is fighting to defend? What hopes has he of diverting the stream of history the way *he* wants it to go? ... Mr Orwell, like all the other supporters of the war, shipping magnates, coal owners, proletarians, university professors, Sunday journalists, Trade Union leaders, Church dignitaries, scoundrels and honest men, is being swept along by history, not directing it. Like them, he will be deposited, along with other detritus, where history decides, not where he thinks (*CWGO* 13: 394).

Savage went almost entirely silent for a quarter of a century. He returned to literary criticism in the 1980s with two unforgiving essays on Orwell, contending that just before the outbreak of war 'he went into reverse, denied his pacifism and reverted to the Kiplingesque militarism of his early upbringing or conditioning' (Ford 1983 8: 137):

> ... he [had] held to a notion of individual morality which he expressed vaguely as 'decency', and which was buttressed to some extent by allegiance to a political movement, the ILP, which was at least derivatively moral in its belief in human, or working-class brotherhood, and its rejection of militarism and war. By ... welcoming the resurgent militarism of World War II, Orwell cut his link with conscience and morality... (Savage 1980: 39).

Orwell had already reviewed at length for the *Adelphi* Alex Comfort's first, pre-anarchist novel, *No Such Liberty* (1941) and, while conceding that it was 'a good novel as novels go at this moment', had taken it apart as a pacifist 'tract'. Comfort retaliated fiercely in the *Partisan Review* controversy, beginning: 'I see that Mr Orwell is intellectual-hunting again...' Orwell retorted that Comfort was 'hoping for a Nazi victory because of the stimulating effect it would have upon the arts' (*CWGO* 13: 39, 395, 397). But this strange, lonely man – Anthony Burgess (1987: 290-291) recalls him appearing in the Fitzrovia pubs 'to down a silent half ', standing on the edge of the group – who always exhibited great kindliness and was the epitome of decency, had already – and entirely typically – initiated an emollient private correspondence. Comfort congratulated him on 'The art of Donald McGill', actually thanked him for the abrasive *Adelphi* review ('It made me revise several ideas'), and the next month invited him to contribute to the first issue of *New Road*, of which Comfort was co-editor. Orwell responded with 'Looking back on the Spanish war' (*CWGO* 13: 406, 496-497). 1943, however, saw Orwell answering the Byronic stanzas Comfort had published as 'Obadiah Hornbooke' in *Tribune* with:

**DAVID GOODWAY**

> I'm not a fan for 'fighting on the beaches',
> And still less for the 'breezy uplands' stuff,
> I seldom listen-in to Churchill's speeches,
> But I'd far sooner hear that sort of guff
> Than your remark, a year or so ago,
> That if the Nazis came you'd knuckle under
> And 'peaceably accept the status quo'.
> Maybe you would! But I've a right to wonder
> Which will sound better in the years to come,
> 'Blood, toil and sweat' or 'Kiss the Nazi's bum' (*CWGO* 15: 144).

(The questions Comfort had actually asked in *Partisan Review* were: 'What ... does Mr Orwell imagine the role of the artist should be in occupied territory? He should protest with all his force, where and when he can, against such evils as he sees – but can he do this more usefully by temporarily accepting the status quo, or by skirmishing in Epping Forest with a pocket full of hand grenades?' *CWGO* 13: 396). In private, Orwell complimented Comfort on his virtuosity: 'You ought to write something longer in that genre, something like the "Vision of Judgement"...' (*CWGO* 15: 165). The following year Orwell, now literary editor of *Tribune*, printed further anti-war verses by Comfort, 'The Little Apocalypse of Obadiah Hornbooke', though not replying in kind. He explained to a truculent correspondent that 'I do not ... agree with "Obadiah Hornbooke", but that is not a sufficient reason for not publishing what he writes.... Besides, if this war is about anything at all, it is a war in favour of freedom of thought'. He did not admit that he had actually solicited 'another satirical poem' (*CWGO* 16: 9, 306).

Forty years later, Comfort, like Savage, returned to the *Partisan Review* row unrepentantly but, in contrast to Savage, claiming Orwell as a friend, albeit 'a friend by post' since he only ever met him once (yet this was characteristic of the busy young doctor's literary relationships).[16] For his part, Orwell was certainly a friend to Comfort, broadcasting and printing his poetry and recommending him as one of the most talented young writers (*CWGO* 15: 273-274; XVI: 9; XVII: 75).[17]

It has been suggested that of the *Partisan Review* controversialists it was only Woodcock who discomposed Orwell, since he accused 'the former police official of British imperialism' of returning to 'his old imperialist allegiances' by working at the BBC and 'conducting British propaganda to fox the Indian masses'. Orwell immediately arranged for Woodcock to participate in a broadcast discussion, which led the latter to concede 'that, if I had heard a fair sample of the Indian broadcasts, I might in the past have been a little too angry about them'. Orwell rammed the point home by observing that 'there is no question of getting to the Indian *masses* with any sort of b'cast, because they don't possess radios, certainly not shortwave sets' (emphasis in the original). This exchange was towards the end of 1942 but, although Woodcock was invited to review for *Tribune* after Orwell became its literary editor twelve months later, a firm friendship between the two men only developed after the imprisonment in April 1945 of three of the editors of Freedom Press's *War Commentary* for attempting to subvert members of the armed forces (*CWGO* 13: 395, and 14: 13, 213-214; Woodcock 1970 [1966]: 13-19; Woodcock 1982: 251-255; Newsinger 1998: 15, 97, 100).[18]

Orwell signed a letter of protest to *Tribune* with eight others, including Comfort, Dylan Thomas and Jankel Adler; and was then recruited by Woodcock to become vice-chairman of the Freedom Defence Committee, the only voluntary body in which he was ever active, as he continued to be down to its dissolution in 1949, by which time he was exceedingly ill (and Woodcock had emigrated to Canada). The Freedom Press Defence Committee had been set up in 1944 to fight the case of the *War Commentary* editors. It was then renamed and enlarged to uphold the civil liberties of libertarians, dissident leftists, pacifists, and deserters at a time when the National Council for Civil Liberties was communist-dominated and only inclined to aid the politically correct. Herbert Read was chairman and Woodcock secretary, with the sponsors including Aneurin Bevan, Gerald Brenan, Clifford Curzon, Michael Foot, E. M. Forster, Victor Gollancz, Basil Liddell Hart, Julian Huxley, Augustus John, Harold Laski, Henry Moore, J. Middleton Murry, George Padmore, J. B. Priestley, Bertrand Russell, D. S. Savage, Osbert Sitwell, Graham Sutherland, Julian Symons, Sybil Thorndike and Michael Tippett (*CWGO* 17: 135-136, 263-264, 18: 48-49 and 19: 34, 421-422; Woodcock 1970 [1966]):19-23; Woodcock 1982: 266-267, 283-285; Crick 1980: 344, 388; Read 1945: 13-14).

Through the work of the Freedom Defence Committee, Orwell and Woodcock were drawn close together. Orwell contributed one of his most remarkable essays, 'How the Poor Die' (1946), to Woodcock's *NOW*, the nature of whose contributors to an issue of the first series he had criticised in the *Partisan Review*, and also made a substantial donation to keep the magazine running. Woodcock went on to write for *Politics* the pioneering 'George Orwell, Nineteenth Century Liberal', greatly appreciated by its subject, who judged it as 'much the most serious criticism I have had', as well as, long after Orwell's death in 1950, the fine study, *The Crystal Spirit* (1970 [1966]): 29; *CWGO* 18: 373, 455-467, and 19: 29).[19]

Savage, Comfort and Woodcock were all pacifists in addition to being anarchists; but non-pacifist anarchists were equally opposed to the Second World War – with the exception of Rudolf Rocker, the German anarchist prominent in the Yiddish-speaking movement in London before World War One, and some of the Jewish anarchists around him who, perhaps understandably, supported the Allied governments. Orwell was also friendly with some of the non-pacifist anarchists in London, most notably Vernon Richards and Marie Louise Berneri. Berneri's father, the Italian anarchist philosopher Camillo Berneri, had been assassinated, almost certainly by communists, during the May Days in Barcelona. Richards was one of three *War Commentary* editors sentenced to nine months' imprisonment in 1945, the charge against the fourth editor, Berneri, being, to her disgust, dropped since under English law a wife could not be prosecuted for conspiring with her husband. Woodcock was responsible for the tale, to be adamantly denied by Richards, that at the time Orwell was having difficulty finding a publisher for *Animal Farm*, he offered it to Freedom Press but such was the antagonism to him for his attacks on opponents of the war as 'objectively pro-Fascist' – Berneri especially objected strongly – that the proposal was dropped. The truth may well be that Woodcock sounded out Berneri, his special friend, and given the vehemence of her reaction went no further (Woodcock 1953: 18; Crick 1980: 317; Richards 1998: 70).[20]

Relations between Berneri, Richards and Orwell subsequently warmed considerably, and Orwell, notoriously averse to being photographed, allowed the couple, who were toying with the idea of becoming professional photographers, to get round the problem of Richards's earning a living after release from prison, to take a remarkable series of shots at his flat and theirs and also in the street. Several of these photographs have been much reproduced, but in 1998 Richards, for the first time, published the entire sequence: portrait studies of Orwell, Orwell at the typewriter, dressing and playing with his small son, wheeling Richard in his pushchair, drinking tea, rolling a cigarette, at his workbench, holding a Burmese sword (as well as many pictures of Richard alone).[21]

ORWELL'S CRITIQUE OF ANARCHISM

Although Orwell displayed an empathy with Spanish anarchism, developed warm friendships with most of the prominent British anarchists of the 1940s (if only Derek Savage had lived in London, he too would probably been drawn into Orwell's circle) and participated fully in the work of the Freedom Defence Committee, he was never in his maturity any kind of anarchist – despite having in the early thirties (and possibly before) offered the self-description of 'Tory anarchist'. During the final ten years of his life he was a left-wing socialist and supporter of the Labour Party; yet at the same time he exhibited pronounced anarchist tendencies and sympathies, for he was a libertarian socialist. According to Julian Symons, whom he had accused in the *Partisan Review* row of writing in 'a vaguely

Fascist strain', but who at the time was a Trotskyist, and with whom he became extremely friendly several years later, Orwell remained a libertarian socialist down to his death. Yet Symons believed that 'at the end' his faith in socialism was 'expressed…more sympathetically in the personalities of unpractical Anarchists than in the slide rule Socialists who make up the bulk of the British Parliamentary Labour Party' (*CWGO* 13: 111; Symons 1963: 49).[22]

In 1946, Orwell wrote a series of articles for the *Manchester Evening News* on 'The Intellectual Revolt' in which he identified four major streams in contemporary socio-political thought, all demonstrating his preoccupation with the tension between economic equality and individual liberty: 'The Pessimists. – Those who deny that a planned society can lead either to happiness or to true progress'; 'The Christian Reformers. – Those who wish to combine revolutionary social change with adherence to Christian doctrine', but who also believe that 'any society which sacrifices the individual to the State will perish'; 'The Left-wing Socialists. – Those who accept the principle of planning, but are chiefly concerned to combine it with individual liberty'; and 'The Pacifists. – 'Those who wish to get away from the centralised state and from the whole principle of government by coercion' and who therefore encompassed most anarchists (*CWGO* 18: 41, 57).

Orwell belongs, like Arthur Koestler and Ignazio Silone, with 'the left-wing socialists'. These writers are 'all aware of the need for planned societies and for a high level of industrial development', but they also want 'the older conception of socialism, which laid its stress on liberty and equality and drew its inspiration from the belief in human brotherhood, to be kept alive' (ibid: 62). In the less advanced societies, this tendency is, Orwell says, 'more likely to take the form of anarchism': 'Underneath it lies the belief that human nature is fairly decent to start with and is capable of indefinite development' (ibid). The genealogy of these ideas is to be traced back through 'Utopian dreamers like William Morris and mystical democrats like Walt Whitman, through Rousseau, through the English diggers and levellers, through the peasant revolts of the Middle Ages, and back to the early Christians and the slave rebellions of antiquity' (ibid). In contrast the pacifists and anarchists – Orwell names Aldous Huxley, Read, Comfort and Savage among others – reject the necessity for a high standard of living:

> … the real problem is whether pacifism is compatible with the struggle for material comfort. On the whole, the direction of pacifist thought is towards a kind of primitivism. If you want a high standard of living you must have a complex industrial society – that implies planning, organisation, and coercion – in other words, it implies the state, with its prisons, its police forces, and its inevitable wars (ibid: 68).

In an earlier review of the writings of Gerrard Winstanley, the Digger (1609-1676), he had, however, considered that his thought 'links up with anarchism rather than socialism because he thinks in terms of a purely agricultural community living at a low level of comfort, lower than was then strictly necessary': 'Not forseeing the machine, he states that a man cannot be rich except by exploiting others, but it is evident that, like Mr Gandhi, he values simplicity for its own sake' (*CWGO* 16: 377).[23] But at the time of the *Manchester Evening News* articles Orwell had also let slip: 'I have always suspected that if our economic and political problems are ever really solved, life will become simpler instead of more complex...' (*CWGO* 18: 240).

Elsewhere, in 'Politics vs Literature: An examination of *Gulliver's Travels*', published in *Polemic* in 1946, he objects to:

> ... the totalitarian tendency which is implicit in the anarchist or pacifist vision of society. In a society in which there is no law, and in theory no compulsion, the only arbiter of behaviour is public opinion. But public opinion...is less tolerant than any system of law. When human beings are governed by 'thou shalt not', the individual can practise a certain amount of eccentricity: when they are supposedly governed by 'love' or 'reason', he is under continuous pressure to make him behave and think in exactly the same way as everyone else (ibid: 424-425).

He develops this assault on anarchism and pacifism in 'Lear, Tolstoy and the Fool', of March 1947, by accusing them, with considerable justification, of authoritarianism:

> The distinction that really matters is not between violence and non-violence, but between having and not having the appetite for power. There are people who are convinced of the wickedness both of armies and of police forces, but who are nevertheless much more intolerant and inquisitorial in outlook than the normal person who believes that it is necessary to use violence in certain circumstances ... they will, if they can, get inside [somebody else's] brain and dictate his thoughts for him in the minutest particulars. Creeds like pacifism and anarchism, which seem on the surface to imply a complete renunciation of power, rather encourage this habit of mind (*CWGO* 19: 65-66).[24]

## CONCLUSION

Even this devastating critique of anarchism as totalitarian, intolerant and power-seeking in tendency is extremely anarchistic in its thrust. For, as the major anarchist writer Colin Ward maintained approvingly, Orwell's version of socialism is 'pretty anarchical', and the equally hostile assessment of Isaac Deutscher, who had known him as a fellow journalist for the *Observer*, was that Orwell was 'at heart … a simple-minded anarchist'.[25] His concern above all others, given his first-hand experience of counter-revolutionary Spain, was that the implementation of socialism should not lead to totalitarianism and the extinction of liberty, an obsession that culminated in the dystopia of *Nineteen Eighty-Four*: 'Today the whole world is moving towards a tightly planned society in which personal liberty is being abolished and social equality unrealised' (*CWGO* 18: 71).[26]

Jennie Lee, wife of Aneurin Bevan and to become a Labour minister herself in 1964, observed of Orwell that 'he hated regimentation wherever he found it, even in the socialist ranks', adding the gloss that 'he was not only a socialist but profoundly liberal' (*CWGO* 11: 5). Woodcock similarly considered that he was 'very much nearer to the old-style liberal than to the corporate-state socialists who … lead the Labour Party'. But Woodcock also points out that he was inconsistent and contradictory, recalling from conversations that his conception of a socialist state seemed more like 'a syndicalist federation than a real State in the traditional Socialist model' and that 'his real inclinations' appeared 'to envisage a decentralised society and workers' control of industry – something rather like the Guild Socialist vision, with a great deal of room for individual initiative' (Woodcock 1948: 122, 123-124; Woodcock 1970 [1966]: 31).

In 1946, it was announced in *Freedom* that Orwell was to speak on 20 January to the London Anarchist Group on 'Trends in Russia's Foreign Policy'.[27] *Freedom* did not carry a report on the meeting – although there is no significance in this since that was not the paper's practice – and Peter Davison makes no mention of it (or a lecture with this title) in his edition of *The Complete Works*, let alone prints a text. It is possible therefore, even probable, that the talk never took place but the fact that Orwell was so billed is indicative of his sympathy for and proximity to anarchism.

Answering the concern of some readers of *Animal Farm* that he now rejected revolutionary change, he explained in anarchist fashion:

> I meant *that kind* of revolution (violent conspiratorial revolution, led by unconsciously power-hungry people) can only lead to a change of masters. I meant the moral to be that revolutions only effect a radical improvement when the masses are alert and know how to chuck out their leaders as soon as the latter have done their job.... What I was trying to say was, 'You can't have a revolution unless you make it for yourself…' (*CWGO* 18: 507, Orwell's emphasis).[28]

And in a letter, written a year before his death, Orwell maintained, just like any good anarchist: 'The real division is not between conservatives and revolutionaries but between authoritarians and libertarians (Davison and Taylor 2003).[29]

NOTES

[1] Unless otherwise attributed details of Orwell's life are drawn from Crick or the chronologies at the beginning of each volume, 10-20, of Peter Davison's magnificent edition, *CWGO* (a version of which appears in his brief but authoritative study, Davison, 1996: xv–xxvii). While Meyers (2000), Bowker (2003) and Taylor (2003) are all accomplished literary biographies, Crick's outstanding work remains essential for the politics. Anarchist concerns find no place in the latest biography, Colls (2013), an interesting consideration of Orwell's 'Englishness'

[2] See also Rees 1961: 29, 48; *CWGO* 5 (*The Road to Wigan Pier*): 137. For the *Adelphi* and its circle, see Crick 1980: 160-161; *CWGO* 10: 181-182; and Newsinger 1999: 22-23

[3] Cf. Pritchett 1990: 97. Carpenter and Wilde each have a chapter in Goodway (2012)

[4] Cf. Michael Sayers's testimony cited by Bowker 2003: 174

[5] Taylor 1981 is an able and very helpful guide to the slippery topic of Orwell's socialism

[6] Cf. *CWGO* 11: 51

[7] Cf. ibid: 93. See also the interesting reminiscences of Bob Edwards, Introduction, to George Orwell, *Homage to Catalonia*, London: Folio Society, 1970: 8; and Stafford Cottman's recollections, 'In the Spanish trenches', in Coppard and Crick 1984: 151-152

[8] See Stansky and Abrahams, 1979: 187, 225-226, for a summary of the importance of Spain in Orwell's career

[9] For Orwell's account and analysis of the May Days, see *CWGO* 6: chap. 9, and app. 2. For the anarchist perspective (with which he concurred), see Richards 1983 [1953] chaps 12-14, and Richards (ed.) 1987

[10] See also Brockway 1947: 303; McArthur n. d.; Buchanan 1997; Newsinger 1998. McGovern, n. d., conveys the ILP's reaction to the events in Spain

[11] International Institute of Social History, Amsterdam: Goldman Archive (GA), 27 A, letters from Eileen Blair to Goldman, 17 March, 12 April, 10 May 1938, and from Goldman to Eileen Blair, 21 March, 8, 14 April, 17 May 1938; GA, 33 A, letter from Goldman to Eileen Blair, 3 May 1938; *CWGO* 11: 131 (letter of 2 April 1938). Orwell thought, mistakenly, that Spender was also a SIA sponsor, presumably believing that since Auden was (temporarily) Spender would be too. For the SIA, see Goodway (ed.) 2008: 21, 82-86, 178 and Goodway 2012: 128-129

[12] See also GA 27 A, letter from Goldman to Rose Pesotta, 3 May 1938, and Davison, 1996: 86. According to Woodcock 1970 [1966]: 103, only 900 copies were sold during Orwell's lifetime. But Orwell told Vernon Richards in March1949 that Secker had no copies left (*CWGO* 20: 60)

[13] Davison does not include Orwell's previous letter to Sayers (of 29 November 1945) in his selection: it has only been reproduced in Taylor 2010. See also *CWGO* 19: 90

[14] See also *CWGO* 11: 53

[15] Crick's claim that Orwell joined the pacifist Peace Pledge Union (PPU) in December 1937 is disproved by Davison, who shows that it was merely a matter of Eileen Blair buying PPU pamphlets (*CWGO* 11: 104)

[16] Alex Comfort, '1939 and 1984: George Orwell and the vision of judgment', in Stansky (ed.) 1983: 17 (reprinted in David Goodway (ed.) *Against Power and Death: The Anarchist Articles and Pamphlets of Alex Comfort*, London: Freedom Press, 1994: 157)

[17] See also *CWGO* 15: 75, 135

[18] A photograph of Woodcock with the other participants in the broadcast is reproduced on the cover of Orwell and Angus 1970 2: 11, and also in Fetherling 1998, while the transcript is printed in *CWGO* 14: 14-25

[19] 'George Orwell, Nineteenth Century Liberal' was collected in Woodcock 1948, chap. 7. For the two men's friendship, see Woodcock 1970 [1966]: 23-45; Woodcock 1982: 285-293

[20] Woodcock 1953 is reprinted in full in both Fetherling 1980: 147, and Coppard and Crick 1984: 200-201. Fredric Warburg accepted *Animal Farm* in August 1944 (*CWGO* 16: 358), a fact that causes severe problems for Crick's account

[21] See also *CWGO* 19: 486-487, and 20: 36, 60, 81-82, 84, 140; Goodway 2015: 236-238 Richards's *Freedom* obituary of Orwell is reprinted as 'Orwell the Humanist' in Richards 1998

[22] See also Barker 1978: 147, 151

[23] See also *CWGO* 19: 109-110

[24] See also the comparison of Swift and Tolstoy, *CWGO* 18: 425-426

[25] Interview by David Goodway with Colin Ward, 29 June 1997; Deutscher 1969 [1955]): 47-48. See too the synopsis of Woodcock's response to 'Politics vs Literature', *CWGO* 18: 431. There are also Colin Ward's five articles, based on impressively wide reading for the time, 'Orwell and anarchism', first published in *Freedom* in 1955 and reprinted in Richards 1998: 15-45

[26] Cf. *CWGO* 17: 403

[27] *Freedom*, 12 January 1946

[28] Cf. the comments by O'Brien on power and the Party in *Nineteen Eighty-Four* (*CWGO* 9: 275-77)

[29] Davison and Taylor 2003; Davison (ed.) 2006: 116

## REFERENCES

Barker, Rodney (1978) *Political Ideas in Modern Britain*, London: Methuen

Bowker, Gordon (2003) *George Orwell*, London: Little, Brown

Brockway, Fenner (1947) *Inside the Left: Thirty Years of Platform, Press, Prison and Parliament*, London: New Leader

Buchanan, Tom (1997) The death of Bob Smillie, the Spanish Civil War, and the eclipse of the Independent Labour Party, *Historical Journal*, Vol. 40, No. 2

Burgess, Anthony (1987) *Little Wilson and Big God*, London: Heinemann

Colls, Robert (2013) *George Orwell: English Rebel*, Oxford: Oxford University Press

Coppard, Audrey and Crick, Bernard (1984) *Orwell Remembered*, London: Ariel Books

Crick, Bernard (1980) *George Orwell: A Life*, London: Secker & Warburg

Davison, Peter (1996) *George Orwell: A Literary Life*, Basingstoke: Palgrave

Davison, Peter (ed.) (1998) *The Complete Works of George Orwell* (*CWGO*), 20 volumes, London: Secker & Warburg

Davison, Peter (ed.) (2006) *The Lost Orwell: Being a Supplement to 'The Complete Works of George Orwell'*, London: Timewell Press

# DAVID GOODWAY

Davison, Peter (ed.) (2010) *George Orwell: A Life in Letters*, London: Harvill Secker

Davison, Peter and Taylor, D. J. (2003) Like autumn in a garden: New light on the friendship between George Orwell and Malcolm Muggeridge, *Times Literary Supplement*, 30 May

Deutscher, Isaac (1969 [1955]) *Heretics and Renegades: And Other Essays*, London: Jonathan Cape

Fetherling, Doug (ed.) (1980) *A George Woodcock Reader*, Ottawa: Deneau & Greenberg

Fetherling, Douglas (1998) *The Gentle Anarchist: A Life of George Woodcock*, Vancouver: Douglas & McIntyre

Ford, Boris (ed.) (1983) *The New Pelican Guide to English Literature*, Harmondsworth: Penguin, 8 vols

Goodway, David (ed.) (2008) *The Letters of John Cowper Powys and Emma Goldman*, London: Cecil Woolf

Goodway, David (2012) *Anarchist Seeds beneath the Snow: Left-Libertarian Thought and British Writers from William Morris to Colin Ward*, Oakland, CA: PM Press, second edition

Goodway, David (2015) Freedom, 1886-2014: An appreciation, *History Workshop Journal*, No. 79, spring: pp 233-242

Heppenstall, Rayner (1960) *Four Absentees*, London: Barrie & Rockliff

McArthur, Dan (n. d.) *We Carry On: Our Tribute to Bob Smillie*, London: ILP Guild of Youth

McGovern, John (n. d.) *Terror in Spain*, London: Independent Labour Party

Meyers, Jeffrey (2000) *Orwell: Wintry Conscience of a Generation*, New York: W.W. Norton

Newsinger, John (1998) The death of Bob Smillie, *Historical Journal*, Vol. 41, No. 2

Newsinger, John (1999) *Orwell's Politics*, Basingstoke and London: Macmillan Press

Orwell, Sonia, and Angus, Ian (eds) (1970) *The Collected Essays, Journalism and Letters of George Orwell*, Harmondsworth: Penguin, 4 vols

Pritchett, V. S. (1990) *Lasting Impressions: Selected Essays*, London: Chatto & Windus

Read, Herbert (1945) *Freedom: Is It a Crime? Two Speeches*, London: Freedom Press Defence Committee

Rees, Richard (1961) *George Orwell: Fugitive from the Camp of Victory*, London: Secker & Warburg

Richards, Vernon (1983 [1953]) *Lessons of the Spanish Revolution (1936–1939)*, London: Freedom Press, third edition

Richards, Vernon (ed.) (1987) *The May Days: Barcelona 1937*, London: Freedom Press

Richards, Vernon (ed.) (1998) *George Orwell at Home (and among the Anarchists): Essays and Photographs (GOHA)*, London: Freedom Press

Savage, D. S. (1980) The case against George Orwell, *Tract*, No. 31, autumn

Stansky, Peter (ed.) (1983) *On Nineteen Eighty-Four*, Stanford, CA: Stanford Alumni Association

Stansky, Peter, and Abrahams, William (1979) *Orwell: The Transformation*, London: Constable

Symons, Julian (1963) Orwell: A reminiscence, *London Magazine*, No. 3, Spring

Taylor, D. J. (2003) *Orwell*, London: Chatto & Windus

Taylor, D. J. (2010) The road to being Orwell, *The Times*, 17 April

Taylor, Richard (1981) George Orwell and the politics of decency, Jowitt, J. A. and Taylor, R. K. S. (eds) *George Orwell*, Bradford Centre Occasional Papers, No. 3, October

Woodcock, George (1948) *The Writer and Politics*, London: Porcupine Press

Woodcock, George (1953) Recollections of George Orwell, *Northern Review*, Montréal, August-September

Woodcock, George (1982), *Letter to the Past: An Autobiography*, Don Mills, Ontario: Fitzhenry & Whiteside

Woodcock, George (1970 [1966]) *The Crystal Spirit*, Harmondsworth: Penguin

## NOTE ON THE CONTRIBUTOR

David Goodway taught sociology, history and Victorian studies to mainly adult students from 1969 until the University of Leeds closed its School of Continuing Education in 2005. For twenty-five years he has written principally on anarchism and libertarian socialism, publishing collections of the writings of Alex Comfort, Herbert Read, 'Maurice Brinton' and Nicolas Walter and of the correspondence between John Cowper Powys and Emma Goldman; *Talking Anarchy* with Colin Ward (second edition, 2014); as well as *Anarchist Seeds Beneath the Snow: Left-Libertarian Thought and British Writers from William Morris to Colin Ward* (second edition, 2012). But his first book was *London Chartism 1838-1848* (1982) and he has most recently published *The Real History of Chartism* (2013) and an edition of George Julian Harney's late journalism, *The Chartists Were Right* (2014).

PAPER

# Only Donkeys Survive Tyranny and Dictatorship:
## Was Benjamin George Orwell's Alter Ego in *Animal Farm*?

**TIM CROOK**

*This paper examines the representation of Benjamin, the donkey in Orwell's* Animal Farm *– the novel and later radio and dramatic adaptations. It places this study in the context of Orwell's ambivalent fascination with animals and his handling of animal themes in many of his writings. In addition, the paper considers the position of the donkey in the broader culture and whether Benjamin served as Orwell's alter ego in the novel. George Orwell constructed the original prose of* Animal Farm *with an omniscient voice writing in the third person. When he had the opportunity to adapt the novel for BBC Radio in 1946, with transmission in early 1947, he chose not to focalise the narrative structure through any of the characters. This paper argues that this was the correct decision in terms of style and the representation of Orwell's politics.*

Keywords: *Animal Farm*, Benjamin, donkey, radio, dramatisation

A WRITER WHO LOVED ANIMALS

The success of *Animal Farm* (1945) depends to a large extent on the anthropomorphic representation of the animal characters and the extent of sympathy and identification that human prose readers and radio drama listeners have for them. The quality of animal characterisation could be due to Orwell's love of animals, which is well recorded in Orwell's oeuvre as well as in his biography and criticism.[1]

In Burma, serving with the Imperial Police Force from 1922-1927, when he was known by his real name, Eric Arthur Blair, he kept a menagerie, as recalled by Roger Beadon who 'was surprised to find Blair's house in a mess, with "goats, geese, ducks, and all sorts of things floating about"' (Wadhams 1984: 24). Moreover, animals seemed to animate Orwell. This is evident in archive images of him. Peter Davison, referring to a picture of him in the company of a dog and cat in Southwold (Davison 2006: 236), described him as to be in 'a surprisingly relaxed mood' and 'looking unusually fit and healthy' (ibid). Orwell looks even happier nursing a pet rabbit in the garden of Francis and Mabel Fierz's home in the 1930s (Stansky and Abrahams 1979: 51). Throughout his life Orwell's sympathy with the animal world is marked by an investment of affectionate characterisation. Orwell's favourite goat at his cottage in Wallington was called 'Muriel' who was a valuable source of milk. It had such an important role in his life that in his diary entry for 15 April 1939 he thought it important to note that Muriel was 'behaving as though on heat' (Orwell 2010: 139). Muriel would be accorded the honour of having a minor part in *Animal Farm*. His dog, described as 'a very friendly and intelligent animal, a medium-size, grey, unclipped poodle' (Wadhams 1984: 118) was named 'Marx' and on the hottest day for 70 years, 12 April 1939, Orwell recorded in his diary: 'Tried Marx with a live baby mouse. He smelt & licked it but made no move to eat it' (Orwell 2010: 139). Orwell was more adept at training Marx to hunt rabbits (Rodden and Rossi 2012: 73).

Orwell had an intense curiosity about the natural world and the creatures within it even when killing them as a teenager with a catapult at Eton. Sir Roger Mynors co-edited with the younger Orwell a magazine called the *Election Times* at Eton. However, his strongest recollection of their friendship was about their passion for unorthodox biology: 'One day Eric Blair killed a jackdaw with a catapult on the roof of the college chapel, which was entirely illegal, and we then took it round to the biology lab and dissected it (Wadhams 1984: 19). Slitting the unfortunate bird's gall bladder produced a dreadful smell. Many years later Orwell was photographed looking deadly and aiming a catapult in Morocco in 1938 (Davison 2006: 240) though the target was not included in the camera frame. He was also pictured milking a Moroccan goat with great concentration (ibid).

As Adam Stock argues: 'An abiding love of the natural world permeates all of George Orwell's writing' (Stock 2012: 46) and he further suggests that his 'complex conception of "nature" was bound up with his aesthetic sensibility, his politics, as well as the darker aspects of his character' (ibid). Orwell's intellectual and political curiosity extended to the animal world even in the midst of disaster and life-threatening situations. In 1947, during the notorious Corryvreckan whirlpool incident off the Isle of Jura (when Orwell with family members almost drowned), his niece Lucy Dakin (now Bestley) remembered that after their boat's engine had been sucked into the treacherous waters and they were dependent on her brother Henry using the oars: '…at that point a seal popped its head up and looked at us. And Eric said: "Curious thing about seals, very inquisitive creatures." And I thought: "I honestly don't think this is the sort of time to be talking about seals"' (Wadhams 1984: 190-191). After being upturned, nearly drowning and finding themselves marooned and soaked on a nearby island, she recalled Orwell tramping off in search of something to eat and returning half an hour later saying: '"Extraordinary birds, puffins. They make their nests in burrows." And then on the subject of food he said: "I did see some baby seagulls, but I didn't have the heart to do anything about it"' (ibid: 191-192).

Orwell always had a fundamental sympathy for animals and their suffering and he was prepared to admit that it took greater priority over his concerns for the plight of human beings. On his sojourn in Marrakech (1938-1939), he wrote:

> Yet I suppose I had not been five minutes on Moroccan soil before I noticed the overloading of the donkeys and was infuriated by it. There is no question that the donkeys are damnably treated. The Moroccan donkey is hardly bigger than a St Bernard dog, it carries a load which in the British army would be considered too much for a fifteen-hands mule, and very often its pack-saddle is not taken off its back for weeks together. But what is peculiarly pitiful is that it is the most willing creature on earth, it follows its master like a dog and does not need either bridle or halter. After a dozen years of devoted work it suddenly drops dead, whereupon its master tips it into the ditch and the village dogs have torn its guts out before it is cold. This kind of thing makes one's blood boil… (Orwell 1971a: 431).

It could be argued that this observation and experience in 1938 may well have informed the depiction of the role of donkeys in the natural world through *Animal Farm*'s irascible old Benjamin. Intriguingly it is the horse Boxer who is worked to death and despatched to an ignoble end in a knacker's yard van, whereas Benjamin is the donkey who lived a very long time. When Benjamin was given the line: 'None of you has ever seen a dead donkey' (Orwell 1998: 19) there may well have been an Orwellian internal irony operating here in that he had seen far more than he cared to.

Orwell's love of animals even extended to those that despised him, particularly when he had been looking at the hindquarters of a gazelle and 'thinking of mint sauce': 'The gazelle I was feeding seemed to know that this thought was in my mind, for though it took the piece of bread I was holding out it obviously did not like me. It nibbled rapidly at the bread, then lowered its head and tried to butt me, then took another nibble and then butted again' (Orwell 1971a: 427).

Orwell revealed that it was his experience of country living in Wallington where he kept animals and ran a small provisions shop that helped conceptualise the idea of *Animal Farm* as a combined beast fable and political satire. He explained in his preface for the 1947 Ukrainian edition of the novel:

> I saw a little boy, perhaps ten years old, driving a huge cart-horse along a narrow path, whipping it whenever it tried to turn. It struck me that if only such animals became aware of their strength we should have no power over them, and that men exploit animals in much the same way as the rich exploit the proletariat (Orwell 1998: 113).

As he explained in his essay 'Why I Write' (1946): '*Animal Farm* was the first book in which I tried, with full consciousness of what I was doing, to fuse political purpose and artistic purpose into one whole' (Orwell 1969: 104-105).

Orwell could always find a political and social angle when writing about animals and birds.[2] In his essay 'The English People' (1947), he observed it would seem that only in England during the Second World War could one find '"Animals" A. R. P. (Air Raid Precautions) Centres, with miniature stretches for cats, and in the first year of the war there was the spectacle of Animal Day being celebrated with all its usual pomp in the middle of the Dunkirk evacuation' (Orwell 1971b: 18). In 1946, in his celebrated essay 'Some thoughts on a common toad', he wrote of being delighted to 'have seen a kestrel flying over the Deptford gasworks, and I have heard a first-rate performance by a blackbird in the Euston Road. There must be some hundreds of thousands, if not millions, of birds living inside the four-mile radius, and it is rather a pleasing thought that none of them pays a halfpenny of rent' (Orwell 1971c: 173).

In Orwell's world, animals were given human names and vice-versa. His first wife, Eileen, signed herself off in correspondence with friends as 'Pig' (Davison 2006: 65) which Davison found ironic given that 'Eileen's pet name should have been that of the animals Orwell pilloried in *Animal Farm*' (ibid: 68). Pigs certainly did not get a particularly good press in *Animal Farm*. Even the heroic Snowball is depicted with corrupt and exploitative tendencies; a significance Orwell was anxious to emphasise in a discussion he had with Julian Symons:

> He pointed out to me that Trotsky, who in the book was Snowball, was potentially just as big a villain as Stalin, who was Napoleon, although he was the victim of Napoleon, because the first note of corruption was struck, Orwell said – and this is so if you look back at the book – when the pigs secretly have the cows' milk added to their own mash. And Snowball consented to that first act of inequality (Wadhams 1984: 150-151).

**TIM CROOK**

In real life, there is no evidence that Orwell liked pigs very much. The main trade at the village shop he began to run in Wallington, near Royston, in April 1936, with Eileen was sliced bacon. Moreover, Orwell's son Richard has a somewhat traumatic memory of the Barnhill pig's demise: 'I knew something awful was going to happen and that it had something to do with the pig. A little later I heard terrible shouts and awful squeals. There was a lot of drama that day. Then, once the pig was dead, we ate it quite cheerfully. We had it smoked for bacon. It fed us for quite a long time (ibid: 194). Orwell's dislike of pigs is also indicated in the 1939 largely autobiographical novel *Coming Up For Air* when the central character, George Bowling, is frightened by an apparent herd of galloping pigs, though the 'huge flood of pig-faces' turned out to be 'schoolchildren in gas-masks' (Meyers 1975: 132).

There is certainly more evidence that Orwell's 'love of animals' was not universal. Avril Blair's future husband, Bill Dunn, recalled an incident when Orwell 'known as being very gentle to animals' (Crick 1992: 525) stamped his boot on to the neck of a huge adder snake, 'got out his penknife and ... just ripped it right open ... quite deliberately' (ibid). Dunn was surprised that such 'a very gentle, kindly sort of man' (ibid) could be capable of such violence. But Crick observed there 'was this sadistic streak in Orwell's character – which usually he mastered' (ibid). The future BBC producer of Orwell's radio adaptation of *Animal Farm*, Rayner Heppenstall, knew it well. He shared a flat with Orwell in Kentish Town in 1935 and when returning home drunk and disorderly one night was beaten up by his older flatmate who set about him with a shooting-stick: 'I looked at his face. Through my private mist I saw in it a curious blend of fear and sadistic exultation' (ibid: 275). Orwell also administered corporal punishment with harsh authoritarianism when teaching at a private school in Hayes in 1933. Former pupil Geoffrey Stevens recalled getting 'six of the best': 'I remember I couldn't sit down on it for at least a week. They were really bad bruises. I had a job to sit in the bath' (Wadhams 1984: 53-54).[3]

George Orwell himself became known as 'Donkey George' because of what Davison described as his 'reputation for being "gloomy" and forbidding' (Davison 2006: 236). Davison argues that friends called him that after 'his grumbling donkey, Benjamin, in *Animal Farm*' (ibid). One of Orwell's biographers, Bernard Crick, attributes the nickname to Celia Kirwan and her twin sister Mamaine: 'Thinking of wise old Benjamin in *Animal Farm*, she and Mamaine used to refer to him as Donkey George' (Crick 1982: 483).

ANIMAL METAPHORS AND REPRESENTATION IN ORWELL'S LITERATURE

Richard Lance Keeble has written of the great amount of humour in Orwell's writing: 'One of my favourite pieces of Orwellian journalism, which never fails to amuse me, is his essay "Some Thoughts on the Common Toad" of 1946' (Keeble 2016). Keeble appreciates Orwell's 'gentle, witty dig at Anglo-Catholics' when he says that 'after his long fast, the toad has a spiritual look, like a strict Anglo-Catholic towards the end of Lent' (ibid). Keeble highlights Orwell's rumination about the spawning of toads: '…because it is one of the phenomena of spring which most deeply appeals to me, and because the toad, unlike the skylark and the primrose, has never had much of a boost from the poets' (Orwell 1971c: 173).

Orwell recalled in 'Why I Write' that his first poem written at the age of four or five was 'a plagiarism of Blake's "Tiger, Tiger"' (Orwell 1969: 99) and he continued to write 'bad and usually unfinished "nature poems" in the Georgian style' (ibid). His first published poem at the age of 11 appeared in the *Henley & South Oxfordshire Standard* on 2 October 1914 and was a patriotic call to arms 'Awake! Young Men of England'. Significantly, the first two lines: 'Oh! Give me the strength of the lion, The wisdom of Reynard the fox' (Orwell 2015: 1) pay homage to the tradition of the beast fable.

Richard Rees, the editor of *Adelphi* magazine, was both an admirer and friend and believed Orwell's highest ambition was to be a great poet. It is may also be very significant that he recalled the importance of the mythological use of the anthropomorphic donkey in the poem 'On a Ruined Farm near the His Master's Voice Gramophone Factory' that he agreed to publish in his magazine in 1934 (Orwell 2015: 34-35). Rees recalled:

> He looked at the past with horror for its record of injustice and cruelties, but always with a certain nostalgia as well. And he looked to the future with misgivings. He compared himself to Buridan's ass: 'Between two countries, both-ways torn / And moveless still, like Buridan's donkey / Between the water and the corn' (Wadhams 1984: 50).

The legend of Buridan's ass has been pervasive as a metaphor for the destructive dilemma of conflicting choice since the Middle Ages. It satirises the moral determinist philosophy of Jean Buridan where there is the paradox of a donkey or ass dying when placed midway between the temptations and vital sustaining needs of hay and water. The metaphor constitutes the final verse of Orwell's poem and it could be argued it sets up the prescient problem of paradoxical double-think in political action and speech in the troubled context of the twentieth century. The characterisation of Benjamin in *Animal Farm* would place the sagacious donkey in the unbearable stasis of knowing and predicting and at the same time failing to act on his wisdom and intelligence. However, unlike Buridan's ass, Benjamin was clearly intelligent enough to help himself to the hay and the water.

**TIM CROOK**

Orwell successfully fused political writing with literary art to great effect in his 1936 anti-imperialist essay 'Shooting an Elephant'. It is assumed that the essay is a documentary prose account of a personal experience that deeply resonated with somebody so sympathetic to the dignity and life-force of so great and noble creature as an elephant that has to be executed for the banal expedience of sustaining colonial hierarchy.[4] Orwell wrote poignantly when contrasting the rifle he used as 'a beautiful German thing with cross-hair sights' (Orwell 1969: 30) and the dreadful impact it had on the morale of his victim which undergoes 'a mysterious, terrible change. He looked suddenly stricken, shrunken, immensely old' (ibid). The elephant is transformed after the third shot, his death symbolising the oppression of the Burmese people under British imperialist rule:

> ...in falling he seemed for a moment to rise, for as his hind legs collapsed beneath him he seemed to tower upwards like a huge rock toppling, his trunk reaching skywards like a tree. He trumpeted, for the first and only time. And then down he came, his belly towards me, with a crash that seemed to shake the ground even where I lay (ibid: 31-32).

George Woodcock observes: 'The elephant, like a rock, like a tree, becomes identified in that splendid, trumpeting moment of downfall with the whole world of nature, and its crash shivers the solidity of the very earth on which its killer lies' (Woodcock 1970: 69). Woodcock also examines Orwell's use of animal allegory in his first novel *Burmese Days* (1934) written many years before *Animal Farm* was conceived: 'Orwell's feelings for the world of non-human beings (which must have provided at least one link of sympathy with Buddhist Burma) was thoroughly exemplified ... where animals appear not only as images, but also as unconscious participants in the action of the novel' (ibid: 81). Woodcock analyses the novel as providing a literary 'conspiracy of the land whose agents, in animal forms, intervene at crucial moments to help determine the fates of the human characters' (ibid).

Orwell provides a vivid and poetic description of the central character Flory's unsuccessful attempt to shoot a pariah dog keeping him awake in the middle of night in a pack baying the moon on the maidan. This draws Woodcock's observation: 'The pariah dog, distrusted by its fellow animals, has no place in the other world of men. Flory, the solitary, distrusted by his fellow white men, has no place in the other world of animals and the Asians who resemble them' (ibid: 83).

Woodcock was also impressed that Orwell did not change sides at any point during the plot of *Animal Farm* (ibid: 157). The narrative voice or point of view of the reader was 'always nearest to that of the unprivileged animals, and perhaps nearest of all to that of Benjamin, the sad and cynical old donkey who sides with no factions and always says that "life would go on as it had always gone on – that is, badly"' (ibid). Woodcock is, therefore, confirming that Benjamin was in some way a manifestation of an aspect of Orwell that the author's friends so affectionately recognised. But Woodcock argues that Benjamin was not the novel's driving narrative point of view. He was only saying that as a character the cynical donkey came closest to being so. This means that Orwell may well have intended to deploy Benjamin with a dramatic story-telling purpose that could have chimed with the personal political epiphanies he had undergone when joining the poor and down-and-outs in London and Paris (1927-1929), the working class miners in Wigan (1936) and the anarchists and socialists of the POUM militia fighting Franco's Fascists during the Spanish civil war (1937).

John Rodden praises Orwell's ability to present a variety of political viewpoints to specific families of the animal kingdom. He argues: 'If the sheep represent blind conformity and the high-strung hens are easily agitated, then Boxer the horse stands for the hard work, endurance and patriotic loyalty of the working-class' (Rodden 2007: 141). Rodden is another significant critic who equates Benjamin the donkey with Orwell's political attitude: 'Though equally tenacious, [he] remains stoically apart from all utopian ideas. There is perhaps a touch of Orwell himself in this creature's timeless scepticism' (ibid).

## INFLUENCES OF ANTHROPOMORPHIC LITERATURE AND THE CULTURAL ROLE OF THE DONKEY

*Animal Farm* has been constantly compared to *Gulliver's Travels* (1726) by Jonathan Swift. Orwell's friend Malcolm Muggeridge said the 1945 beast fable satire was worthy of Swift: 'It is a masterpiece. You can't flaw it. That book, like *Gulliver's Travels*, will always be of interest to people. It's beautifully worked out. I think George was better writing about animals than about human beings, because the people in his novels aren't really convincing – but the animals were perfectly convincing! I think he had sympathy with them' (Wadhams 1984: 151-152). In fact, Orwell had read *Gulliver's Travels* at least seven times throughout his life and his devotion to the text began the night before his eighth birthday (Stansky and Abrahams 1972: 35). *Gulliver's Travels* had centre stage in his 1946 essay 'Politics vs. Literature' (Orwell 1971c: 241-261) in which he wrote that Swift was 'a Tory Anarchist, despising authority while disbelieving in liberty, and preserving the aristocratic outlook while seeing clearly that the existing aristocracy is degenerate and contemptible' (ibid: 253). His concluding sentence: 'The durability of *Gulliver's Travels* goes to show that if the force of belief is behind it, a worldview which only just passes the test of sanity is sufficient to produce a great work of art' (ibid: 261) could be said of *Animal*

Farm itself. It was the third and fourth books of *Gulliver's Travels* that gave Orwell the model of Swift's 'brilliant reversal of the role of horses and human beings' (Rodden 2007: 135). He was able to fashion the dipsomaniacal Farmer Jones as one of Swift's Yahoos, symbolising the decadent Czarist regime that neglected the repressed and rebellious serfs – shown as starving beasts of burden.

John Rodden and John Rossi acknowledged the childhood influences of Orwell's early reading: 'Late Victorian and Edwardian England produced a rich collection of such animal stories as Kipling's *Jungle Book*, where the boy Mowgli could speak to the animals. Kenneth Grahame's *Wind in the Willows*, featuring the eccentric Toad of Toad Hall and his friends, appeared while Orwell was a schoolboy' (Rodden and Rossi 2012: 74). Orwell's childhood friend and kindred literary spirit Jacintha Buddicom recalled that the young Eric Blair 'particularly liked' Beatrix Potter's *The Tale of Pigling Bland* (of 1913) in which pigs walked upright (ibid) and read it over and over again. Rodden argues that Orwell's inspiration was drawn 'as much from the vogue of animated cartoons in the previous decade, featuring Mickey Mouse, Porky Pig and Donald Duck, as from any literary source' (Rodden 2007: 134-135) though the fables of Aesop or La Fontaine offered the model of 'brief parables attached to pointed morals' (ibid). Orwell's biographer Gordon Bowker argues that Orwell would have been influenced by his studies of Aristophanes' fables at Eton, and 'Another likely source of inspiration was Thurber, with whose political fables he was familiar' (Bowker 2003: 308). The tale of 'A Very Proper Gander' who is expelled from a farm by 'malign rumour-mongers' was a case of 'slippery' language control being turned to 'cruel political ends' (ibid).

Orwell is also likely to have been influenced by the literary legend conceived by William Shakespeare in *A Midsummer Night's Dream*, where the character Bottom has his head converted into that of a donkey. Orwell also referred to *Don Quixote* by Cervantes in some of his critical essays (Orwell 1971b: 321) and would have undoubtedly appreciated the role of Sancho Panza's loyal and heroic donkey Dapple. The exquisite melancholy of Eeyore in A. A. Milne's *Winnie The Pooh* first appeared in book publication in 1926. Moral values and the qualities of wisdom are associated with the donkey through Biblical fables such as Balaam's ass. Donkeys also feature in cross-cultural traditions of carnival throughout the world where they often perform a mocking and subversive role of power reversal.

THE ROLE OF BENJAMIN IN *ANIMAL FARM* AS PROSE AND AUDIO DRAMA

Orwell created two literary forms for *Animal Farm*: the prose novella and the radio dramatisation script for the BBC's first broadcast in 1947. They are different forms of literature and offer different textures of narrative and dramatic representations of his animal characters.

Orwell was no novice in the art of radio dramatisation. He was a confident and assured radio playwright and had two years' experience as a producer of dramatic and cultural programming at the BBC between 1941 and 1943 (Crook 2012: 198-200). He had significant practical experience of adapting prose literature for the sound medium and had theorised about the relative merits of narrative voice and dialogic drama in published criticism of BBC programmes such as Louis MacNeice's *The Rescue*, in 1945 (ibid:104 and Crook 2015: 202-203). *Animal Farm* was written with an almost daily soap opera ritual of reading and listening with his wife Eileen when she was still producing *Kitchen Front* programmes for the BBC. This exchange operated like an active radio drama workshop as Eileen's Ministry of Food colleague Lettice Cooper recalled: 'He read it aloud to her every night in bed as he was writing it – the piece that he'd done that day. ... And she used to tell us about it every morning, and she would quote bits out of it when we were having our coffee at Selfridge's across the road from the office' (Wadhams 184: 131).

Orwell's problem with his BBC adaptation was that his producer, Rayner Heppenstall, had no faith in the style of his narrative-linked script which he later described as having 'a certain lameness' (Orwell 1998: 122) and Orwell's biographer, Bernard Crick, described as 'a very stilted version' (Crick 1992: 493). When Heppenstall commissioned Orwell, he asked for 'as complete a dramatisation as possible, "with connecting narrative reduced to little more than statements of time and place"' (Orwell 1998: 118). Orwell resisted because, as he later wrote to Heppenstall: 'I must say I don't agree about there being too much narrator. If anything I thought there should have been more explanation' (ibid: 121). Heppenstall set about hacking at Orwell's radio drama script as though he were displacing revenge for his friend's previous 1935 attack on him with the shooting stick. Davison calculated that the producer excised 490 lines, 253 of which had been spoken by the narrator (ibid: 120). Davison observed: '...it is significant that the script was cut quite sharply to less than the full time allowed for the broadcast. About 150 lines more than necessary were cut' (ibid).

There is no evidence that Heppenstall had given his writer the courtesy of consultation. Rather, Heppenstall defied Orwell's artistic intention to add dialogic lines in his radio dramatisation that politically and artistically clarified a key turning point in his satire – the decision by the ascendant pigs, including Snowball, to appropriate the cow's milk and harvested apples. Daniel J. Leab, in *Orwell Subverted*, described this as censorship and as much of a perversion of the integrity of Orwell's original novel as the distortion

PAPER

achieved in the notorious Halas and Batchelor cartoon released in 1954 that had been funded by the US Central Intelligence Agency (Leab 2007: 139). Demonstrating the skill of a radio playwright who could write realistic and effective dialogue, Orwell had added the following exchange:

> Clover: Do you think that is quite fair to appropriate the apples?
> Molly: What, keep all the apples for themselves?
> Muriel: Aren't we to have any?
> Cow: I thought they were going to be shared out equally. (Lines 259-262, Orwell 1998: 153).

Davison comments: 'The significance of these lines was lost on the BBC producer, Rayner Heppenstall' (Orwell 2001: 233). In fact, Heppenstall was so determined to prove his point about the alleged inadequacies of Orwell's adaptation that two years after his death, he commissioned Peter Duval Smith to write a version with minimal narrative engagement that he further revised for broadcast in 1957 (Crick 1992: 648, note 29). The *Observer*'s radio critic, Giles Romilly, thought the Duvall Smith/Heppenstall version was 'sensitive, respectful and just' (*Observer* 1952). But he did complain that, with so much more dialogue than the original book, it rendered the characterisation of Napoleon as 'too much of a stadium martinet: he lacked insinuation and would have been ousted by even the stupidest horse' (ibid). He also thought the script had 'cut away some of the hard political skin of its original' and 'regretted the absence of the cat, one of Orwell's most animal animals' (ibid).

In 2013, the award-winning BBC Radio Drama department director, Alison Hindell, produced a new dramatisation of *Animal Farm* from Orwell's original adaptation script. The success of the production vindicates Orwell's decision aesthetically to balance narration with dramatic dialogue in order to fuse his original political and artistic purposes. The 2013 BBC version cast a female-voiced narrator and demonstrated that the balance of telling and showing the story enabled the essential deployment of irony that lies at the heart of the fable. Having a voice outside the characters and dramatic action gives the listener and, indeed, the original reader the chance to appreciate the dislocation of knowledge and observation between the diegetic world of the characters and the non-diegetic world of the audience.

There is also the opportunity to point the audience to indirect focalised meaning when the narrator can describe in the third person some aspect of a dialogic character's interiority and point of view. The original 1947 Orwell scripted radio dramatisation had been a success. Despite the liberties in editing exercised by the producer, Orwell was able to report that his domestic listening group at home in Canonbury Square, Islington, north London, 'all seemed to think it was good' (Orwell 1998: 120), and there had been good press notices. A critic and sinologist present grasped the intentions of the satire within the first few minutes. And the *Manchester Guardian*'s radio critic said the production had been splendid: 'One does not remember having heard a "fantasy" which took so strong a hold of the imagination' (*Manchester Guardian* 1947).

Orwell made the right decision not to adopt any of the animal characters as the omniscient narrative voice.[5] Orwell harnessed the potential of the effective double vision in animal allegory very effectively. As Ellen Leyburn argues, the form provides the writer with 'the power to keep his reader conscious simultaneously of the human traits satirized and of the animals as animals' (cited in Lee 1969: 107). If Benjamin had been the all-seeing, all-knowing narrator and audience confidante, the dramatisation would have lost the animal allegory's potential to prescribe 'two levels of perception which interact to purvey the irony in comparisons and contrasts' (ibid). Benjamin is the cynic of the farm and as Robert A. Lee observed: 'In his cynicism, Benjamin will come to see but be incapable of changing the reality of the revolution' (ibid: 111).

Foisting Benjamin with the function of narrative voice in a fable as subtle and politically allusive as *Animal Farm* would have also dissipated the integrity of his allegorical role. He would have had to have been more than the morose, pessimistic and indifferent bystander. Dramatisations of *Animal Farm* in other forms have lamentably failed to harness or express Orwell's aims and purposes. The 1954 Halas and Batchelor film not only substituted an alternative ending, but deracinated the animal characters of any human dialogue thus defeating the entire purpose of the original satirical fable (see Leab 2007). Peter Hall's 1984 theatrical dramatisation drained the original story of its exquisite irony, introducing an insipid and risible boy narrator who continually told the audience what it could already see. Hall's subversion of Benjamin's original characterisation with the ludicrous line: 'I shall protest. For the first time in my life I shall protest. (He confronts the PIGS.) You pigs have gone far enough' (Hall 1993: 59) before the sheep begin bleating 'Four legs good, two legs better!' defeats the entire purpose of developing Benjamin as the indifferent cynic who intervenes too late when his friend Boxer is about to be sent to his slaughter.

**PAPER**

In the novel, Benjamin is first characterised by narrative description as 'the oldest animal on the farm, and the worst tempered' (Orwell 1998: 2). He was cynical, and never laughed because there was nothing to laugh at' (ibid). In the radio dramatisation, Orwell skilfully introduces the donkey's first vocalisation with the word: 'Fleas' in answer to Major's peroration on 'Tell me, comrades,

TIM CROOK

what is the worst enemy that we animals have to contend with?' (ibid: 128). This is an elegant characterisation of Benjamin's selfish preoccupation with using his tail to keep the fleas off him while the old Berkshire boar is trying to inculcate his animal comrades with the idea that their worst enemy is Man. Benjamin is developed as a character unimpressed with political change; even revolution: 'I think that donkeys live a long time' (ibid 135) and: 'Everything happens sooner or later. On the other hand nothing ever changes except names' (ibid: 136). He lives by the motto that he is a survivor because 'None of you has ever seen a dead donkey' (ibid).

WAS BENJAMIN ORWELL'S ALTER AGO?

As the revolution decays into gradual exploitation, dictatorship and disillusionment, Benjamin can only contribute cynical observations such as 'Quite a coincidence, is it not?' (ibid: 156), and: 'You know I never meddle in such matters' when he can read how 'animalist' commandments are changing. Moreover, he is convinced that the only reason donkeys live a long time is 'that they never talk politics' (ibid: 174). While the witty all-knowing cynicism of Benjamin could represent Orwell's personal bitter-sweet experience of the abuse of political power, Orwell cannot be dismissed as an apolitical bystander who intervened and protested too late. Orwell as an individual had the political courage to speak out even to the extent that it undermined his relationship with his first publisher Victor Gollancz and made him a hate figure for many on the political left. But it is the horror and carnage of the show trial confessions and bloody executions at Animal Farm where Benjamin is shown physically ineffectual and politically irresponsible. He becomes the time-honoured passive bystander keeping silent for his own survival and wellbeing. It is the Benjamins of this world that Protestant pastor Martin Niemöller addressed with his poem that started: 'First they came for the Socialists, and I did not speak out – Because I was not a Socialist' and ended: 'Then they came for me – and there was no one left to speak for me' (Stein 2003: cover).

Orwell's characterisation raises a wider political metaphor about choice and the dilemma for Buridan's ass is, therefore, not hay or water but impartiality or activism. Orwell presents Benjamin as a symbol of political defeatism. The poetic and desperately pessimistic observation that 'things never had been, nor ever could be much better or much worse – hunger, hardship, and disappointment being, so he said, the unalterable law of life' (Orwell 1998: 87) is a complicity in the apolitical that will condemn him to tragedy and shatter his golden heart when the Pigs arrange for his devoted and broken friend Boxer to be converted into dog meat. His cry and call for action: 'Fools! Fools! Don't you see what is written on the side of that van?' (ibid: 180) is too late. The playful irony of animal fable darkens into the political tragedy and Orwellian 'heinous sin of irresponsible intelligence' (Lee 1969: 124). As Lee confirms: 'We know too much about Orwell's social beliefs from other contexts to assume that Benjamin speaks for Orwell' (ibid) and all of Orwell's political writing and activism counter the posture of 'assuming that only the very worst is inevitable in life, that change for the better is a delusion, and that the only alternative is a retreat into a social self-pity' (ibid: 124-125).

Orwell acted and intervened. He was agitational when undercover with the poor and homeless, observing Lancashire miners and their work and fighting against Fascism in the Spanish civil war to the extent of taking a bullet in the neck. In his essay 'Inside the Whale' (1940) about the American novelist Henry Miller, he wrote: 'In the world of 1935 it was hardly possible to remain politically indifferent' (Shelden 1992: 239). He had been told by Miller that going to Spain was 'sheer stupidity' and had found the novelist's selfishness shamelessly irresponsible (ibid: 274), so much so that he would later characterise Miller's position 'as a "willing Jonah" comfortably riding out storms in the warm belly of the whale' (ibid: 275). Benjamin might live a long time, but his conscience will be forever troubled. Knowing without action is the delusion of the fool. Politically, *Animal Farm* is about a society that cannot control its own language and Orwell says it is 'doomed to be oppressed in terms which deny it the very most elemental aspects of humanity' (Lee 1969: 127). Benjamin understands, but raises the issue so late his intelligence only serves to write his own epitaph.

CONCLUSION: MUCH MORE THAN JUST A 'LITTLE BOOK'

*Animal Farm* is much more than Orwell's self-deprecating descriptions of it as his 'little book' (Orwell 2006: 110) or 'little squib' (Wadhams 1984: 111). The ironic ambiguities also meant, as William Empson warned, that it had a huge capacity for being misunderstood: 'It is a form that inherently means more than the author means, when it is handled sufficiently well' (cited in Crick 1992: 492). Orwell was so surprised that it was being placed in the children's section of bookstores, he patrolled them personally to reposition the title on its proper shelf (Rodden and Rossi 2012: 79). The Queen, though, was able to obtain a copy by sending her footman to an anarchist bookshop (ibid).

Orwell properly retained authorial narrative focalisation away from his characters in his prose and audio-dramatic forms. Giving Benjamin the centre of consciousness would have distorted the complexity of Orwell's many political and artistic purposes. As John Newsinger concludes, up until his death Orwell retained political hope of a third way independent of both Russia and America, despite a considerable pessimism about the future (Newsinger 1999: 153-154). Benjamin exists more powerfully as the witness who does not speak; a metaphor for the journalist who tells lies by omission and politicians in power who look away.

TIM CROOK

NOTES

[1] Orwell said in his 1947 essay/memoir 'Such, Such Were the Joys' that: 'Most of the good memories of my childhood, and up to the age of about twenty, are in some way connected with animals' (Orwell 1971c: 395-396)

[2] Bernard Crick was also impressed with how Orwell could fuse powerful sociological writing with animal metaphor. In *The Road to Wigan Pier*, Orwell juxtaposed his memorable description of seeing from his train 'the usual exhausted face of the slum girl who is twenty-five and looks forty, thanks to miscarriages and drudgery' catching his eye with 'the most desolate, hopeless expression' he had ever seen with the image of two crows 'in a bare patch beside the line' courting and copulating (Crick 1992: 287)

[3] In 'Such, Such Were the Joys' Orwell describes the humiliating abuse of beatings he received while at St Cyprian's preparatory school in Eastbourne which began at the early age of eight over bed-wetting (Orwell 1971c: 379-384). It is also intriguing that he should observe approvingly later on in the essay that by 1947 'Beating, too, has become discredited, and has even been abandoned at many schools' (ibid 418)

[4] Crick has always been equivocal about whether 'Shooting the Elephant' was documentary truth or fiction (Crick 1992: 165-166). In a later revised edition of his biography he devoted several more pages of analysis to new research accounts continuing 'the elephant question' debate (ibid 586-589)

[5] I, however, was so convinced that Benjamin was the authorial voice or Orwell's alter ego that I decided to make the donkey the main narrative voice and point of view of a radio dramatisation for UK independent radio in 1988. My decision, I now realise, was creatively, artistically and politically flawed. I had been inspired by the ironic potential of a recording I had acquired of a donkey braying loudly. The sound seemed to symbolise an ambiguity of perception. I felt I could be listening to an agonising cry of deep existential despair, or ecstatic hilarity

REFERENCES

**Books**

Bowker, Gordon (2003) *George Orwell*, London: Little Brown

Crick, Bernard (1982) *George Orwell: A Life*, Harmondsworth, Middlesex: Penguin

Crook, Tim (2012) George Orwell: Cold War radio warrior?, Keeble, Richard Lance (ed.) *Orwell Today*, Bury St Edmunds, England: Abramis pp 102-122

Crook, Tim (2015) George Orwell and the radio imagination, Keeble, Richard Lance (ed.) *George Orwell Now!*, New York: Peter Lang pp 193-208

Davison, Peter (2007) *The Lost Orwell*, London: Timewell Press

Hall, Peter (1993) *The Play of George Orwell's* Animal Farm *Adapted by Peter Hall*, London: Heinemann Plays

Leab, Daniel J. (2007) *Orwell Subverted: The CIA and the Filming of* Animal Farm, Pennsylvania: The Pennsylvania State University Press

Keeble, Richard Lance (2016) 'There is always room for one more custard pie': Orwell's humour, Keeble, Richard Lance and Swick, David (eds) P*leasures of the Prose: Journalism and Humour*, Bury St Edmunds: Abramis pp 10-25

Lee, Robert A. (1969) *Orwell's Fiction*, London: University of Notre Dame Press

Meyers, Jeffrey (1975) A *Reader's Guide to George Orwell*, London Thames and Hudson

Newsinger, John (2002) *Orwell's Politics*, Oxford: Palgrave

Orwell, George (1969) *Selected Writings*, Bott, George (ed.) London: Heinemann Education Books Ltd

Orwell, George (1971a) *The Collected Essays, Journalism and Letters of George Orwell, Volume 1: An Age Like This 1920-1940*, Orwell, Sonia, Angus, Ian (eds) Harmondsworth, Middlesex: Penguin

Orwell, George (1971b) *The Collected Essays, Journalism and Letters of George Orwell, Volume 3: As I Please 1943-1945*, Orwell, Sonia and Angus, Ian (eds) Harmondsworth, Middlesex: Penguin

Orwell, George (1971c) *The Collected Essays, Journalism and Letters of George Orwell, Volume 4: In Front of Your Nose 1945-50*, Orwell, Sonia and Angus, Ian (eds) Harmondsworth, Middlesex: Penguin

Orwell, George (1998) *Collected Works of George Orwell, Volume 8: Animal Farm*, Davison, Peter (ed.) London: Secker & Warburg

Orwell, George (2001) *Orwell and Politics*, Davison, Peter (ed.) London: Penguin Classics

Orwell, George (2010) *Diaries*, Davison, Peter (ed.) London: Penguin Classics

Orwell, George (2015) *The Complete Poetry*, Venables, Dione (ed.) England: Finlay Publishers for the Orwell Society

Oxley, B. T. (1976) *George Orwell: Literature in Perspective*, London: Evans Brothers Limited

Rodden, John (2007) *The Cambridge Companion to George Orwell*, Cambridge: Cambridge University Press

Rodden, John (2009) *George Orwell: The Politics of Literary Reputation*, London: Transaction Publishers

Rodden, John and Rossi, John (2012) *The Cambridge Introduction to George Orwell*, Cambridge: Cambridge University Press

Shelden, Michael (1992) *Orwell: The Authorised Biography*, London: Minerva

Stansky, Peter and Abrahams, William (1972) *The Unknown Orwell*, London: Paladin Grafton Books

Stansky, Peter and Abrahams, William (1979) *Orwell: The Transformation*, London: Constable

Stein, Lou (2003) *Hitler Came For Niemöller: The Nazi War against Religion*, London: Pelican

Stock, Adam (2012) Of pigs and men: The politics of nature in the fiction of George Orwell, Keeble, Richard (ed.) *Orwell Today*, Bury St Edmunds, Suffolk, Abramis pp 46-61

Wadhams, Stephen (1984) *Remembering Orwell*, Harmondsworth, Middlesex: Penguin

Woodcock, George (1970) *The Crystal Spirit: A Study of George Orwell*, Harmondsworth, Middlesex: Penguin

**Newspapers**

Broadcasting review (1947) Our Radio Critic, *Manchester Guardian*, 18 January

Broadcasting *Animal Farm* (1952) By Our Radio Critic, *Manchester Guardian*, 25 February

Pigs and poets (1952) Romilly, Giles, *Observer*, 9 March

**Radio**

BBC Radio Four (2013) *Animal Farm* adapted from his own novel by George Orwell, directed and produced by Alison Hindell, 26 January

**Websites**

Keeble, Richard Lance (2016) Orwell, the university and the university of life, 10 January. Available online at http://www.orwellsociety.com/orwll-the-university-and-the-university-of-life/, accessed on 16 July 2016

## TIM CROOK

**Unpublished manuscript**
Crook, Tim (1988) Dramatisation of George Orwell's *Animal Farm*, for Independent Radio Drama Productions, IRDP archive, Department of Media and Communications, Goldsmiths, University of London. (Although commissioned, this script did not achieve production due to rights restrictions applying in the late 1980s.)

## NOTE ON THE CONTRIBUTOR

Tim Crook is a Professor in the Department of Media and Communications at Goldsmiths, University of London where he has originated and co-organised an annual George Orwell Studies conference. He is also Visiting Professor of Broadcast Journalism at Birmingham City University, chair of the Professional Practices Board of the Chartered Institute of Journalists and a member of the committee of the Orwell Society. He has been researching and writing a book for Ashgate titled *George Orwell on the Radio*. His chapter 'George Orwell: Cold War radio warrior?' was published in the volume *Orwell Today* in 2012 and 'George Orwell and the Radio Imagination' in the volume *George Orwell Now* in 2015.

PAPER

# 'The End was Contained in the Beginning':

## Orwell's Kyauktada and Oceania

### FIRAS A. J. AL-JUBOURI

*Preceding his masterpieces* Animal Farm *(1945) and* Nineteen Eighty-Four *(1949), George Orwell's* Burmese Days *(1934) critiqued colonialism and its authoritarian temperament. In Burma, Orwell was awakened to the evils intrinsic to colonial societies that are built on deeply-felt and institutionally-sanctioned racism, corrupt government officials and relentless economic exploitation. This paper presents the first detailed analysis of the commonalities between* Burmese Days *and* Nineteen Eighty-Four. *Although comparisons have been drawn between the two novels before, they neither substantiate the significance of Orwell's colonial experience in shaping his long-term dislike of authority nor accentuate the complexities of colonialism as an exploitative system that is dystopian in nature. This paper provides an alternative ideological and thematic connection examining the affinities between the two novels that marked the beginning and end of Orwell's fictional writing: his first anti-colonial chronicle and his last dystopia.*

Keywords: *Burmese Days, Nineteen Eighty-Four,* imperialism, dystopia

PERSPECTIVE

If ever there was an author whose life and work blended with the utmost intensity, that author would be George Orwell (1903-1950), the pseudonym adopted by Eric Arthur Blair in 1933. He was a writer whose subject matter was determined by the character of his age. He acquired an emotional outlook that challenged totalitarianism and championed the common people and is renowned for his critical appraisal of political power that rests on force and fraud. He cultivates a natural, simple style to share his experiences of colonial life, which were his source of art and inspiration, in his first fiction *Burmese Days* (1934) and it later found its greatest expression in his dystopia *Nineteen Eighty-Four* (1949). Orwell served in the Indian Imperial Police in Burma for five years (1922-1927): 'When I came home on leave in 1927 I was already half determined to throw up my job, and one sniff of

## FIRAS A. J. AL-JUBOURI

English air decided me. I was not going back to be a part of that evil despotism' (2001b [1937]: 137-138). The evil of despotism became a theme that enthralled his thoughts and actions and infused his writing throughout the following two decades.

The earliest references to the themes and symbols in *Nineteen Eighty-Four* are found in his 'As I Please' column contributions in *Tribune*. On 4 February 1944, three years before writing and five years before publishing *Nineteen Eighty-Four*, Orwell wrote that 'the really frightening thing about totalitarianism is not that it commits "atrocities" but that it attacks the concept of objective truth: it claims to control the past as well as the future' (*Collected Works of George Orwell, CWGO* 16: 89). Two months later in the same column, he also added that totalitarianism was 'visibly on the up-grade' in many parts of the world: 'Out in the street the loudspeakers bellow, the flags flutter from the rooftops, the police with their tommy-guns prowl to and fro, the face of the Leader, four feet wide, glares from every hoarding' (ibid: 172). These images starkly resemble the streets of Oceania where the posters displaying the 'blackmoustachio'd face' of Big Brother 'gazed down from every commanding corner' and the 'helicopter [police patrol] skimmed down between the roofs ... snooping into people's windows' (Orwell 2013 [1949]: 4). Winston is 'thirty-nine' in 1984 which makes his birth date roughly in 1945 and his recollections are paradoxically those of the physical horrors of a war and its human degradation that continued beyond its actual end in 1945 (ibid: 3). Reviving these emotional memories furnish the background of Oceania. Thus, far from being a picture of the totalitarianism of the future, *Nineteen Eighty-Four* is a realistic picture of the totalitarianism that culminated throughout the previous decade and remained a constant concern for Orwell.

Moreover, on 18 May 1944, Orwell sent a letter to Noel Willmett, who had asked 'whether totalitarianism, leader-worship etc. are really on the up-grade' given 'that they are not apparently growing in [England] and the USA'. Orwell's reply revealed some of the most defining themes and metaphors of his final fiction *Nineteen Eighty-Four*

> [Any dictator] can't say that two and two are five, because for the purposes of, say, ballistics they have to make four. But if the sort of world that I am afraid of arrives, a world of two or three great superstates which are unable to conquer one another, two and two could become five if the fuhrer wished it. That, so far as I can see, is the direction in which we are actually moving, though, of course, the process is reversible. ...
>
> On the whole the English intelligentsia have opposed Hitler, but only at the price of accepting Stalin. Most of them are perfectly ready for dictatorial methods, secret police, systematic

falsification of history etc. so long as they feel that it is on 'our' side. Indeed the statement that we haven't a Fascist movement in England largely means that the young, at this moment, look for their fuhrer elsewhere. One can't be sure that that won't change, nor can one be sure that the common people won't think ten years hence as the intellectuals do now. I *hope* they won't, I even trust they won't, but if so it will be at the cost of a struggle (italics in the original) (*CWGO* 16: 191).

Again, the letter refers explicitly to four important themes of *Nineteen Eighty-Four*: three great superstates ruling the world yet 'unable to conquer one another', the metaphor for mind control when 'two and two could become five if the fuhrer [Big Brother or O'Brien] wished it', the 'systematic falsification of history' and the italicised 'hope' that refers to the common people and directly alludes to Orwell's statement, '*if there is hope*, wrote Winston, *it lies in the proles*' (italics in the original) (Orwell 2013 [1949]: 80). These examples were Orwell's earliest direct reference to the ideas and themes that he later expounded and examined in *Nineteen Eighty-Four*. However, this paper proposes older origins for *Nineteen Eighty-Four*, going back to Orwell's first real brush with authoritarianism and power politics: his service in the British Imperial Police in Burma, an experience that shaped his understanding and hatred of oppression and colonial exploitation and instilled a fear of power politics that became more real as the ideologies of the 1930s gave way to the totalitarian war, atrocities and dictatorships of the 1940s.

ORWELLIAN BLUEPRINTS: THE COLONIAL ORIGINS OF ORWELL'S DYSTOPIA

For five years in Burma, Orwell dressed in uniform with shining black boots, was armed with guns and a sense of moral superiority; hence, he represented the authority, power and reputation of the Imperial Police Force and kept this part of the British Empire in line. However, the reality of his job and what he represented exposed the dark side of authority. Ranajit Guha explains that Orwell went to the East 'without knowing much about it or what to expect there and was shocked to see how tyrannical British rule was in South Asia, how cruelly it oppressed its subjects, and how strongly the latter resented the raj' (1997: 489). Consequently, he promptly returned to England and resigned. Just as quickly, he began his career as a writer and used the pen-name 'George Orwell' as a pseudonym. He dressed as a tramp and walked into the poorest parts of London to document the stories of the down-and-outs.

Orwell based his first novel, *Burmese Days*, on his encounters in the Far East. The Burmese experience was both morally exhausting yet politically enlightening. In *The Road to Wigan Pier* (of 1937) he declares: 'I was in the Indian Police for five years, and by the end of that time I hated the imperialism I was serving with a bitterness which I probably cannot make clear.' He goes on to explain his role as an accomplice in tyranny: 'It is not possible to be part of such a system without recognising it as an unjustifiable tyranny' (Orwell 2001b [1937]: 134). Orwell elsewhere calls imperialism 'an evil thing' (*CWGO* 10: 501). In a letter to Geoffrey Gorer, dated 15 September 1937, Orwell explains the relationship between Fascism and imperialism:

> Fascism ... is only a development of capitalism, and the mildest democracy ... is liable to turn into Fascism when the pinch comes. ... [British] rule in India ... is just as bad as German Fascism. ... If one collaborates with a capitalist-imperialist government in a struggle 'against Fascism', i.e. against a rival imperialism, one is simply letting Fascism in by the back door (*CWGO* 11: 80).

The above statement provides the basis of Orwell's animosity towards totalitarian tendencies in the politics of his day. He was not terrified of standing against tyranny and exploitation, whether with his pen or with his rifle as he did in Spain; what horrifies him is that power politics would infect the minds of those whose job it is to expose it, the intelligentsia. 'The power-worship which is the new religion of Europe,' Orwell states in 1941, 'has infected the English intelligentsia' (*CWGO* 12: 394). In his essay 'Rudyard Kipling' (1942), Orwell highlights the growing significance of power and Kipling's colonial character: 'No one, in our time, believes in any sanction greater than military power; no one believes that it is possible to overcome force except by greater force. There is no "law", there is only power.' He also emphasises that imperialism is a stage that precedes Fascism and totalitarianism when he declares that 'those who pretend otherwise are either intellectual cowards, or power-worshippers under a thin disguise, or have simply not caught up with the age they are living in. Kipling's outlook is pre-Fascist'. Hence, the force of imperialism can only be conquered by the greater force of totalitarianism. In addition, Orwell considers Kipling as 'the prophet of British Imperialism in its expansionist phase' and 'the unofficial historian of the British Army' arguing that 'all his confidence, his bouncing vulgar vitality, sprang out of limitations which no Fascist or near-Fascist shares' (*CWGO* 13: 152). In the last years of his life, Orwell was involved with the evils of totalitarian power; in the first years, he was involved with the evil power of imperialism.

The years between the First and Second World Wars proved to be pivotal for Orwell and his exploration of the themes of colonialism and totalitarian power politics. Daniel Bivona asserts: 'British imperial rule generally during this inter-war period was undertaken in a "bad faith" which was deepened by the growing incompatibility between the desire to be powerful and the desire to seem noble'

(2001: 158). Orwell's *Burmese Days* dramatises this 'bad faith' of the Empire, written by a novelist who was also a colonialist deeply entangled with advancing the very imperialist view the novelist in him rejects. He conceives the Empire as a bureaucratic juggernaut indifferently crushing both the colonised and those British officials employed in its service beneath its wheels.

Orwell's literary reputation achieved its highest renown towards the end of his life with the publications of *Animal Farm* (1945) and *Nineteen Eighty-Four* (1949) turning him into one of the most esteemed prophetic writers of the twentieth century. Together with *Burmese Days*, these three novels essentially narrate the story of Burma's modern history. The history of the country starts with *Burmese Days*, which narrates the country's era under British colonialism. Soon after independence from Britain in 1948, a military dictator sealed Burma from the outside world, initiated socialism and through bad planning, corruption, mismanagement and dictatorship reduced Burma into an extremely poor country. A similar situation is narrated in Orwell's *Animal Farm*, an allegorical tale about a socialist revolution gone wrong in which a group of pigs revolt against the human farmers yet through corruption, manipulation deceit and ruthlessness run the farm into ruin. Lastly, in *Nineteen Eighty-Four*, Orwell's account of a depressing dystopia draws a distressingly truthful picture of Burma in the twentieth and twenty-first centuries, a country governed by one of the world's most coldblooded and determined dictatorships. Emma Larkin suggests that 'Orwell wrote not just one novel about the country, but three: a trilogy comprised of *Burmese Days*, *Animal Farm* and *Nineteen Eighty-Four*' (2011: 2). In her book *The Origins of Totalitarianism*, Hannah Arendt locates the origins of 'totalitarianism' in the troubled colonies (1951: 185). Similarly, Sant Singh Bal believe that in Orwell's *Nineteen Eighty-Four*, Oceania's political hierarchy is essentially colonial in nature, 'an alien elite [Inner Party] governing the great mass of white "natives"' (1981: 75). While Christopher Hitchens adds another influence to Orwell's dystopian prophecy, which is the Spanish Civil War. He considers the 'two crucial epiphanies' that influenced Orwell's political mind-set to be those 'in the torrid and sultry climates of Burma and Catalonia' (2003: 2).

In both *Burmese Days* and *Nineteen Eighty-Four*, the protagonists' failures in their attempts to challenge the authoritarian establishment and to maintain meaningful relationships reflect the difficulties of sustaining nonconformity and common decency. In *Burmese Days*, the central character, John Flory, is portrayed as a critic of the colonial system; he is also a solitary figure who lapses in and out of allegiance to the system he abhors. In *Nineteen Eighty-Four*, the main protagonist, Winston Smith, is also an ardent critic of the system, yet endeavours to serve it as best he can. Both

PAPER

FIRAS A. J. AL-JUBOURI

Flory and Winston nurture their weakened sense of identity by avoiding contact with others. They operate in their environments in restricted ways. The physical maladies Orwell gives them – false teeth, varicose veins, or birthmarks – are trivial handicaps but they reinforce their alienation from the real world, which is made starker by their unorthodox political aspirations.

Mark Connelly sees both protagonists as 'remarkably alike' (1987: 41). Flory's world, which is on the outskirts of an empire, is congruous with Winston's London of Airstrip One, which is one region of a bigger part of the world called Oceania, both signifying tyranny. Both are middle-aged and have an instinctive dislike for their peers, the mainstream ideology, and the moral degradation that isolation imposes on them. Yet both are cogs in the wheels of despotisms, doing their part either in advancing colonial exploitation through Flory's timber company or in enhancing totalitarian expediency through Winston's rewriting and refabricating of history in the Ministry of Truth. Friendless and unloved, they seek escape in gin and prostitutes. Both seek to rebel, to assert their individuality, and both are eventually destroyed.

Orwell's dystopia ironically substantiates the essential theses of *Burmese Days* – the terrors of Oceania are made more efficient than those of Kyauktada, but the desperation and despair of the individual in those societies remain qualitatively the same. Flory warns of a time when 'all the gramophones [will be] playing the same tune' (2001a [1934]: 40), foreshadowing Orwell's fears of the 'lies that streamed out of the telescreens', the orthodoxy of Newspeak and the slogans of *Nineteen Eighty-Four* (2013 [1949]: 85). Hence, Flory's torment is fated to drive him to the suicide which is orchestrated from the beginning to conform to the story's dramatic end and, more importantly, to its structural outline. In the same vein, Winston Smith's final surrender is a result of desperation, ending with the death of his soul and literal death of the body, which are similar forms of self-sacrifice since the novel ends with: 'He had won the victory over himself. He loved big brother' (ibid: 342). The major difference lies in the state of the soul before deliverance: Flory dies with resentment and shame while Winston dies with repentance and satisfaction.

On the other hand, the anti-hero U Po Kyin, Sub-divisional Magistrate of Kyauktada in Upper Burma, is an autocrat of totalitarian proportions, presented as a personification of Big Brother in Kyauktada, one who represents the native counterpart of O'Brien. U Po Kyin climbed the ladder of success by exploiting the reputations and ruin of others: 'His brain, though cunning, was quite barbaric, and it never worked except for some definite end.' He symbolises the shortcomings of progressive imperialism wherein it invariably sabotages its own undertaking by driving a deep wedge between different sectors of the colonial people. Being a thoroughly corrupt Sub-divisional Magistrate, he accepts bribes and uses gangs to enforce his will upon others. He shares in the proceeds of robberies which take place in the district and hence his supporters remain loyal. No accusation can stand against his cunning; they are simply discredited 'with strings of suborned witnesses, following this up by counter-accusations which left him in a stronger position than ever' (2001a [1934]: 4, 3). Hence, he kept the British respectful and satisfied and his fellow Burmese subjugated and apprehensive. He was a large, fifty-six year-old-man 'yet shapely and even beautiful in his grossness. ... His face was vast, yellow and quite unwrinkled, and his eyes were tawny'. U Po Kyin rose to status through trickery, forgery and brutality: 'He was practically invulnerable, because he was too fine a judge of men ever to choose a wrong instrument, and also because he was too absorbed in intrigue ever to fail through carelessness or ignorance' (ibid: 1, 3). O'Brien is a prominent member of the Inner Party. He is a 'large, burly man with a thick neck and a coarse, humorous, brutal face. In spite of his formidable appearance he had a certain charm of manner' (2013 [1949]: 13). Winston suspects he is very intelligent and may share his subversive views of society. When O'Brien discloses that he does have radical thoughts, Winston is eager to join him in a secret underground movement led by Emmanuel Goldstein, the Brotherhood. The group aims to overthrow the Party. Winston does not understand that O'Brien is covertly loyal to the Inner Party and that the secret underground group is solely a trap made by the Party to detect potential insubordinates. O'Brien deceives Winston and later becomes his interrogator and intimidator. It is he who discloses to Winston that the true, harsh reality of the Party is to maintain power for power's sake. Like U Po Kyin, O'Brien cares only for power.

However, the analogy between Orwell's initial experience of authoritarianism and later prediction of totalitarianism is both deeply connected with, and broadly representative of, his personal journey to dystopia. The idea of representing a colonial society as a totalitarian regime reflects Orwell's antagonism and frustration towards the empire and colonial appropriation. Kyauktada represents all that Oceania stands for. As George Woodcock states: 'The white society of Upper Burma, as Orwell portrays it, is the earliest prototype of the ruling elite of Oceania which he described fourteen years later in *Nineteen Eighty-Four*' (2005: 62). Yet, the parallels established by Orwell's critics fail to highlight the bigger picture, the political connections between colonialism and totalitarianism: the roots of *Nineteen Eighty-Four* as a dystopia are embedded in Burmese soil. Orwell did note an equivocal connection between colonial despotism and dystopian totalitarianism on account of historical and political expediency. In 'Shooting an Elephant' (1936), Orwell confessed the following: 'I did not even know that the British Empire is dying, still less did I know that it is a great deal better than the younger empires that are going to supplant it' (*CWGO* 10: 501). In the letter to Noel Willmett, Orwell makes a similar connection between British imperialism and the rise of totalitarianism, which is based on a choice of evils: 'I know enough of British imperialism not to like it, but I would support it against Nazism or Japanese imperialism, as the lesser evil' (*CWGO* 16: 191). Yet, what makes one dying empire better than those that are going to supplant it? And when does the lesser evil become the bigger evil that Orwell associates with Nazism (totalitarianism) and Japanese imperialism since both are essentially evil regardless of size and magnitude? The following sections will explore the relationships between *Burmese Days* and *Nineteen Eighty-Four* to elaborate on Orwell's view of imperialism as a lesser evil than totalitarianism.

THE IDEOLOGICAL AND ECONOMIC AFFINITIES: KYAUKTADA AND OCEANIA

In *Burmese Days* and *Nineteen Eighty-Four*, geopolitical necessities dictate economic strategies. The main objective of British colonialism was primarily economic: to exploit natural resources and to create dependence on foreign materials even if it meant ruining or disabling the existing native economy. In fact, in his conversation with Dr Veraswami, who is an intelligent and educated Madrasi Brahmin service doctor and devotedly pro-British, Flory makes this colonial motif quite clear:

> 'My dear doctor ... how can you make out that we are in this country for any purpose except to steal? It's so simple. The official holds the Burman down while the businessman goes through his pockets. Do you suppose my firm, for instance, could get its timber contracts if the country weren't in the hands of the British? Or the other timber firms, or the oil companies, or the miners and planters and traders? How could the Rice Ring go on skinning the unfortunate peasant if it hadn't the Government behind it? The British Empire is simply a device for giving trade monopolies to the English – or rather to gangs of Jews and Scotchmen' (2001a [1934]: 38).

Orwell's allusion to the 'official' and the 'businessman' are illustrative of his views on the economy in Burma and wherever land is taken by force and exploited by fraud. Veraswami's answer only affirms the paradox of the discussion: 'You say you are here to trade? Of course you are. Could the Burmese trade for themselves? Can they make machinery, ships, railways, roads? They are helpless without you.' Clearly, Veraswami believes in the 'white man's burden' colonial motif. He argues that in colonial hands, the forests are 'improved', arguing that 'while your businessmen develop the resources of our country, your officials are civilizing us, elevating us to their level, from pure public spirit. It is a magnificent record of self-sacrifice' (ibid: 39). More importantly, Flory makes the point that 'trade monopolies' and racism are not uniquely characteristic of the British; they can be disguised under ethnic or nationalistic preferences and pretexts. Michael Shelden points out that Orwell had been pressured by his publisher, Harper's, to change the main characters in *Burmese Days* from officials to businessmen in order to 'reduce the libel danger' (1995: 202).[1] In a letter to Dr W. M. C. Harrowes, dated 15 November 1946, Orwell states that 'Harper's asked me to make some small alterations ... the chief one was to change a few characters from government servants into business men so as to make the book less directly an attack on British imperialism' (*CWGO* 18: 485). However, Shelden and Harper's failed to perceive that the focus on businessmen, in fact, augments Orwell's trenchant criticism of imperialism by increasing the emphasis on its economic basis. Flory's emphasis on economic exploitation as the primary motivation behind British imperialism is underpinned by the fact that the prominent protagonists in the story, Flory, Ellis and Lackersteen, are businessmen rather than 'government servants'.

The Party's economic strategy in *Nineteen Eighty-Four* exists to serve a higher political and dictatorial purpose. It is not so much dedicated to exploiting foreign natural resources as to keeping the workforce busy and in servitude, and to stalling or stopping any kind of general economic development and prosperity. Its strategy is more attuned to a future totalitarian structure that is flawless and timeless: to exhaust the surplus of natural resources, exploit the work force but keep chronic shortage and to maintain a state of war that ensures the stability of Big Brother. The Ministry of Plenty is wholly responsible for the economic affairs of Oceania. It administers continuous rationing and the distribution of goods, and exploits the media for such purposes. The chocolate rations, for example, inspired 'demonstrations to thank Big Brother for raising the chocolate ration to twenty grammes a week. And only yesterday, [Winston] reflected, it had been announced that the ration was to be *reduced* to twenty grammes a week' (italics in the original) (2013 [1949]: 67).

Emmanuel Goldstein's book, *The Theory and Practice of Oligarchical Collectivism*, reflects on the shortcomings of past totalitarian regimes and provides adroit strategies for creating and maintaining totalitarianism.[2] In this book, Orwell outlines his vision of the future, depicting a world governed by three super-states contesting, by war, the possession of wealth and plenty for the ruling clique:

> A rough quadrilateral with its corners at Tangier, Brazzaville, Darwin and Hong Kong, containing within it about a fifth of the population of the earth. It is ... a bottomless reserve of cheap

labour. Whichever power controls equatorial Africa, or the countries of the Middle East, or Southern India, or the Indonesian Archipelago, disposes also of the bodies of ... millions of ... hard-working coolies. The inhabitants of these areas, reduced more or less openly to the status of slaves, pass continually from conqueror to conqueror, and are expended like so much coal or oil in the race to turn out more armaments, to capture more territory, to control more labour power, to turn out more armaments, to capture more territory, and so on indefinitely (ibid: 216, 217).

The extract outlines the method of exploiting labour and expending materials 'indefinitely'. This kind of strategy, where the end is justified by a continuous and circular means, beguiles and overwhelms the exploited and renders them incapacitated and exhausted both physically and morally. This endless exploitation of 'cheap labour' is the same form of slavery that Ellis uses to justify his exploitation and abuse of the Burmese, whom he considers 'a set of damn black swine who've been slaves since the beginning of history' (2001a [1934]: 22). Abusing 'cheap labour' also illustrates the irony of acquiring comfort through political deception, which can be traced back to the incongruous ideology of British colonial policies:

> The high standard of life we enjoy in England depends upon our keeping a tight hold on the Empire, particularly ... India and Africa. Under the capitalist system, in order that England may live in comparative comfort, a hundred million Indians must live on the verge of starvation – an evil state of affairs (2001b [1937]: 148)

The need to gain economic and cultural monopoly and 'comparative comfort' through the decimation and deprivation of other weaker nations is the parent of all totalitarian evil. The 'tight hold on the Empire' which squeezes wealth out of India and Africa and creates an 'evil state of affairs' is taken to another level in Oceania, where the iron fist of totalitarian power controls a 'rough quadrilateral' of oppressed colonies with bottomless reserves of disposable coolies who are endlessly exploited to maintain a certain way of life. Winston's visit to O'Brien's flat attests to the 'comparative comfort' the Inner Party members acquire for being authoritarian:

> The whole atmosphere of the huge block of flats, the richness and spaciousness of everything, the unfamiliar smells of good food and good tobacco, the silent and incredibly rapid lifts sliding up and down, the white-jacketed servants hurrying to and fro – everything was intimidating. ... The passage down which he led them was softly carpeted, with cream-papered walls and white wainscoting, all exquisitely clean. ... Winston could not

remember ever to have seen a passageway whose walls were not grimy from the contact of human bodies (2013 [1949]: 194, 195).

However, the exploitation and subjugation of the masses needs to be justified ideologically. In both *Burmese Days* and *Nineteen Eighty-Four*, Orwell justifies how political ideology demarcates economic expediency: stealing and scuttling in one, and sustaining and subduing in another. Flory suggests that the British have intentionally crippled those Indian and Burmese industries that might compete against their own. Colonialism enforces the stagnation of the colonies so that they become weak and easily exploited, while the colonial power grows strong and maintains its benefits and prestige indefinitely:

> 'We've never taught a single useful manual trade to the Indians. We daren't; frightened of the competition in industry. We've even crushed various industries. Where are the Indian muslins now? Back in the forties or thereabouts they were building sea-going ships in India, and manning them as well. Now you couldn't build a seaworthy fishing boat there. In the eighteenth century the Indians cast guns that were at any rate up to the European standard. Now, after we've been in India a hundred and fifty years, you can't make so much as a brass cartridge case in the whole continent. The only Eastern races that have developed at all quickly are the independent ones. I won't instance Japan, but take the case of Siam' (2001a [1934]: 39).

Unmistakably, Orwell is intensifying his direct attack on the empire, calling it a 'trade' monopoly having no real purpose but to 'steal' and, in the process, crush any possible 'competition in industry'. Franz Fanon concludes that Europe is literally responsible for 'the creation of the Third World' in the sense that its materials, wealth and labour are from the colonies, where 'the sweat and corpses of blacks, Arabs, Indians, and Asians' have fuelled the 'opulence' of Europe (2004: 58, 53).

In the last article he published in Paris, in *Le Progrès Civique*, 'How a nation is exploited: The British Empire in Burma' (1929), which was translated from the French in the *Collected Works*, Orwell provides a brief history of Burma. Although he states that his article will discuss 'the good and bad sides of British administration in Burma from an economic and a political standpoint', the article focuses more on the negative rather than the positive side, if any, of colonialism (*CWGO* 10: 144). He notes that Burma is 'one of the richest [countries] in the world' since it 'abounds in natural resources which are only just beginning to be exploited'. Accordingly, Orwell ironically notes that 'thanks to the process euphemistically known as "peaceful penetration", which means, in plain English, "peaceful annexation", the British have gained possession of it: a state of affairs that is the "logical result of any imperialist policy"' (ibid: 143). Orwell then examines the various ways through which the Burmese are being exploited but then merely stresses that this is happening because they are unaware of it:

> It is true that the British seized the mines and the oil wells. It is true that they control timber production. It is true that all sorts of middlemen, brokers, millers, exporters, have made colossal fortunes from rice without the producer – that is the peasant – getting a thing out of it.
>
> It is also true that the get-rich-quick businessmen who made their pile from rice, petrol etc. are not contributing as they should be to the well-being of the country, and that their money, instead of swelling local revenues in the form of taxes, is sent abroad to be spent in England.
>
> If we are honest, it is true that the British are robbing and pilfering Burma quite shamelessly.
>
> But we must stress that the Burmese hardly notice it *for the moment*. Their country is so rich, their population so scattered, their needs, like those of all Orientals, so slight that they are not conscious of being exploited (italics in the original) (ibid: 145).

The phrase 'it is true' is repeated four times in the above passage to emphasise the economic exploitation and the benefits of 'peaceful penetration', while 'for the moment' is italicised to imply the inevitable agitations and problems that are looming once the Burmese discover the reality of colonialism and exploitation. Thus, Orwell argues that 'British politics in Burma is the same as in India' where, 'industrially speaking', both countries were 'deliberately kept in ignorance'. This means that the Burmese can only produce 'basic necessities, made by hand' and not, for example, motorcars rifles, clocks, electric-light bulbs and they 'would be incapable of building or sailing an ocean-going vessel'. At the same time, they have been made dependent on 'certain machine-made articles' made by the English factories and consequently, the products 'find an important outlet in a country incapable of manufacturing them herself' (ibid: 146).

Orwell also argues that education for the natives can provoke sedition and rebellion: 'The most dangerous enemies of the government are the young men of the educated classes. If these classes were more numerous and were *really* educated, they could perhaps raise the revolutionary banner. But they are not' (italics in the original). The last phrase, 'they are not', is a comforting one that ironically guarantees the fact that presently, no substantial education is provided for the common natives except for those who were 'educated in England, and belong ... as a result to the small class of the well-to-do'. He goes on to assure the colonialists that 'because there are no educated classes, public opinion, which could press for rebellion against England, is non-existent' (ibid: 145). Orwell concludes by stating that the Burmese relationship with the British Empire is that of 'slave and master': while the master's control is 'despotic', 'self-interested' and needs to end (ibid: 146).

Similarly, in Oceania, the colonial strategy evolves to prescribe economic principles and to inscribe degradation, inertia and ignorance upon society, a strategy that is sanctioned and justified by the Party slogan 'Ignorance is Strength' through which they overcome the maladies of imperialism (2013 [1949]: 6). The natives of Burma are analogues to the proles in Oceania. If one was to replace the word proletarian for natives the meaning would still be the same:

> From the proletarians nothing is to be feared. Left to themselves, they will continue from generation to generation and from century to century, working, breeding, and dying, not only without any impulse to rebel, but without the power of grasping that the world could be other than it is. They could only become dangerous if the advance of industrial technique made it necessary to educate them more highly; but, since military and commercial rivalry are no longer important, the level of popular education is actually declining. What opinions the masses hold, or do not hold, is looked on as a matter of indifference. They can be granted intellectual liberty because they have no intellect. In a Party member, on the other hand, not even the smallest deviation of opinion on the most unimportant subject can be tolerated (ibid: 240).

Another problem of imperialism is also cunningly handled where all races and people are equal in the eyes of Big Brother, albeit the survival and continuity of despotic, self-interested authority is what counts. Admission to the Outer or Inner Party, for example, is by examination that is taken at the age of sixteen and not by heredity or skin colour:

> Nor is there any racial discrimination, or any marked domination of one province by another. Jews, Negroes, South Americans of pure Indian blood are to be found in the highest ranks of the Party, and the administrators of any area are always drawn from the inhabitants of that area. In no part of Oceania do the inhabitants have the feeling that they are a colonial population ruled from a distant capital. Oceania has no capital, and its titular head is a person whose whereabouts nobody knows. Except that English is its chief lingua franca and Newspeak its official language, it is not centralized in any way. Its rulers are not held together by blood-ties but by adherence to a common doctrine (ibid: 238-239).

Furthermore, the Party hinders technological progress in certain areas and wealth, and encourages ignorance, which were hallmark characteristics of the colonial 'Third World'. It encourages mechanisation and progress but only when constrained to create a hierarchical society and to help safeguard the Party and the state. Thus, the need for a totalitarian strategy that maintains poverty, progress and mechanisation simultaneously: 'The problem was how to keep the wheels of industry turning without increasing the real wealth of the world. Goods must be produced, but they must not be distributed. And in practice the only way of achieving this was by continuous warfare' (ibid: 220). The colonial policy Orwell discusses in *Burmese Days*, of keeping others illiterate and their economy backward in order to keep them vulnerable, is further modified in *Nineteen Eighty-Four* to ensure that the wheels of industry kept turning without increasing the wealth of the nations. The answer to the problem is to create and sustain a state of indefinite war to expend labour:

> War is a way of shattering to pieces, or pouring into the stratosphere, or sinking in the depths of the sea, materials which might otherwise be used to make the masses too comfortable, and hence, in the long run, too intelligent. Even when weapons of war are not actually destroyed, their manufacture is still a convenient way of expending labour power without producing anything that can be consumed (ibid: 220).

Indeed, there are other sinister intentions behind the act of continuous war: to instil poverty, ignorance and hierarchy in society:

> In principle the war effort is always so planned as to eat up any surplus that might exist after meeting the bare needs of the population. In practice the needs of the population are always underestimated, with the result that there is a chronic shortage of half the necessities of life; but this is looked on as an advantage. It is deliberate policy to keep even the favoured groups somewhere near the brink of hardship, because a general state of scarcity increases the importance of small privileges and thus magnifies the distinction between one group and another (ibid: 220-221).

Thus, the production and distribution of goods and wealth in Oceania is effectively constrained to keep the general living standards at bare minimum. It is sabotaged intentionally so that scarcity and being on 'the brink of hardship' make small and irrelevant privileges seem grand and significant, which in turn affirm class differences 'between one group and another'.

Orwell's rejection of colonial appropriation is undertaken not only to focus on the economic agenda with theft as his central metaphor, but also to reflect the growth of his political understanding of totalitarian trends and sinister administrative agendas, ideas that he grappled with for the rest of his life.

## CONCLUSION

Orwell's first and last novels share much that connects the main characters and motifs. John V. Knapp asserts that, in *Burmese Days*, 'Orwell has given us the *experience* of living in a totalitarian regime where human beings are assumed to be political objects' (italics in the original) (1981: 297). In *Nineteen Eighty-Four*, for the Inner Party, as well as for the white minority in Kyauktada, subjugation, standardisation and submission guarantee semblances of security, stability and superiority. However, the deviant individual who does not conform threatens colonial or totalitarian order and has to be either re-indoctrinated and/or killed by those whom he threatens. The research has highlighted the major affinities between colonialism and totalitarianism, an association that is implied by a letter Orwell wrote to Katharine, Duchess of Atholl, on 15 November 1945, in which he refused an invitation to speak on the platform of the League of European Freedom because he was not prepared to associate himself with a Conservative organisation that supported imperialism:

> I cannot associate myself with an essentially Conservative body which claims to defend democracy in Europe but has nothing to say about British imperialism. It seems to me that one can only denounce the crimes now being committed in Poland, Jugoslavia etc. if one is equally insistent on ending Britain's unwanted rule in India. I belong to the Left and must work inside it, much as I hate Russian totalitarianism and its poisonous influence in this country (*CWGO* 17: 385).

It was hypocritical to denounce Russian intervention in Poland, claiming to defend democracy in Europe, without equally condemning British imperialism. He saw both the colonial and the totalitarian projects as having a common ideological matrix.

Orwell's Burmese experience was a major turning point in his life because he witnessed the manipulative roles of the colonialists and understood their impact on both the colonialists and the colonised. This experience, argues Stephen Ingle, shaped Orwell's 'political perspective' and provided him with a 'framework of analysis of the relationship between the rulers and ruled' (2006: 40). Identifying the totalitarian elements in colonialism and establishing Kyauktada as a forerunner of Oceania signifies how close both works are. This finding is especially relevant, for it sheds light on the significance of Orwell's post-*Nineteen Eighty-Four* writing projects. Throughout Orwell's career, stray images and thoughts from his colonial experience kept finding their way into his writing. Only a few

## FIRAS A. J. AL-JUBOURI

months before he died he was trying to write another book about Burma – a short novel called *A Smoking-Room Story*. Writing about Burma again soon after the publication of *Nineteen Eighty-Four* demonstrates the significance of the thematic and political parallels between the two periods in Orwell's life, beginning with a profound sense of disillusionment and ending with a total vision of dystopia.

### NOTES

[1] Orwell's first publisher Victor Gollancz (1893–1967) thought *Burmese Days* was libellous and publishing it would be taking 'one big risk'

[2] The book accounts for the long history of treachery of Party intellectuals by Party intellectuals. Goldstein is a Party intellectual and the Brotherhood he leads mimics the Big Brother they opposed

### REFERENCES

Arendt, Hannah (1951) *The Origins of Totalitarianism*, London: Harcourt

Bal, Sant Singh (1981) *George Orwell: The Ethical Imagination*, New Delhi: Arnold-Heinemann

Bivona, Daniel (2001) *British Imperial Literature, 1870-1940: Writing and the Administration of Empire*, Cambridge: Cambridge University Press

Connelly, Mark (1987) *The Diminished Self: Orwell and the Loss of Freedom*, Pittsburgh: Duquesne University Press

Davison, Peter (1998) (ed.) *The Complete Works of George Orwell*, 20 Vols, London: Secker & Warburg

Fanon, Franz (2004) *The Wretched of the Earth*, trans. by Richard Philcox, commentary by Jean-Paul Sartre and Homi K. Bhabha, New York: Grove Press

Guha, Ranajit (Spring 1997) Not at home in Empire, *Critical Inquiry*, Vol. 23, No. 3 pp 482-493

Hitchens, Christopher (2003) *Orwell's Victory*, London: Penguin

Ingle, Stephen (2006) *The Social and Political Thought of George Orwell: A Reassessment*, Oxford: Routledge

Knapp, John V. (1981) Orwell's fiction: Funny, but not vulgar!', *Modern Fiction Studies*, Vol. 27 pp 294-301

Larkin, Emma (2011) *Finding George Orwell in Burma*, New York: Penguin

Orwell, George (2001a [1934]) *Burmese Days*, London: Penguin

Orwell, George (2001b [1937]) *The Road to Wigan Pier*, London: Penguin

Orwell, George (2013 [1949]) *Nineteen Eighty-Four*, London: Penguin

Shelden, Michael (1995) *Orwell: The Authorised Biography*, London: Minerva

Woodcock, George (2005) *The Crystal Spirit: A Study of George Orwell*, Montreal, Canada: Black Rose

### NOTE ON THE CONTRIBUTOR

Firas A. J. Al-Jubouri was awarded a PhD in English Literature from Newcastle University. He taught English Literature and Academic Writing at several academic institutions such as Ahlia University (Bahrain) and taught an IELTS course as a prerequisite for PhD students registered at Brunel University London. His areas of research and teaching interests are the dystopian genre (George Orwell) and the twentieth century English novel. He has published a monograph on George Orwell entitled *Milestones on the Road to Dystopia*. He now teaches at the American University of Sharjah (UAE).

# 'The Lesser Evil':
## Orwell and America

### JOHN NEWSINGER

*George Orwell is often assumed to have been uninterested in the United States with his thinking immune to any American influences. This neglects his interest in American literature, in particular with the work of Mark Twain, Jack London and Henry Miller. During the Second World War, he came under the influence of the US magazine,* Partisan Review, *for which he wrote his 'London Letters'. Even though he considered the US politically backward, in the post-war years he came to the reluctant conclusion that if the choice was between a world dominated by Soviet Union or the US, he would prefer the States, although he hoped for a socialist revival as offering an alternative.*

Keywords: George Orwell, United States of America, American literature, American servicemen, *Partisan Review*, James Burnham

There has been so little written about George Orwell's attitude towards and thinking about the United States of America that one may be forgiven for believing that he was pretty much oblivious to the country.[1] Admittedly, he never visited there (although he planned to before death cut him short) and he never wrote a *Homage to California*, a *Down and Out in New York and Chicago*, nor even an *Animal Ranch*.

Nevertheless, it will be argued here that the United States was in a number of ways an important influence on him. This influence can be usefully broken down into four categories: first, the literary and cultural influence; second, the impact of US servicemen in Britain during the war, what Orwell called the 'Occupation'; third, his relationship with the New York intellectuals and the journal *Partisan Review* during and immediately after the war; and lastly his post-war thinking regarding the ideas of James Burnham, conflict with the Soviet Union and the British Labour government's alliance with, indeed dependence on, the United States.

## JOHN NEWSINGER

### 'IMAGINARY COUNTRY': ORWELL AND TWAIN

In November 1946, Orwell published an article in *Tribune*, the leftwing Labour Party weekly journal, where he reminisced about the 'books one reads in childhood' and how they 'create in one's mind's eye a sort of false map of the world' (*CWGO* 18: 493).[2] One of the 'imaginary countries' that he 'acquired early in life was called America'. While some of the books that this 'imaginary' America derived from can still be taken seriously (he mentions *Tom Sawyer* and *Uncle Tom's Cabin*), the most important have been generally forgotten (among those he mentions is John Habberton's *Helen's Babies*, of 1876). While the English 'are accustomed to thinking of American society as more crude, adventurous and, in a cultural sense, democratic than our own', a view that derives from 'Mark Twain, Whitman and Brett Harte', this was not the only 'America' that was being imagined. There was also the literature portraying the society of 'the more populous eastern states' where, he argues, 'a society similar to Jane Austen's seems to have survived longer than it did in England'. In books such as *Helen's Babies* and Louisa May Alcott's *Little Women* (of 1868-1869), we find people who are 'uncorrupted. They have something that is perhaps best described as integrity, or good morale'. While very different, Twain's memoir *Life on the Mississippi* (of 1883) and *Little Women*, do have one thing in common: 'an underlying confidence in the future, a sense of freedom and opportunity'. This literature was the product of a society that was, he insists, better than Europe. Indeed, he gets quite carried away, positively eulogising nineteenth century America as:

> ... a rich, empty country which lay outside the mainstream of world events, and in which the twin nightmares that beset nearly every modern man, the nightmare of unemployment and the nightmare of state interference, had hardly come into being. There were social distinctions, more marked than those of today, and there was poverty ... but there was not, as there is now, an all-pervading sense of helplessness ... the civilisation of nineteenth-century America was capitalist civilisation at its best (*CWGO* 18: 495-497).

The situation began to change after the Civil War, but even so for some decades, at least, life in America 'was much better fun than life in Europe'. And he goes on to contrast this nineteenth century American literature read by people of his generation with what the United States offers children in 1946. No one today would claim 'that American books are the best ones for children', and he singled out for especial disdain the 'comics' where 'sinister professors manufacture atomic bombs in underground laboratories while Superman whizzes through the clouds, the machine-gun bullets bouncing off his chest like peas, and platinum blondes are raped, or very nearly, by steel robots and fifty-foot dinosaurs' (*CWGO* 18: 496). We shall return to Orwell's prejudice (not too strong a word) against American comic books later. What is clear, however, is his acknowledgement of the importance of this construction of an 'imaginary' America in what he describes as the at least partial 'Americanisation' of British children, including himself, that was once accomplished by books, but was now primarily accomplished by films. Now, of course, this recognition of American influence on the construction of English childhood was written at a time when British dependence on the US was absolutely undeniable, a factor that may have shaped his reminiscence, but it is still of considerable interest.

One American writer whom Orwell remained attached to throughout his life was Mark Twain. Not only was Twain an early childhood influence, but in February 1934 Orwell was actually considering writing a short book on the man and his writings to coincide with his centenary the following year (*CWGO* 10: 335). This interest persisted so that, in June 1948, he was to write to Edmund Wilson in the States asking him to send a copy of Van Wyck's book, *The Ordeal of Mark Twain*, of 1920, which he could not get in Britain (*CWGO* 19: 252, 415). And in November 1943, once again in *Tribune*, he had discussed Twain's writings (*CWGO* 16: 5-7). The occasion was the publication by the Everyman Library of new editions of *Tom Sawyer* and *Huckleberry Finn*. According to Orwell, Twain was born into 'the golden age of America, the period when the great plains were opened-up, when wealth and opportunity seemed limitless, and human beings felt free, indeed *were* free, as they had never been before and may not be again for centuries' (italics in the original). For him, Twain's 'best and most characteristic books', *The Innocents at Home* (1869), *Roughing It* (1872) and *Life on the Mississippi* showed how 'human beings behave when they are not frightened of the sack' (*CWGO* 16: 5).

Unfortunately, Twain's promise as a social critic was not realised. While he had 'in him an iconoclastic, even revolutionary vein which he obviously wanted to follow up', he never did, becoming instead 'that dubious thing a "public figure", flattered by passport-officials and entertained by royalty'. This decline, according to Orwell, 'reflects the deterioration in American life that set in after the Civil War'. This was 'the age of cheap immigrant labour and the growth of Big Business'. The United States became a plutocracy. Twain even for a time gave up writing and went into business himself. He 'gave himself up to the prevailing fever, and made and lost vast sums of money'. For Orwell, Twain's flaw was 'his inability to despise success'. Nevertheless, at least several of Twain's books are 'bound to survive', not least because 'they contain invaluable social history', a somewhat ungenerous assessment, one might think, of a writer who clearly fascinated him (*CWGO* 16: 5-7).

When Orwell wrote of people being really free in pre-Civil War America, he not only ignored the position of women but also somewhat more astonishingly the position of black slaves, both men and women. Twain's parents, as Orwell observes, did 'own one or perhaps two slaves', but the significance of slavery is nowhere acknowledged. Indeed, the Civil War is not seen as putting an end to slavery, but rather as inaugurating the reign of Big Business, which was undoubtedly true, but the conflict cannot be reduced to that. Orwell was never to get to grips with the reality of the oppression of African Americans. He opposed what he knew of it. In September 1944, for example, he wrote a review of D. W. Brogan's *The American Problem* where he criticises him for only giving 'a few pages to the Negroes' and only mentioning in 'a couple of parentheses … that millions of Negroes are both half-starved and disenfranchised' (*CWGO* 16: 406-407).

Nevertheless, a good case can be made that he never really understood the magnitude of the oppression of African Americans, its routine violence and occasional appalling savagery, nor its full significance for American society. It is a matter of some regret that Orwell never penned 'A Lynching' to accompany his 'A Hanging'. One can only speculate on how he would have responded to the lynching of Claude Neal in October 1934, for example. Neal was an African American accused of rape and murder and was lynched in Marianna, Florida. His lynching was widely advertised, attracting an audience of between 2-3,000 men, women and children. He was brutally beaten, castrated and fed his own genitals, branded all over with hot irons, had his fingers and toes cut off, before being hanged and shot to death. His corpse was taken down, dragged behind a vehicle, mutilated some more and then strung up outside the town courthouse. Neal's torment was accompanied by the burning down of the homes and businesses of many of the town's black inhabitants. Altogether that year, fifteen African Americans were lynched. This was how the 'Negro' was oppressed in the United States.[3]

## 'LOYALTY TO THE EXPLOITED CLASSES': ORWELL AND JACK LONDON

The American writer who had the most influence on Orwell was arguably Jack London. On 3 March 1943, he broadcast a short talk on Jack London for the BBC. The programme was intended for an audience in India. Orwell singled out *The Iron Heel* (1908) for praise because even though it was 'a very poor book, much below Jack London's average', it showed that the capitalist class would not just let itself be expropriated, but 'would hit back. They wouldn't simply lie down'. This was a crucial insight which had been borne out by Hitler and the Nazis. As he put it: 'Who now will dare say that something like this hasn't happened over great areas of the world, and may not continue to happen unless the Axis is defeated' (*CWGO* 15: 6).

He was to return to this theme a number of times. On 8 October 1945, Orwell broadcast a Forces Educational programme on the BBC on Jack London (*CWGO* 17: 297-305) and later was to write the Introduction to a new edition of London's *Love of Life and Other Stories*, that was published early in 1946 (ibid: 351-357). In his radio broadcast, he emphasised London's socialist politics, that 'above all things he was a Socialist' and that 'the basis of all his best work is a feeling of indignation against the cruel, sordid misery in which the modern world often forces people to live'. Orwell does not discuss London's 'animal books' (such as *Call of the Wild*, of 1903, and *White Fang*, of 1906) but, instead, concentrates on his 'Socialistic books', singling out the dystopian novel, *The Iron Heel*, in particular. In 1934, all over Europe there was 'a sudden search for copies of this book, which had become a rarity'. Now people wanted to get hold of the book because it was 'in some ways a surprisingly accurate forecast of Fascism'.

Orwell particularly praised London for his recognition that 'the capitalist class would not just let itself be abolished ... and would stop at nothing in defence of its possessions'. To protect its wealth and power the capitalist class would, if necessary, resort to an 'organised reign of terror'. Indeed, Orwell told his servicemen and women listeners that Chapter XXI of *The Iron Heel* was 'one of the best statements of the outlook of a ruling class ... that has ever been written'. Nevertheless, as far as he was concerned, London's best books were those novels and short stories 'in which his Socialist convictions have been digested, so to speak, and are not on the surface'. He recommended *The Valley of the Moon*, *When God Laughs*, *The Road*, *The Jacket*, *The Iron Heel* and *Before Adam* 'if you can get hold of them. ... If you read those six books, you've read the best of Jack London' (ibid: 302-303, 305).

Orwell opens his Introduction to *Love of Life and Other Stories* (1905) by telling his readers that 'Love of Life' was one of the last stories that Nadezhda Krupskaya read to her husband, Lenin, when he was dying and that he greatly enjoyed it. He then goes on to praise *The Iron Heel* as 'not a good book', but as one that 'on several points ... was right where nearly all other prophets were wrong'. London, he writes:

> ... imagines a proletarian revolution breaking out in the United States and being crushed, or partially crushed, by a counter-offensive of the capitalist class; and, following on this, a long period during which society is ruled over by a small group of tyrants.... But the book is chiefly notable for maintaining that capitalist society would not perish of its 'contradictions...' (ibid: 352).

**PAPER**

**JOHN NEWSINGER**

Once again, he praised 'London's understanding of the nature of a ruling class', and most especially the way that he knew 'instinctively that the American business-men would fight when their possessions were menaced'. How does he explain that London had this insight whereas most on the left believed the capitalist class would surrender without a fight? London, he argues, could foresee Fascism because he had 'a Fascist streak in himself, or at least a marked strain of brutality' (ibid: 353).

This excursion into amateur psychology is not convincing. Rather than deriving from his own temperament, London's insight came from his understanding of the US capitalist class of his own day and the violence that they were prepared to use to resist unionisation, let alone socialism. While he was writing *The Iron Heel*, there was a determined attempt to judicially murder the leaders of the Western Federation of Miners, Bill Haywood and Charles Moyer. Indeed, London contributed to their defence fund and campaigned on their behalf.[4] Unionisation in the States was often resisted with lethal force and many employers maintained their own armed company police and spy networks as well as making use of notorious private detective agencies such as the Pinkertons. It was the brutal reality of class relations in the United States that informed *The Iron Heel*. One last important point with regard to *The Iron Heel* is that it was an important literary influence on Orwell's own *Nineteen Eighty-Four* (1949), portraying, as it does, the readiness of a ruling class to make use of a terrorist state in order to hold on to power. Certainly, Fredric Warburg, in his publisher's report on *Nineteen Eighty Four*, argued that Orwell 'must acknowledge a debt to Jack London's *Iron Heel*' although he felt that 'in verisimilitude and horror he surpasses this not inconsiderable author' (*CWGO* 19: 479).

Orwell insisted that despite his increasing success and wealth, London 'never faltered in his loyalty to the exploited classes' and that even when already 'a successful and famous man he could explore the worst depths of poverty in the London slums' and produce *The People of the Abyss* (1903), 'which still has sociological value'. He does acknowledge that there were occasions when London succumbed to 'race mysticism', but relates this to the dominant strain of Darwinism of the time, rather than to the racism of white America (*CWGO* 17: 354, 355).

### 'UNHEROIC': ORWELL AND HENRY MILLER

A dramatic contrast with Orwell's enthusiasm for Jack London was his enthusiasm for Henry Miller. In his essay, 'Inside the Whale' that was published in March 1940, Orwell praised Miller's *Tropic of Cancer* (1934) and *Black Spring* (1936) as novels 'about the man in the street' although he does regret 'that it should be a street full of brothels' (*CWGO* 12: 88). When T*ropic of Cancer* was first published, 'the Italians were marching into Abyssinia and Hitler's concentration camps were already bulging'. This did not seem 'to be a moment in which a novel of outstanding value was likely to be written about American deadbeats cadging drinks in the Latin Quarter', but this was Miller's achievement (ibid: 87).

In the essay, Orwell rehearses the view of US history that informs his understanding of Twain, celebrating the mid-nineteenth century when 'American men felt themselves free and equal, *were* free and equal, so far as that is possible outside a society of pure communism' (italics in the original) (ibid: 90). Miller still sees himself as 'free and equal' but by means of 'a sort of mystical acceptance of the thing-as-it-is'. As he points out, today this means accepting world of concentration camps, putsches, torture, purges, machine guns, political murders, tinned meat and Hollywood films. But, nevertheless, Miller's passive acceptance actually enables him 'to get nearer to the ordinary man than is possible for more purposive writers'. As literature has become increasingly concerned with political issues, there has been less and less room 'for the ordinary man than at any time during the last two centuries'. Miller represents a turn away from politicised writing. He had recognised that there was no hope, that 'most certainly we are moving into an age of totalitarian dictatorships' and he responded by adopting a 'passive attitude', giving himself 'over to the world process'. Orwell goes a long way towards endorsing this stance (ibid: 91).[5]

This very much represented Orwell's pessimism at this stage of the 'phoney war' and of the Hitler-Stalin Pact. He had earlier resisted Miller's *passivism* when he met him on his way to fight in Spain in 1936 and he was soon to throw himself into the fight for a 'People's War' and an English Revolution.[6] By December 1942, he published an article, 'The End of Henry Miller' in *Tribune* where he argued that 'the period of wars and revolutions' had reopened and Miller's response was to run away. What a book he could have written about life for the ordinary man in Paris under German occupation, but 'if the Germans were in Paris Miller would inevitably be somewhere else'. That somewhere else was Greece, where Miller made clear that he never wanted to set eyes on America again, but as soon as Greece was under threat, he 'left for America'. Miller's writing was determinedly about 'the unheroic', which Orwell considered one of his great strengths as a writer, but now 'we live in what is, however unwillingly, a heroic age'. For Orwell, Miller's brief moment had been and gone (*CWGO* 14: 217-218).

Orwell's interest in American literature continued right up until his death. We find him dismissing James Cain's *The Postman Always Rings Twice* (1934) as 'an awful book' in February 1949 and recommending Norman Mailer's *The Naked and the Dead* (1948) as 'awfully good, the best book of the last war yet' in July of that same year (*CWGO* 20: 35, 146).

## 'DISGUSTING AMERICAN COMICS'

Which leaves us with Orwell's quite ferocious hostility to American comics. On 3 January 1946, he wrote to Dwight Macdonald in the US, apologising for not delivering the article on this subject that he had promised for his journal, *Politics*. He had intended contrasting them with 'the American books and papers which I, like most people about my age, was partly brought up on'. He had sketched the piece out already, but unfortunately whatever work he had done has never been found (*CWGO* 18: 11). He had already made his position clear, however, in a short discussion published the previous May in the *Leader* magazine. He looked, in particular, at Marvel Comics that seemed 'mainly given over to "scientification" – that is, steel robots, invisible men, prehistoric monsters, death rays invasions from Mars, and such-like'. They were 'very disquieting', in his opinion, tending 'to stimulate fantasies of power' and really only concerned with 'magic and sadism'. It was all 'a riot of nonsensical sensationalism, with nothing of the genuine scientific interest of the H. G. Wells stories'. It was all just so much 'poisonous rubbish' (*CWGO* 17: 221). He returned to the subject in his 'As I Please' column in *Tribune* on 27 December 1946 where he discussed a comic one of his readers had sent to him. On the front page there was 'either an ape-like lunatic, or an actual ape dressed up as a man, strangling a woman so realistically that her tongue is sticking four inches out of her mouth'. His reader asked whether this was suitable reading for children and Orwell makes clear that it should be kept out of their hands. He is against any ban, but somewhat dishonestly suggests as an alternative looking into the use of precious dollars 'to pay for this pernicious rubbish' with the clear intention of stopping their importation (*CWGO* 18: 523-524).

His cultural conservatism, on this particular occasion, seems to derive from his more general concern that the ethos of Jack the Giant Killer was being supplanted in popular literature by that of Jack the Dwarf Killer. While one cannot blame him personally for my generation of post-war children being deprived of Marvel comics until their teens and, instead, being subjected to Dan Dare and the *Eagle*, he was certainly in tune with the cultural prejudices that were responsible.[7]

It is also worth noting that Orwell was a consumer of Hollywood films and that for a time he worked as a film reviewer for *Time and Tide* in 1940-41. Of the 45 films he reviewed, 37 were made in the US. As John Tulloch has pointed out, his attitude was 'mainly dismissive' and that even when 'he admits that an American film is powerful, his judgement is heavily qualified by contempt for what he presents as its materialist values' (Tulloch 2012: 97).

'OCCUPIED TERRITORY'

The American entry into the Second World War prompted Orwell into discussing British attitudes towards the United States in the 'London Letter', published in the American left-wing journal, *Partisan Review* There had been no increase in 'pro-American sentiment – the contrary if anything'. Indeed, it had 'brought out the immense amount of anti-American feeling that exists in the ordinary low-brow middle class'. As far as the middle class were concerned, Americans were 'boastful, bad-mannered and worshippers of money, and are also suspected of plotting to inherit the British Empire'. He knew people who automatically switched the radio off when any American news came on. This was 'the jealousy of the ordinary patriotic middle class'. As for the working class, they had no 'cultural hostility' to the Americans; indeed, they were 'being more and more Americanised in speech through the medium of the cinema', but they 'nearly always dislike Americans when in actual contact with them' (*CWGO* 13: 108-109). Exploring the British response to the arrival of increasing numbers of American servicemen in Britain was to become one of Orwell's regular concerns.

In his January 1943 'London Letter', he told his left-wing readers in the States that since his previous 'Letter' 'there has been an obvious growth of animosity against America' (*CWGO* 14: 293). Even the left intelligentsia were beginning to realise that 'the USA is potentially imperialist and politically a long way behind Britain'. People were saying that 'whereas Chamberlain appeased Germany, Churchill appeases America'. Indeed, he went on to insist that it was a fact that the British ruling class was being propped up by the United States, given 'a new lease on life it would not otherwise have had'. People were blaming the US 'for every reactionary move, more even than is justified'. As for British workers, there was 'widespread anti-American feeling'. This was, at least in part, because the common people 'nearly everywhere are xenophobe'. Popular goodwill towards the Soviet Union depended on the fact that few British people had ever met any actual Russians! Even the British women seemed to have gone off the Americans who were only ever seen with 'tarts or near tarts' – an observation that my mother, her sisters and their friends would certainly have taken great exception to! Indeed, people 'seem to prefer the Negroes to the white Americans'. What did he put this hostility down to? Essentially it was resentment about the pay and food that the American soldiers received. On '10 shillings a day and all found', the whole US Army was a 'middle class' army and not lower middle class at that. And, he went on, there was also 'very bitter anti-British feeling' among US servicemen. The Americans had 'the profoundest contempt for England', regarding the English as 'no good at anything except running away'. On another occasion (*Tribune*, 20 May 1944), he was to observe that for many American soldiers, the 'salient fact' about Britain was that 'the girls here walk out with niggers' (*CWGO* 14: 293-294; *CWGO* 16: 230).

He thought this mutual dislike would only become politically significant if Germany was defeated and a protracted war in the Far East ensued. For most British people this would be a war for 'the rubber companies and the Americans'. Now that the tide had turned in the war and the British ruling class felt secure and increasingly confident, 'its real war aims', hitherto 'unmentionable' would become apparent. Once the British people realised what a 'dreary world ... the American millionaires and their British hangers-on intend to impose upon us', there would be growing opposition that would probably feed off anti-American sentiment. Most people, Orwell told his American readers, favoured 'some kind of United States of Europe, dominated by a close alliance between Britain and the USSR'. He still thought there was the possibility that 'radical change will again become possible', although at the moment, 'the reactionaries are tightening their grip everywhere'. As we shall see, he was eventually to acknowledge in the pages of *Partisan Review* that his hopes for radical social and political change, indeed for a revolution, in Britain were misjudged (*CWGO* 14: 295-296).

Orwell himself was not immune to anti-Americanism, although he made at least some effort to hide it from his *Partisan Review* readers. Even so, he complained in one of his 'London Letters' that 'some provincial towns have been almost taken over by the American troops' who walked around with 'a look of settled discontent' (*CWGO* 13: 522). Writing some eighteen months later in *Tribune*, on 3 December 1943, he actually complained that 'it is difficult to go anywhere in London without having the feeling that Britain is now Occupied Territory'. This somewhat extreme observation was prompted, at least in part, by an encounter with two drunken American soldiers in a tobacconist (*CWGO* 16: 12). He also writes, presumably from personal experience, that the claim made by some Americans that more US soldiers than British were killed in the First World War can, on occasion, 'cause a violent quarrel'. There was, he goes on, no popular anti-Americanism in Britain until US soldiers arrived in the country and the situation was not helped by their pay being five times that of a British soldier. As far as most British people were concerned, the only American soldiers with any manners 'are the Negroes'. A number of readers responded to this contribution by writing to the newspaper in defence of the Americans (*CWGO* 16: 14-17).

His subsequent 'London Letter' comes across as somewhat apologetic in this respect, although whether in response to this criticism is impossible to say. A number of American soldiers, *Partisan Review* readers, have got in touch with him and he has let one of them spend the night at his flat. Orwell confesses, after discussing with this young man, how he has been received in Britain, to a certain sadness at the lack of hospitality shown to the Americans by ordinary British people. He wants the magazine's readers to know that while British people at the best of times are not very hospitable to strangers, this is compounded by 'the fact that rations are not easy to stretch and that after years of war people are ashamed of the shabby interiors of their houses' (*CWGO* 16: 160).

Orwell continued the discussion of the impact of American soldiers in his 'As I Please' column in *Tribune* on 11 August 1944, warning that a creeping 'colour bar' was being introduced in dance halls, restaurants and hotels in deference to the prejudices of white Americans. People had 'to be vigilant against this kind of thing and to make as much public fuss as possible' (ibid: 328-329). Certainly, the racism of white Americans seems to have heightened his awareness of the oppression of African Americans. He wrote, once again in *Tribune*, of how in the States, 'Negroes are still pushed out of skilled jobs, segregated and insulted in the Army, assaulted by white policemen and discriminated against by white magistrates. In a number of Southern States they are disenfranchised by means of a poll tax'. This was, however, part of 'a world-wide problem of colour' that 'simply cannot be solved inside the capitalist system'. The living standards of the 'not white' had to be bought up to that of the whites, even if this meant 'temporarily lowering our own standards'. In the interim, the least the individual could do was 'to avoid using insulting nicknames' which was hardly adequate (ibid: 23-24).

'LONDON LETTER'

Orwell's relationship with the US magazine *Partisan Review* is vital to any understanding of his political development in the 1940s. Elsewhere, I have described it as his 'American connection' (Newsinger 1999: 90-100). The magazine had started in 1934 under the auspices of the US Communist Party, but had been re-launched in 1936 as a 'literary Trotskyist' magazine. In its new incarnation, it was fiercely hostile to Stalinism and showed a broad sympathy for Leon Trotsky's ideas while rejecting any organisational affiliation with American Trotskyism. When war broke out in Europe in 1939, the magazine adopted a strong anti-war position with one particular editor, Dwight Macdonald, leading the way.

Despite Orwell's strong support for the war, his campaigning for the conflict to be transformed into a revolutionary war led to Orwell being invited to take over their 'London Letter' slot. He sent off his first contribution in January 1941 and it appeared in the March-April issue. Up until the summer of 1946, Orwell despatched another fourteen 'London Letters'. The significance of these epistles should not be underestimated. Most critical

**JOHN NEWSINGER**

and biographical attention focuses on his relationship with and contributions to *Tribune*, but what his 'London Letters' and other contributions to *Partisan Review* show is that his political thinking cannot be reduced to a species of Labourism. This is not to deny the importance that the Labour Party came to have in his thinking, but rather that his socialism was something more than Labourism and that he certainly never regarded the Labour Party, even when most supportive of it, as a vehicle for the socialist transformation of Britain (see Newsinger 2017, forthcoming). One reason why this is not more widely acknowledged is precisely because *Partisan Review* was an American magazine. His contributions remained virtually unknown in Britain until the publication of the four-volume edition of his *Collected Essays, Journalism and Letters*, edited by Sonia Orwell and Ian Angus and first published in 1968 (Orwell and Angus 1968). There was, in the 1940s, no British equivalent of *Partisan Review*, no British 'literary Trotskyist' magazine, and no London equivalent of the 'New York intellectuals'. If there had been, then Orwell would certainly have contributed to such a magazine and would have inevitably been part of such a circle of intellectuals, both fiercely anti-Stalinist and to the left of the Labour Party. Indeed, one can easily see him as more comfortable as the literary editor of such a magazine than as the literary editor of *Tribune*.

There is only space here to examine one of Orwell's 'London Letters' in any detail. His July-August 1942 contribution was entitled 'The British Crisis' by his editors (*CWGO* 13: 302-308). In it, he argued that the British people were, at last, ready for radical change. As he explained, he did not mean 'that people in significant numbers are crying out for the introduction of Socialism, merely that the mass of the nation wants certain things that aren't obtainable under a capitalist economy'. People wanted 'more social equality, a complete clean-out of the political leadership, an aggressive war strategy and a tighter alliance with the USSR'. What was required was some sort of 'war communism'. Since the fall of Singapore, Churchill's position has been 'shaky', indeed, 'I wouldn't give Churchill many more months of power'. Part of the problem, as far as he was concerned, was that for most people 'Socialism' was identified with the 'discredited Labour Party', a Labour Party that had no 'guts' and was led by a 'tame cat' like Attlee. He thought Stafford Cripps (Minister of Aircraft Production 1942-1945) might be the man to give leadership to the general desire for radical change, although he wisely qualified this with the fear that Cripps might, in fact, turn out to be just 'a second-rate figure ... a sort of bubble blown by popular discontent'. At this point in time, he still argued that a revolutionary outcome was possible, that one 'can after all discern the outlines of a revolutionary world war'. Defeats in the Far East had 'gone a long way towards killing the old conception of imperialism'. What had been missing in Britain so far was a 'revolutionary party' and 'able leftwing leadership'. He told his American readers that Cripps might provide the necessary leadership, but he still thought that 'a new political party will have to arise if anything is to be changed' (ibid).

By the time of his next 'Letter' that appeared in the March-April 1943 issue, he was already admitting that the crisis was over and the 'forces of reaction have won hands down' (*CWGO* 14: 292).

Orwell put a lot more into his 'London Letters' than just his, in retrospect, wildly over-optimistic judgements of the unfolding political situation. He discussed the conditions of life in wartime Britain, the problem of anti-semitism, the Home Guard, the impact of US servicemen, the activities of the Communist Party (its 'anti-Trotskyist pamphlets ... are barely distinguishable from those of the Spanish Civil War period, but go somewhat further in mendacity'), rationing, popular attitudes towards the Soviet Union and, of course, the contribution the Poles have made 'towards solving our birth-rate problems' (*CWGO* 13: 518, 522). And, in the 'London Letter', of winter 1944, he acknowledged that his hopes for revolution had clearly been wrong. His mistake derived from 'a political analysis which I had made in the desperate period of 1940 and continued to cling to long after it should have been clear that it was untenable'. He had also assumed that without a socialist revolution of some kind in Britain, the war would be lost. 'There were,' as he observes, 'excuses for this belief, but still it was a very great error. For after all, we have not lost the war, unless appearances are very deceiving, and we have not introduced Socialism.' In Britain, 'there has been no real shift of power and no increase in genuine democracy', while the United States was actually moving further 'away from Socialism'. As he acknowledged, 'I over-emphasized the ant-Fascist character of the war, exaggerated the social changes that were actually occurring, and under-rated the enormous strength of the forces of reaction' (*CWGO* 16: 412-414).

Two more points are worth making here regarding *Partisan Review*. First, as I have argued elsewhere (Newsinger 1999), the magazine, and one editor in particular, Dwight Macdonald,[8] had an important influence on the writing of *Nineteen Eighty-Four* by introducing Orwell to the theory of bureaucratic collectivism. It is this that provided the basis for Goldstein's *The Theory and Practice of Oligarchical Collectivism* in the novel and, indeed, for the novel's portrayal of Oceania (ibid: 124-128). Second, when Orwell was asked by the editors to contribute to a series on 'The Future of Socialism', his contribution, 'Toward European Unity', that appeared in the July-August 1947 issue, did not celebrate the Labour government in London as showing the way towards socialism in any respect whatsoever. He did support Attlee's government, but he did not see it as introducing socialism. As he

**JOHN NEWSINGER**

made clear, he thought the prospects for socialism were extremely grim, which is hardly a resounding vote of confidence in the socialist credentials of a Labour government with an overwhelming majority. Nevertheless, one had to work towards the establishment of 'democratic socialism ... throughout some large area'. Socialism, Orwell acknowledged, 'cannot properly be said to be established until it is world-wide', but, in the interim, 'a Socialist United States of Europe seems to me the only worth-while political objective today'. One of the obstacles to this was that Britain was 'almost a dependency of the USA' (*CWGO* 19: 164-165).

### 'DISHONESTY IS THE BEST POLICY': ORWELL AND JAMES BURNHAM

As the war came to an end, Orwell found himself intellectually grappling with the immense changes that were taking place in the world. Much of this concern took the form of a debate with the American political thinker James Burnham, a former Trotskyist, who was moving sharply to the right. Burnham and his *The Managerial Revolution* (1941) are often seen as one of the intellectual inspirations for *Nineteen Eighty-Four*, but this was not, in fact, the case. In his Marxist days, Burnham had been one of the advocates of the theory of bureaucratic collectivism which certainly was an influence, but Orwell was very critical of his later trajectory. He lambasted him in *Tribune* on 14 January 1944. Burnham's thesis in *The Managerial Revolution* was that capitalism was finished, socialism was impossible and that what was taking place was the emergence of a new ruling class across the world, the Nazis in Germany, the communists in Russia and 'the business executives' in the US. This new ruling class 'expropriates the capitalists, crushes the working class movements and sets up a totalitarian society'. He forecast German victory over Britain and Russia and the division of the world into three super states, Germany, the US and Japan, 'making ceaseless war upon one another' and keeping 'the working class in permanent subjection'. Now, Orwell acknowledged that 'collectivism is not inherently democratic' and that class rule was not ended merely 'by formally abolishing private property', but as he pointed out, Burnham's specific prophecies had all proven false soon after they were made: Germany and Japan were both on the way to crushing defeat. His major criticism, however, was that Burnham was 'trying to spread the idea that totalitarianism is unavoidable, and that we must therefore do nothing to oppose it' (*CWGO* 16: 60-61).

He followed this assault up a few days later with a hostile review of Burnham's new book, *The Machiavellians* (1943), that appeared in the *Manchester Evening News* on 20 January 1944. Here, Orwell was absolutely scathing about where Burnham was headed. He described him as having achieved a 'rather short-lived renown' with *The Managerial Revolution* 'by telling American business-men what they wanted to hear'. Now, in his new book, Burnham argues that 'Democracy is impossible, though useful as a myth to deceive the masses' and that 'Society is inevitably ruled by oligarchies who hold their position by means of force and fraud'. He looks forward to 'the emergence of a new ruling class, who will rule "scientifically" by the conscious use of force and fraud, but who will to some small extent serve the common good because they will recognise that is to their own interest to do so'. Stripped of its intellectual apparatus, Burnham's argument is that 'Dishonesty is the best policy'. Orwell dismissed him as a false prophet (ibid: 72-74).

How important Orwell thought it was to counter Burnham's influence was shown when he returned to the attack with his 'Second Thoughts on James Burnham', published in the third issue of the journal, *Polemic*, of May 1946. This essay was reprinted as a pamphlet, *James Burnham and the Managerial Revolution*, by the Socialist Book Centre later in the year. It was also published in Chicago in the United States the following year in the *University Observer: A Journal of Politics* (*CWGO* 18: 284). Here, Orwell once again accused Burnham of seeing all historical change as merely the replacement of one ruling class by another with the masses always 'thrust back into servitude'. He then proceeded to dissect Burnham's various prophecies, pointing out that 'when they were verifiable', they invariably 'turned out to be wrong'. In explaining Burnham's mistakes, he makes the point that 'one cannot leave out of account the fact that Burnham is an American' with the 'characteristic prejudices and patches of ignorance' that one would expect! Nevertheless, Orwell does acknowledge that throughout the world, for the last fifty years or so, 'the general drift has almost certainly been towards oligarchy'. He ends, however, by proclaiming that Burnham's supposed 'realism' amounts to nothing more than a dream of a 'huge, invincible, everlasting slave empire' and that this is so much nonsense, 'because slavery is no longer a stable basis for human society' (*CWGO* 18: 269, 277, 279, 280, 283).

Orwell had not yet finished with Burnham. In March 1947, he wrote a review of his *The Struggle for the World* (1947) for the US magazine, *The New Leader*. Here he admitted that he might have got Burnham wrong. Rather than being some sort of apologist for an inevitable totalitarianism, Burnham was, in fact, the exponent of a US 'world empire'. The only alternatives were 'domination by Communism or domination by the United States' and Burnham was now emerging as the champion of American domination. He now had an 'essentially a conservative program', indeed, in important respects, a positively 'reactionary ... program'. It involved the ruthless suppression of dissent and possibly 'a preventive war in the very near future, while the Americans have atomic bombs and the Russians have not'. As part of this new US imperial order, Burnham advocated 'the fusion of Britain with the United States'. According to Orwell, given that Britain had been pretty much a dependency of the United States for some years already, this might actually take place 'almost of its own accord'. If Burnham was right and the only alternatives were Russian or American domination, then 'the European peoples may have to accept American domination'. Nevertheless, he hoped Burnham was being too pessimistic and while he recognised that the best alternative of a 'Socialist United States of Europe has not as yet much magnetism', he suggested other possibilities if war could be avoided in the short-term. 'One is,' he suggested, 'that the Russian regime may become more liberal and less dangerous a generation hence' and another was that 'the great powers will be simply too frightened of the effects of atomic weapons ever to make use of them.' One other point that Orwell made, in an important discussion, was that while the leadership of local Communist Parties throughout the world were undoubtedly 'Quisling' in their attitude towards the Soviet Union, this was not true of their broader memberships so that Burnham's advocacy of domestic repression was a mistake. And indeed, Orwell was to oppose any importation of McCarthyism into Britain (CWGO 19: 98-99, 102-05).

'THE LESSER EVIL': 'WE SHOULD CHOOSE AMERICA'

In the 'London Letter' that came out in the winter of 1944, Orwell wrote of the United States being 'the most powerful country in the world and the most capitalistic' (CWGO 16: 412). He regarded the US as politically backward, even though he insisted that support for capitalism on the part of Americans was not 'something unalterable, a sort of racial characteristic like the color of eyes or hair' and still hoped that one day 'a powerful Socialist movement might for the first time arise in the United States' (CWGO 19: 166). The United States was certainly not seen as offering any way forward for the world. But, in a world dominated by the United States it would be possible to continue the fight for a better future, whereas in a world dominated by the Soviet Union, this would be impossible. From this point of view, the US was the 'lesser evil'. He was absolutely clear in his own mind that in the event of having to choose a side between even the politically backward US and the totalitarian Soviet Union, he would take the American side. He argued in an unpublished article written for Tribune some time towards the end of the summer of 1947 that: 'In the end the choice may be forced on us. We are no longer strong enough to stand alone, and if we fail to bring a western European union into being, we shall be obliged, in the long run, to subordinate our policy to that of one Great Power or the other … everyone knows in his heart that we should choose America' (ibid: 182).

CONCLUSIONS

In retrospect, Orwell's exaggerated fear of Soviet aggression and ambitions of world domination (although he in no way exaggerated the domestic horrors of Stalinism in either the Soviet Union or in its East European satellites), led him to not only make clear that he would support the Americans if it came to war, but also to involve himself in the fighting on the ideological front in the early stages of the Cold War.

This led to his involvement with the British secret state. His involvement was slight but nevertheless compromising. While his relationship with the Labour government's covert propaganda agency, the Information Research Department (IRD), is well-known, involving his handing over of the names of individuals he considered sympathetic to the Soviet Union and as such, not to be approached by the IRD, it is worth noting here that the lists of fellow-travellers he compiled included Americans. Among those listed were Louis Adamic, Walter Duranty, Scott Nearing, Paul Robeson, Upton Sinclair, Orson Welles, Anna Louise Strong, John Steinbeck and Edgar Snow (*CWGO* 20: 242-257).

His pessimism regarding the prospects for socialism together with the ferocity of his anti-Stalinism towards the end of his life led to his involvement in a thoroughly disreputable exercise. His actual conscription as a one-dimensional Cold Warrior, however, was only to be accomplished posthumously.[9]

NOTES

[1] One exception is Christopher Hitchens's brief engagement with the question in his *Orwell's Victory* where he describes America in a typically overdone fashion as 'the grand exception to Orwell's prescience about the century in which he lived' (2001: 75)

[2] *CWGO* refers throughout to the 20-volume *Collected Works of George Orwell*, edited by Peter Davison, London: Secker and Warburg, 1998

[3] Newsinger 2012: 118-119

[4] Clymer 2003: 134-145

[5] Miller described 'Inside the Whale' as Orwell's 'left-handed attack on me' in a letter to Anaïs Nin that he sent from California in April 1944 (Stuhlmann 1975: 347)

[6] See Newsinger 1999: 61-86

[7] The Communist Party actually ran a campaign against the importation of American horror comics into Britain. See Barker 1983

[8] Macdonald resigned from *Partisan Review* when it became pro-war, but despite their disagreement over this issue, he remained the member of the editorial board who was closest to Orwell. See Newsinger 1999: 125-127, 147-150

[9] See, in particular, Shaw 2004 and Leab 2007

# JOHN NEWSINGER

## REFERENCES

Barker, Martin (1983) *A Haunt of Fears*, London: Pluto

Clymer, Jeffory (2003) *America's Culture of Terrorism: Violence, Capitalism and the Written Word*, Chapel Hill

Hitchens, Christopher (2002) *Orwell's Victory*, London: Penguin Books

Leab, Daniel J. (2007) *Orwell Subverted: The CIA and the Filming of* Animal Farm, University Park, PA: Pennsylvania State University Press

Newsinger, John (1999) *Orwell's Politics*, London: Palgrave Macmillan

Newsinger, John (2012) *Fighting Back: The American Working Class in the 1930s*, London: Bookmarks

Newsinger, John (2017, forthcoming) *'If there is hope': Orwell and the Left*, London: Pluto

Orwell, Sonia and Angus, Ian (1968) *George Orwell's Collected Essays, Journalism and Letters*, Harmondsworth: Penguin

Shaw, Tony (2004) Cinematic propaganda during the Cold War: A comparison of British and American movies, Connelly, Mark and Welch, David (eds) *War and the Media: Reportage and Propaganda 1900-2003*, London: I. B. Tauris pp 162-181

Stuhlmann, Gunther (ed.) (1975) *Henry Miller: Letters to Anaïs Nin*, London: Peter Owen

Tulloch, John (2012) Sceptic in the palace of dreams: Orwell as film reviewer, Keeble, Richard Lance (ed.) *Orwell Today*, Bury St Edmunds: Abramis pp 79-101

ARTICLE

# The Edges of the Empire:
## The Symbolism of Bladed Weapons in Orwell's *Burmese Days*

**DON ARP, JR.**

*Many cultures around the world have a unique style of national weapon that can have a pervasive role in daily activities and can be a significant aspect of cultural tradition and identity. Often, these cultural weapons are bladed implements such as knives, daggers, and swords. Given the status of these weapons, they often figure significantly in both the mythologies internal to the culture and in depictions and explorations of that culture by outsiders. Such is the case in Orwell's novel* Burmese Days, *in which he uses two national weapons, the Gurkha kukri and the Burmese dah, to symbolise the opposing sides of colonial conflict. The dah is the weapon of the oppressed while the kukri is the tool of Empire. These weapons, especially the dah, play subtle yet significant roles in advancing and sustaining the symbolic structure of the novel.*

Keywords: *Burmese Days*, sword, weapon, symbolism

Around the world, unique weapon forms are often associated with specific regions and cultures. These weapons play a pervasive role in daily activities and can be a significant aspect of cultural tradition and identity. George Orwell even said (2000 [1945]: 7): 'It is a commonplace that the history of civilization is largely the history of weapons.' Swords and bladed weapons, in particular, play fundamental and expansive roles in human culture. The British explorer, Sir Richard Francis Burton, once wrote (1987 [1884]: xv): 'The history of the sword is the history of humanity.' The impact is much deeper than simply history: 'Swords have played an integral role in a large number of mythologies' (Peterson and Dunworth 2004: 52)

As a result, these weapons easily lend themselves to serving larger scale symbolic functions, as seen in Orwell's novel, *Burmese Days* (1934). In the novel, two such national weapons, the Gurkha kukri and the Burmese dah, each symbolise an opposing side in the struggles gripping colonial Burma. The kukri represents the ready violence, might, and glee of subjugation wielded by the British authorities. Against this tool of empire, is the dah. The dah represents the adjacent possible – the unrealised potential of violence – of the oppressed Burmese and is the item that provides a sense of identity and an edge to strike against the Empire. For, as Orwell notes, 'a simple weapon – so long as there is no answer to it – gives claws to the weak' (2000 [1945]: 7) The roles played by these weapons throughout the novel provide a cultural grounding for the larger themes, contributing to the 'intricate symbolic structure' of the book (Lee 1969: 820).

THE EMPIRE'S BLADE: THE KUKRI

By the 1930s, the fierce Gurkha warriors of Nepal had been a part of the British military, either the British East India Company Army or the British army proper, for more than a hundred years. The emblem of the Gurkha is the kukri, a formidable weapon in appearance, with a large, curved blade, sharpened on the concave edge. It is omnipresent in Gurkha culture, serving interchangeably as a tool and weapon of war.

> With few exceptions, they carry in their girdle their national 'khukri,' or curved knife, a well-balanced instrument, which they know full well how to use. It is in general use for all domestic purposes; also a heavy one is used in warfare and for slaughtering buffaloes, and they have been known to sever a buffalo's neck at a single blow with such a knife (Anonymous 1896: 18).

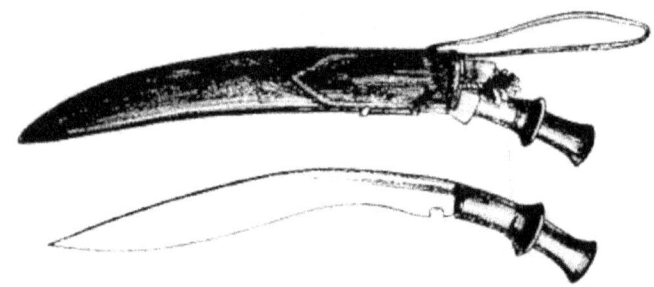

Figure 1. A traditional Gurkha kukri

The kukri makes one appearance in *Burmese Days*. In response to reports of possible unrest, the local law enforcement presence, Westfield, a man eager for violence against the Burmese, sets out to quell the unrest, with unsatisfying results. 'Westfield and the dozen constables he had taken with him to Thongwa – jolly round-faced Gurkha boys, pining to use their kukris on somebody – found the district depressingly peaceful' (1974 [1934]): 112). It is interesting that the only appearance of this fierce blade, a weapon employed to police the Empire, describes its users as 'jolly' but also that the kukris seemed to have never left their sheaths.

The image of the kukri presents a conflicted identity: a fierce tool of Empire that is, in practice, rather impotent. It seems the kukri, although a proud symbol of Gurkha identity, was relegated to the role of inspiring fear rather than actually perpetrating violence. Such a role brings to mind a line from Orwell's celebrated essay of 1941 'The Lion and the Unicorn: Socialism and the English Genius'. When discussing British military marching, he wrote: 'It belongs to a society which is ruled by the sword, no doubt, but a sword which must never be taken out of the scabbard' (Orwell 1961: 255). From this perspective, perhaps it can be argued that Burma was to be ruled by the kukri that must never exit its sheath.

THE BURMESE BLADE: THE DAH

Just as the kukri is the national blade and cultural symbol of the Gurkha, the dah is the national weapon of Burma. 'There is in Burma a kind of a large knife called a dah which is a useful agricultural as well as a domestic implement, and in most of the murders the dah plays a prominent part' (Maung 1928: 13).

Figure 2. The Burmese dah

In appearance the dah 'has a passing affinity in shape with the Japanese sword, although there is no comparison in quality. The blade is slightly curved, single-edged and usually tapers to a point ...' (Wilkinson 1993: 198) Further, although intricate examples do exist, the dah has the appearance of a common field tool: 'The hilt is guardless, sometimes with a plain, almost tubular wooden grip' (ibid). One British hunter noted: 'The Burmese dah answers all purposes, from chopping wood to clearing the jungle' (Evans 1911: 212).

Although the dah was an agricultural tool, it was also a serious weapon. When assessing the locals' strength in the Anglo-Burmese War of 1895-1896, one British officer noted: 'At close quarters the dah, a species of broadsword, is in the hands of the Burmese a formidable weapon' (Ritchie and Evans 1894: 81).

The dah appears regularly in *Burmese Days*, although its appearances can be grouped under three distinct themes. Examining these thematic appearances shows the symbolism the weapon has to the story and Orwell's overall message. Further, the examination of these themes lays the groundwork for elevating the dah from simple agricultural tool to the more complicated level of artifact and social object. The dah is an artifact, or an object with a 'particular cultural function' (Matusitz 2014: 207). But the dah is also a social object or 'an object of which the meaning is shared by a community' (ibid). How the dah appears as both an artifact and a social object in *Burmese Days* shows the rather complex and situational identity of the sword and its place in the society that used it.

NATIVE IDENTITY

The reader first sees the dah in depictions of everyday life, the customary frame in which one would see the dah on a day-to-day basis in the colony. It seems that whenever one sees a Burmese in the jungle, the dah is in hand: 'The Burman left his cart and pushed through the jungle, slicing the creepers with his dah' (Orwell 1986 [1934]: 58). And age was not a restriction on dah usage: 'six shock-headed youths came down the path, carrying dahs over their shoulders' (ibid: 162). The dah is a key facet of native Burmese identity.

What is perhaps most interesting in the images of the everyday usage of the dah is how unconcerned the British appeared to be with the presence of the sword. In all practicality, the white inhabitants of Kyauktada were outnumbered by a populace armed with swords. Examples showing this indifference also show the potential danger of the blade in the hands of the Burmese. While on the hunt, the Burmese around Flory and Elizabeth are described as '…each with his broad dah laid along his forearm' (ibid). As the party progresses through the jungle, the dah is employed to cut an obstacle whose size is equated to a wrist: 'A bamboo the thickness of a man's wrist had fallen and hung across the path. The leading beater severed it with an upward flick of his dah' (ibid). Although the Burmese posed no real danger to Flory and Elizabeth, they were in the jungle, surrounded by sword-bearing Burmese who no doubt suffered under colonial oppression. As Orwell writes: 'In the distance there was such a tumult of yells and the rattle of dahs against tree trunks that one could hardly believe six men could make so much noise' (ibid: 170).

It is interesting to note that the dah's place as a symbol of the Burmese is reinforced by its absence in the hands of the Europeans, save for one: Flory. While at his lumber camp, Flory is seen with his dah in the jungle: 'In his idleness he flung his dah at them [birds], scaring them away' and 'He loitered a little way into the jungle, flicking at creepers with his dah' (ibid: 215). This is interesting in that Flory, of all the Europeans, is the only one at times sympathetic to the Burmese and, at least in the eyes of some of the Europeans, more aligned with the Burmese than the British.

## MOCKED SYMBOL

The dah, inasmuch as it is a proud symbol of the Burmese, is also mocked by those most critical of Burmese culture: the Europeans and those Burmese wanting to be accepted by the Europeans. During their respite in the Chinese shop after the failed festival outing, Flory and Elizabeth are surrounded by various goods, which are described as being 'foreign-looking, queer and poor', with a collection of dahs falling under that description (ibid: 127). The dahs in the shop were most likely simple, working tools, but they are dismissed in the description.

Similarly, the dah's ability as a weapon is questioned by Ma Kin, U Po Kyin's wife. In recounting his plan to cause unrest and use his response to gain favour with the Europeans and entrance into the club, Ma Kin states: 'They are very foolish, those villagers. What can they do with their dahs and spears against the Indian soldiers? They will be shot down like wild animals' (ibid: 138). This mocking of the dah as a weapon is fair based on the realities of modern warfare, but as will be seen, the dah is used to make a strike against the Empire.

## A WEAPON AGAINST EMPIRE

Despite it being wrongly mocked as a weapon, the dah is used to strike back in revenge at the Empire and injure the European community. During the short-lived rebellion, the forest officer, Maxwell, shoots and kills a Burmese. In revenge, Maxwell is killed with dahs: 'It was the body of Maxwell, cut almost to pieces with dahs by two relatives of the man whom he had shot' (ibid: 237). Here Orwell takes the simple tool and raises it beyond the mundane as it commits a murder not of a Burmese, but of a European: 'The murder of a white man is a monstrosity, a sacrilege…' (ibid: 238).

After the killing of Maxwell, the dah is seen, although never used, during the violent protests that culminate with the surrounding of the European Club, where it is reported that 'all the villagers are outside! Big stick and dah in their hands… ' (ibid: 245). Even though it is not used, the threat of the dah is ever-present. As the Europeans watch the crowd, they see 'here and there a curved dah glittering' (ibid: 246). Clearly in this setting, Orwell meant the dah to signify the capacity for violence and to build tension that the Europeans might meet their fate at the edge of the blade. Despite the killing of Maxwell, some post-protest perspective explains that a blade was never swung at a European during the riots because the Burmese were more realistic about the consequences: 'Probably the Burmans had not used their dahs for fear of provoking rifle-fire' (ibid: 251). This statement gives the Burmese more tactical credit than Ma Kin was willing to do earlier in the novel. This inequity in arms also illustrates the oppression Orwell saw in the Empire: 'I think the following rule would be found generally true: that ages

DON ARP, JR.    in which the dominant weapon is expensive or difficult to make will tend to be ages of despotism, whereas when the dominant weapon is cheap and simple, the common people have a chance' (2000 [1945]: 7).

This riot scene, with the Burmese not clashing against European firepower, can be further explored alongside an examination of Orwell's essay 'Shooting an Elephant', first published in *New Writing* in 1936. As de Lange notes (2009: 15): 'The elephant has many symbolic meanings. He is both a symbol of the oppressor and the oppressed.' Or according to Meyers (2000: 72), the elephant 'symbolizes the death throes of the British Empire'. Once the elephant is shot down (there is much debate on whether the animal is completely dead by this point), the Burmese strip the meat from the animal. De Lang (op cit: 15): 'When the Burmese strip the elephant's carcass to the bone Orwell seems to imply that the vicious circle continues when the oppressed now becomes the oppressor.' Yet it is interesting that the Burmese cannot strike back at the Empire, or in this case a symbol of the Empire, until it has been put down by a firearm. As in the scene from *Burmese Days*, it seems the Burmese have a desire to act, but know that no success can be had in a clash between blade and rifle. The one example we do have from the novel, the killing of Maxwell, reinforces this as it was doubtful Maxwell was armed. Apart from Flory's carrying of a dah while in the jungle and the hunting scenes, there is little mention of arms being carried by the Europeans.

But what if the Burmese had raised their dahs in anger and then were shot down by Flory and the armed troops? Flory's quandary is not unlike that of the policeman in 'Shooting an Elephant', as in each case a European has in his control the power of arms and the ability to decide against whom to use it. As Runciman argues (2009: 182): 'He has the power in his hands: he can use it against the elephant, or against the crowd. Regardless of the consequences the fact remains that he has the power in his hands; what is important is what he chooses to do with the power.'

ORWELL AND THE SWORD

The dah held a special significance for Orwell. Bowker notes that '… he took mementoes, too, notably a collection of Burmese swords with which he would decorate his rooms, as he might have decorated it with tiger heads had he better luck in the hunt' (Bowker 2003: 95). Perhaps it was bad luck hunting, but also it seems Orwell sympathised more with the Burmese than the British, and thus a collection of objects that were fundamental to the native identify fit well with him being a failed imperialist.

Orwell clearly saw that swords were antiquated compared to modern rifles. That said, he also recognised the powerful popular mythology held by such weapons. He points this out in an 'As I Please' piece, saying: 'Others besides myself have noted that war, when it gets into the leading articles, is apt to be waged with remarkably old-fashioned weapons' (2000 {1943-1946]: 209). But this appearance also had a linkage with a heroic, almost nationalistic attitude: 'Soon as an heroic attitude has to be struck, the only armaments mentioned are the sword … the spear, the shield…' (ibid).

Another clue on how Orwell saw the bladed weapons in *Burmese Days* is suggested in the way he represented the weapons in the novel (op cit). Interestingly, Burmese and Hindi words are always italicised in the text, so dah always appears in italics. Foreign words, 'some of which might well have been set in italic in a book not so firmly placed in the milieu of *Burmese Days*, have been allowed to stand in roman' (ibid: 312-313). Moreover, the foreign words that stand in roman are the words associated with elements or practices of the British side of imperialism. One word is quite interesting on this list: kukri. On the list, it shares space with memsahib, punkah, sahib, sepoy, and topi, to name a few. Kukri is a word and weapon of Empire. Dah is a word and weapon of the Burmese. It must be noted that *Burmese Days* and, to an extent, 'Shooting an Elephant' are not the only pieces in which Orwell has used a weapon as a symbol of identity. In *Animal Farm* (1945), Napoleon's dominate power position is symbolised by his carrying a whip, the device that was a tool in the eyes of the farmer but a weapon in the eyes of the animals (2003 [1945]: 79).

## CONCLUSION

Cultures the world over often have a specific form of weaponry that holds significant importance for cultural identity and mythology. These weapons may be implements of everyday life, drafted for combat out of necessity and familiarity. Or, they may be weapons of war, designed for a singular martial purpose. Regardless, these weapons are often re-appropriated, both by the culture itself and by outsiders, to embody an essence of identity or belief of the group. This practice makes these weapons powerful symbols in literature. In *Burmese Days*, Orwell uses the Burmese dah and the Gurkha kukri to represent the two sides of colonial conflict in Burma.

The dah is the tool-turned-weapon, an always visible tool that is, at least in the novel, seldom used for violence. That said, it is omnipresent and a source of constant threat to the European inhabitants of Kyauktada. The kukri is a weapon of Empire, used by the Gurkha soldiers of the British army to enforce order in the colonies. In this role, the kukri is the symbol of ever-ready violence and might of the imperial oppressor. In the novel, the kukri is not as complex in its use as the dah. The dah appears in several capacities where it represents native Burmese identity, is a mocked symbol of perceived native inferiority, and at last raises to be a weapon against the Empire. Serving as both an artifact and a social object, the dah well serves to advance the symbolic structure of the novel.

And between the two weapons, it is the dah that actually draws blood, the kukri resting impotent in a sheath. For Orwell, weapons represented much about a culture and its perceived advancement, but they also held sway in forming an identity. As seen in other works, Orwell uses weapons to serve as a badge of identity. Interestingly, from his time in Burma, Orwell's most significant souvenirs, ones that graced the walls of his various homes, were his collection of Burmese dahs. The role these weapons played in the structure of *Burmese Days* is significant and contributes to the novel's rich symbolic structure.

## REFERENCES

Anonymous (1896) *The Darjeeling Himalayan Railway: Illustrated Guide for Tourists*, London: McCorquodale and Co.

Bowker, Gordon (2003) *Inside George Orwell*, New York: Palgrave MacMillan

Burton, Richard F. (1987 [1884]) *The Book of the Sword*, New York: Dover Publications, Inc.

de Lange, Adriaan M. (2009) Autobiography: An analysis of 'Shooting an Elephant', Bloom, Harold (ed.) *George Orwell*, New York City: Infobase Publishing pp 9-48

Evans, George Patrick Elystan (1911) *Big Game Shooting in Upper Burma*, London: Longmans, Green

Lee, Robert A. (1969) Symbol and structure in *Burmese Days*: A revaluation, *Texas Studies in Literature and Language*, Vol. 11 pp 819-835

Matusitz, Jonathan (2014) *Symbolism in Terrorism: Motivation, Communication, and Behavior*, Lanham: Rowan & Littlefield

Maung, Khim (1928) A Burmese portrait, *The Rotarian*, April pp 12-15

Meyers, Jeffrey (2000) *Orwell: Wintry Conscience of a Generation*, London/New York: W. W. Norton & Company

Orwell, George (2003 [1945] and [1949]) *Animal Farm* and *1984*, Boston: Houghton Mifflin Harcourt

Orwell, George (1974 [1934]) *Burmese Days*, Orlando: Harcourt, Inc.

Orwell, George (2000 {1943-1946]) *George Orwell: 'As I Please', 1943-1946*, Boston: David R. Godine Publisher

Orwell, George (1986 [1934]) *The Complete Works of George Orwell, Volume 2*, Burmese Days (Appendix by Davison, Peter). London: Secker and Warburg

Orwell, George (1961) *The Orwell Reader: Fiction, Essays, and Reportage*, Boston: Houghton Mifflin Harcourt

Orwell, George (2000 [1945]) You and the atom bomb, Orwell, Sonia and Angus, Ian (eds) *George Orwell: In Front of Your Nose, 1946-1950*, Boston: David R. Godine Publisher pp 7-10

Peterson, Amy T. and Dunworth, David (2004) *Mythology in Our Midst: A Guide to Cultural References*, Westport: Greenwood Publishing Group

Ritchie, Anne Thackeray and Evans, Richardson (1894) *Lord Amherst and the British Advance Eastwards to Burma*, Oxford: Clarendon Press

Runciman, David (2009) *Political Hypocrisy: The Mask of Power, from Hobbes to Orwell and Beyond*, New Haven: Princeton University Press

Wilkinson, Frederick (1993) India and Southeast Asia, Coe, Michael (ed.) *Swords and Hilt Weapons*, New York: Barnes & Noble Books pp 186-203

## NOTE ON THE CONTRIBUTOR

Don Arp, Jr., is an independent researcher and writer. He has a Master of Arts in Anthropology (specialising in archaeology) and a Bachelor of Arts with highest distinction, both from the University of Nebraska-Lincoln. He also has a Certificate in Forensic Science from North Central State College in Mansfield, Ohio. He maintains an active research agenda and is published in several fields. Some of the journals that have published his work include *Journal of Forensic Identification*; *Journal of Pidgin and Creole Languages*; *Cuneiform Digital Library Notes* and *Journal of Intellectual Property Law and Practice*.

# ARTICLE

# The Poet Who Wanted to Shoot an Elephant

## GERRY ABBOTT

*Orwell's celebrated essay 'Shooting an Elephant' of 1936 records an event that happened while he served as an Imperial Policeman in Burma between 1922-1927. But did it really happen? A number of Orwell biographers have raised questions. This article argues that evidence from Orwell's own poems, Captain H. R. Robinson's autobiography and other sources suggests that Orwell did actually shoot an elephant while stationed in Moulmein.*

Like many boys of his age, the ten-year-old Eric Blair was fascinated by guns. It was just before the First World War, and years later he reminisced in a newspaper article about the toys available in those days: 'One of the greatest joys of my own childhood were those little brass cannons on wooden gun-carriages' the largest of which 'went off with a noise like the Day of Judgement' (*Evening Standard*, 1 December 1945). He managed to make his own gunpowder, and rejoiced in the fact that in those days 'you could walk into any bicycle shop and buy a revolver' and, indeed, could 'buy for 7s. 6d. a fairly lethal weapon known as a Saloon rifle. I bought my first Saloon rifle at the age of ten, with no questions asked'.

Young Eric developed an unhealthy delight in killing animals, especially with guns. On a visit to the Buddicom family when he was seventeen, his friend Prosper recorded that the two spent about three weeks of that month fishing and shooting near Henley on Thames (Buddicom 1974: 100-101). Creatures later killed by one or other of the boys and mentioned by Eric in two short letters in January 1921 were snipe, woodcock, rats, partridges and rabbits (Davison 1998: 78-79). Prosper's sister Jacintha, in whom Eric was romantically interested, had been appalled when he and Prosper killed a hedgehog: 'The only time I can remember quarrelling with Eric myself was when he and Prosper killed a beautiful hedgehog – an animal for which I have particular affection – and baked it in clay as they had heard gipsies did. I would not speak to them for a week (Buddicom 1974: 21). More strangely, Eric 'used to kill eels by firing at them with a 12 bore shotgun' (Crick 1980: 129), the shotgun being far more violent than the .22 Saloon rifle.

Having left Eton and passed the entry requirements of the Imperial Military Police, Eric prepared to sail to Burma. Before his departure he sent a final poem to Jacintha:

> Friendship and love are closely intertwined,
> My heart belongs to your befriending mind:
> But chilling sunlit fields, cloud-shadows fall –
> My love can't reach your heedless heart at all (Crick 1980: 72).

Sixteen years later, by which time he was writing as George Orwell, he would receive a letter from the University of Buffalo addressing him as a poet and seeking the gift of manuscripts for their collection on modern poetry, and Orwell would reply: 'I am not a poet, only a novelist' (Davison 2000: 155). That word 'only' suggests a rueful admission of his lack of success in writing good poetry. In October 1922, at the age of nineteen, Eric sailed from Birkenhead on the SS *Herefordshire* to take up his first posting in Burma, where he would continue to try his hand at verse, and disembarked in Rangoon a month later.

## CAPTAIN ROBINSON'S POSTING

Almost exactly a year before Eric's arrival, another Military Police officer had taken up his new post in the far north of Burma. Twenty-four-years-old, Captain Herbert Robinson could hardly have been given a posting more remote and daunting than Konglu, a small hilltop town on the north-east frontier near Putao. Getting there meant travelling by train from Rangoon to the railhead town of Myitkyina and then marching for twenty-four days at the head of a line of mules laden with a year's supply of provisions. Once settled in, he was left in single-handed charge of the civil and military affairs of a huge tract of mountainous terrain. Robinson's first year or so in Konglu was in his own words 'interesting if rather lonely ... I never saw another white man and rarely spoke my own tongue' (Robinson 1942: 23-24).

Finding and apprehending law-breakers called for stamina and persistence. In one case it took him an arduous two-week march to find a young woman accused of poisoning her elderly husband. Then on the way back she escaped, had to be re-arrested and was finally imprisoned in Konglu. From the beginning he had found her very attractive and eventually in his own words 'an overwhelming aching and yearning seized my soul, and one night I fell' (ibid: 33). She seems to have been a willing participant in what followed but the fact that she was still manacled and shackled adds a chilling note to his confession.

Soon after this sexual encounter Robinson was visited by a well-known botanist of the time. The plant-hunter Frank Kingdon

**GERRY ABBOTT**

Ward, who happened to be returning from an excursion into China, wandered into Fort Hertz (Putao) and came across the bungalows of the police officers. At this point 'striding across the compound came an Englishman. It was Captain Robinson, of the Military Police' (Kingdon Ward 1924: 254). Kingdon Ward adds an observation that is rather touching, given Robinson's subsequent fate. Unlike the other officers, who loved the good fishing available at Fort Hertz. 'He did not fish. He had never been known to shoot anything, unless it was sitting still, looking the other way' (ibid: 257). The time would soon come when, even sitting still and looking the right way, he would fail to hit the target fair and square.

ERIC BLAIR'S ARRIVAL

Having disembarked in Rangoon, Blair took the mail train to Mandalay where, on a November day in 1922, he was greeted by a group of Burma Police officers among whom was Roger Beadon, a recent arrival. Beadon's impression of Eric was of a man 'sallow-faced, tall, thin, and gangling, whose clothes, no matter how well cut, seemed to hang on him' (Stansky and Abrahams 1972: 150-151). No sooner had Blair settled in to life at the Police Training School than he and Beadon were off in an attempt to hunt for tigers. According to Taylor (2003: 68), Blair asked Beadon if he wanted to come on a tiger shoot, but Beadon claimed that the idea was his own. As he recalled in a 1969 BBC interview:

> I said: 'Would you like to come out for a tiger shoot?' He thought it was a good idea. Heaven knows what made me do it, but I had a Luger Parabellum Automatic and we borrowed the Principal's shotgun and went out about fourteen miles from Mandalay and asked a man if we could borrow his bullock cart because we wanted to go after tiger. The gentleman very kindly produced his bullock cart, it must have been about nine o'clock at night, and as dark as you could make it. We got into the back of the cart and he drove round about, me with my Parabellum cocked and Blair with the other gun. But we didn't see a tiger and I had a sort of feeling that the gentleman in charge of the bullock cart never intended that we should (Coppard and Crick 1984: 63).

Although Eric was by now nineteen, this expedition was clearly a boyish piece of wishful thinking with no hope of success, but it does suggest that he would have no qualms about shooting big game.

Where Jacintha Buddicom had failed to raise Eric's verse to the realms of poesy, Mandalay's ladies of easy virtue had more success. One of them inspired this ironic verse, probably written just after Eric left that city:

### Romance

When I was young and had no sense
In far-off Mandalay
I lost my heart to a Burmese girl
As lovely as the day.

Her skin was gold, her hair was jet,
Her teeth were ivory;
I said 'For twenty silver pieces,
Maiden, sleep with me.'

She looked at me, so pure, so sad,
The loveliest thing alive,
And in her lisping, virgin voice,
Stood out for twenty-five.

The final line of this light-hearted poem nicely demolishes the description of the Burmese girl as *maiden*, *pure* and *virgin*. The poem was undated but was written on Burma government paper. So, too, was a longer and much darker poem of the same period told in the persona of a man of the church who describes how he spent his 'parson's week' – an occasional extended week off-duty. Of the poem's eight stanzas, two will suffice to establish its tone:

### The lesser evil

Empty as death and slow as pain
The days went by on leaden feet;
And parson's week had come again
As I walked down the little street.

      \*\*\*

I thought of all the church bells ringing
In towns that Christian folk were in;
I heard the godly maidens singing:
I turned into the house of sin.

Both poems end with a woman's demand for payment (for both in full, see Crick 1980: 92-93).

## ROBINSON COMES DOWN TO MANDALAY

It was early in April 1923 that Herbert Robinson came down to Mandalay by train from Myitkyina, having received news that his service would be discontinued. It is most likely that he had been cashiered for conduct unbecoming an officer and a gentleman (behaviour that included a reliance on opium) but his own brief explanation was simply that his dismissal was part of the Geddes programme of cuts: 'The Geddes Axe had fallen' (Robinson 1942: 44). While in Mandalay awaiting a passage to England, Robinson was required to complete the formalities concerning retirement from the Indian Army. It was inevitable now that Blair, having arrived about four months earlier, and Robinson would meet; the most likely venue would be the Upper Burma Club, once a part of Mandalay's old gilded palace but by this time a leisure facility established by the British inside the palace precincts. Robinson records: 'One evening towards the end of April I was sitting in the Upper Burma Club discussing my plans with two friends, whom I will call the Poet and the Padre' (Robinson 1942: 60).

We might pause at this point and consider why Captain Herbert Robinson, even though he published his autobiography only after more than twenty years had passed, named no names. There can be little doubt that 'the Poet' was Blair; it is also likely that 'the Padre' was an army chaplain (*padre* being an everyday military term for a man of the cloth) who probably, like Robinson, had disgraced himself; and it seems clear that Blair not only knew him but also wrote about him in *The Lesser Evil*. There appears to have been some agreement, spoken or unspoken, that both Poet and Padre should remain anonymous.

Robinson provides an incidental detail which also suggests that 'the Poet' was Eric Blair: when Robinson, Blair and another man drove out to the nearby hills in another shot at hunting and things went wrong, 'the slight figure of the Poet' came back running and ended up, as one would expect of a man known to have weak lungs, 'too exhausted to think of doing the return trip' (ibid: 114). As Robinson had just observed: 'The Poet was hardly one's idea of a mighty hunter before the Lord. Pale and delicate in appearance, but otherwise healthy enough, he looked what he was – a poet' (ibid: 113). It is at this point that Robinson adds a startling piece of information: 'But poets, like women with child, have peculiar fancies, and this one wanted to shoot an elephant.'

## ROBINSON'S EXIT

Robinson, becoming more and more dependent on opium, set up a smoking den in his lodgings, tried unsuccessfully to kick the habit and when he was at his wits' end decided to shoot himself. Never a good shot even if the target was sitting still, he succeeded only in blinding himself, blowing both eyeballs out of their sockets, and was repatriated in March 1925. Soon after arriving, he entered the Massage School of the National Institute for the Blind and worked in London hospitals as a physiotherapist. In 1942 he published his autobiography. This was reviewed by George Orwell in the *Observer* of 13 September 1942, who, in his phrasing (e. g: 'Those who knew the author in Mandalay' and 'Those who knew Captain Robinson in the old days') indicated his acquaintance with the author. Herbert finally killed himself in March 1965 at the age of sixty-nine.

## BLAIR'S ELEPHANT

After completing his exams in 1924, Eric had been posted to Myaungmya, Twante, Syriam, Insein and, in April 1926, Moulmein. He returned to England in 1927, adopted the pen-name George Orwell and later, having seen three of his prose works published – *Down and Out in Paris and London*, in 1933, *Burmese Days*, in 1934, and *A Clergyman's Daughter*, in 1936 – wrote to the publisher John Lehmann: 'I am writing a book at present and the only other thing I have in mind is a sketch (it would be about 2000-3000 words), describing the shooting of an elephant. It all came back to me very vividly the other day …' and again on 2 June: 'I enclose that sketch I mentioned to you. As I say the incident had stuck in my mind & I wanted to write it, but whether it will be quite in your line I am not certain' (Davison 2000: 483 and 486). This 'sketch' was 'Shooting an Elephant', a narrative in which Orwell describes how, and more importantly why, he shot a runaway elephant during his time in Moulmein.

The phraseology in the two letters above ('It all comes back to me' and 'the incident had stuck in my mind') strongly suggests that the sketch was to be autobiographical, and the narrative is written in the first person. In *Burmese Days*, Orwell had already arranged for the protagonist John Flory (his alter ego) to impress Elizabeth Lackersteen by describing to her 'the murder of an elephant which he had perpetrated some years earlier'. (Note 'murder' and 'perpetrated'.) The Orwell Archive at University College London contains a statement by George Stuart, a railway engineer in Moulmein, in which he says he was in the club when a message arrived and Eric 'went off in his old Ford to pick up a rifle and went in search of the elephant … and he shot this elephant' (Davison 1998: 506 n. 2). The elephant was said to belong to a big timber firm, and Stuart maintained that Blair was posted to Katha as a punishment, the chief of the police service being publicly angry and saying that Blair was a disgrace to Eton. A footnote in Crick (1980: 96) concerns another possible witness: 'One old Burma hand, R. C. Chorley, with whom he went pigeon-shooting in Twante, thinks he remembers reading in the *Rangoon Gazette* that Blair had been called in to shoot a rogue elephant; but he also thinks that he may have read "Shooting an Elephant".' Taylor (2003: 80) points out that there is, indeed, such a report in the *Rangoon Gazette* dated 22 March 1926, but the protagonist was Major E. C. Kenny, subdivisional officer at Yamethin who, 'to the delight of the villagers', shot an elephant that had killed a man. Kenny was not punished but promoted. Both Taylor and Crick doubt whether Blair did kill an elephant, and Crick adds (1980: 96n.) that other authors also wrote 'in a similar, ambiguous, first-person descriptive vein, a then-fashionable genre which blurred any clear line between fiction and autobiography – truthful to experiences but not necessarily to fact'.

THE TRUTH?

What, then, were the facts in this matter? It seems that we are left with a choice of two main interpretations: either (1) that Eric did *not* shoot an elephant in Moulmein, but may have based his 'sketch' on the report of an exploit such as Major Kenny's far to the north in Yamethin; or (2) that 'Shooting an Elephant' is substantially a correct report and that 'the Poet', therefore, did finally get his elephant.

Interpretation (1) would ask us to regard his 'sketch' not as an autobiographical account but as an essay, a vehicle for him to vent his anger at finding himself a victim of the imperialist system he was employed to enforce. In the years between 1926 and 1936, his hatred of imperialism had certainly matured and now needed to be more openly expressed. But interpretation (2) would be more interesting in that it would fit into Blair's stated wish to kill an elephant. The use of 'murder' and 'perpetrated' suggests an acute awareness of his wrongdoing, and this is heightened when in his short 'sketch' he denies the wish three times:

- 'I had no intention of shooting the elephant – I had merely sent for the rifle to defend myself …'
- 'Moreover, I did not in the least want to shoot him.'
- 'But I did not want to shoot the elephant.'

Here, protesting too much, Orwell lays the blame upon the imperialist system and 'the will of those yellow faces behind', while he is 'only an absurd puppet' who shoots the creature 'solely to avoid looking a fool'. Yet the guilt is surely real. I suggest that 'the Poet' did eventually get his elephant; that on watching the great animal's slow death he instantly regretted it; that the police would not want the matter advertised in the *Rangoon Gazette*; and that when the death of the elephant came back to Orwell 'very vividly', he wrote the account as an expiation. This explanation, though hypothetical, fits the facts as we know them and needs to be taken seriously.

## REFERENCES

Buddicom, Jacintha (1974) *Eric and Us*, London: Leslie Frewin

Coppard, Audrey and Crick, Bernard (eds) (1984) *Orwell Remembered*, London: BBC

Crick, Bernard (1980) *George Orwell: A Life*, London: Secker & Warburg

Davison, Peter (ed.) (1998) *George Orwell: A Kind of Compulsion, 1903-1936*, London: Secker & Warburg

Davison, Peter (ed.) (2000) *George Orwell: Facing Unpleasant Facts, 1937-1939*, London: Secker & Warburg

Davison, Peter (ed.) (2010) *The Orwell Diaries*, London: Penguin Books

Kingdon Ward, Frank (1924) *From China to Hkamti Long*, London: Edward Arnold

Orwell, George (1934) *Burmese Days*, New York: Harper Brothers

Orwell, George (1970 [1936]) Shooting an Elephant, Blair, Sonia and Angus, Ian (eds) *The Collected Essays, Journalism and Letters of George Orwell, Volume 1*. Harmondsworth: Penguin Books pp 265-272, originally published in *New Writing* 2

Robinson, Herbert (1942) *A Modern De Quincey: An Autobiography*, London: Harrap

Stansky, Peter and Abrahams, William (1972) *The Unknown Orwell*, London: Constable

Taylor, D. J. (2003) *Orwell: The Life*, London: Chatto & Windus

## NOTE ON THE CONTRIBUTOR

Gerry Abbott started teaching refugees in 1958 while qualifying as a teacher of EFL. After teaching for four years in Thailand and two in Jordan, he was appointed Lecturer in the Teaching of English Overseas, University of Manchester. Secondments took him to Makerere University (with Idi Amin as Chancellor), PDR Yemen, Sarawak, Pakistan, Cameroon and finally Burma, where his house was on the same road as the Burma Police training school that George Orwell had attended. Airlifted from the orchestrated violence of 1988, he retired and, having hitherto published widely on English language teaching, turned his attention to the history and culture of Burma, producing *Inroads into Burma* (OUP, Kuala Lumpur, 1997); *The Traveller's History of Burma* (Orchid Press, Bangkok, 1998); and , with Khin Thant Han, *The Folk-Tales of Burma* (Brill, Leiden, 2000).

# REVIEWS

**Forgotten Places: Barcelona and the Spanish Civil War**
Nick Lloyd
Author, Barcelona, 2015, pp 388
ISBN 978 1 5195 3111 7 (pbk)

This is a wonderful hybrid of a book. At first it is a bit confusing to understand its organisation despite the author's instructions on how to use it. There are various cross-references and numbering of sections. The text can be read in order to find out more about Barcelona and the War and much else mostly about the radical history of the city. But its other purpose is to be carried about in Barcelona itself to provide information and illumination about the city's terrible, dramatic, and heroic history during the Civil War. Nick Lloyd, an Englishman resident in Barcelona, provides guided visits himself, including I understand, a splendid one recently for the Orwell Society.

The book has some grainy illustrations, the most moving of which shows the author reading an excerpt from *Homage to Catalonia* to Richard Blair, George Orwell's son, and Quentin Kopp, the son of Georges Kopp, Orwell's commander in Spain. There is one glorious image, used for the jacket, of the 17-year-old communist militia woman, Marina Ginestà, on the roof of the Hotel Colón, on 21 July 1936, with a borrowed rifle slung over her shoulder. Her look is full of happy hope and confidence. The rest of her life story is told, including her memory of the taking of the image, speaking about it in 2008. 'It is a good picture. It reflects the feeling we had at the time. ... There was euphoria. ... They say that in the Hotel Colón photo I have a captivating look. It's possible because we lived at the same time as the mystique of the proletarian revolution and the images of Hollywood, of Greta Garbo and Gary Cooper' (p. 169).

Approximately the first third of the book is a history of Barcelona and the Civil War, and then the remaining two-thirds is divided into fourteen sections covering the various neighbourhoods of Barcelona, with the chapters divided into numbered sections indicating places but also individuals and events associated with those particular areas. There are many cross-references. Lloyd imagines his readers dipping into the book as needed and not necessarily reading all of the second part. There is a wide historical range including discussions of both earlier periods and later events, such as, for instance, the role of the basing in Barcelona of the American Sixth Fleet after the Second World War. In order to make the various sections of the second part somewhat independent of one another, there is some repetition but it does not become excessive. Many fascinating stories are told, so many of them involving death. There are quite a few anarchists throwing bombs but their violence is easily overshadowed by the numerous accounts of torturing, shootings and executions. The exuberant early days in Barcelona at the time of the outbreak of the rebellion in July 1936, so wonderful in many ways, did also provide the cover for private vendettas and murders. Those on the right were killed and those on the left fought one another during the May Days of 1937, the internecine conflicts between the supporters of the republic, including later torturing to death by Soviet agents, not to mention the innumerable executions after Franco's victory. It is a grim story.

There is much both relevant to and about Eric Blair, George Orwell, in this book making vividly clear, I believe, why his comparatively brief time in Spain, from the end of December 1936 to June,1937, may have been the most important experience in his life. It shaped his ideas and provided the dominating conceptions of his two most influential books, *Animal Farm* and *Nineteen Eighty-Four*. He missed the most glorious days of the transformation of Barcelona starting in July when the city became a workers' paradise. But the city he found when he arrived was still so exhilarating that he felt that this was a new world that he had to fight for. It was what he saw in Spain that made him a convert to socialism as an ideal society. But his experiences in Spain also made him intensely aware of how virtually impossible it was to preserve the positive side of a revolutionary transformation. Because the Western democracies determined to follow a policy of non-intervention, the republic was forced to rely on the Soviet Union to provide arms, paid for by Spanish gold, which led to a mounting domination of Soviet policy.

A reasonable argument could be made that the social revolution and the upheaval it entailed should be postponed in the interests of first winning the war against the rebels. Of course, the tragedy was that even though the revolution was curtailed the war was lost. Bred in the traditions of English empiricism, Orwell, though deeply regretting postponing a much better society, accepted that ideological sacrifices had to be made so that the war might be won. In fact, he had come back from the front in May to look into transferring from the POUM militia to the more efficient communist-dominated International Brigades. But once he found his comrades being attacked in the streets of the city he knew that he had to act with them. Revolutions are what he thought should happen but they seem inevitably to fail. The leaders are almost always corrupted by power. There was then the further tragedy in Barcelona of the fighting in its streets between the factions of the left.

REVIEW

Perhaps deliberately but also appropriately for the readers of this journal, the book ends with a discussion of the site of the Lenin Barracks where Orwell was taken to train and be trained when he joined the POUM militia. There we find the English/Orwellian combination of political commitment and individualism. This last section has quotations from *Homage to Catalonia* and his essay, 'Looking Back on the Spanish War'. There he remembers by name the individuals, his comrades who were offering their lives in the moving hope to create a better world. 'It is probable that all of them are dead' (p. 374). Revolutions are about the masses and the classes but its ultimate aim for an English revolutionary is to improve the quality of the individual life. It was that that was so important for Orwell. His experiences in Spain were crucial for the creation of that vision but also, alas, made him aware of its fragility, of the degree that it is at fatal risk from its enemies, both internal and external. This book, providing so much about Barcelona, makes wonderfully vivid how essential that vision was and is.

Peter Stansky,
Stanford University

**Worktown: The Astonishing Story of the Birth of Mass-Observation**
David Hall
Wiedenfeld & Nicolson, London, 2015, pp 323
ISBN 978 0 2978 7168 2

In 1943, while discussing the ongoing decline of the pub as a cultural institution, George Orwell anticipated the general argument of Richard Hoggart's *The Uses of Literacy* (1957) by claiming that 'the whole trend of the age is away from creative communal amusements and towards solitary mechanical ones' (*CWGO* 14: 321). Specifically, the communal pleasures and elaborate social rituals of pub life were in competition with the 'passive, drug-like pleasures of the cinema and the radio'. However, Orwell was glad to note, the average pub-goer was still putting away between fifteen and twenty pints a week and beer remained a positive good in its own right beyond the need for justification. The occasion for these reflections was an unsigned review for *The Listener* of *The Pub and the People* (1943), a book compiled by the social research organisation Mass Observation, which had been founded in January 1937 by the leftish intellectual circles surrounding the GPO documentary film unit at Blackheath.

Mass Observation, conceived as a programme for the scientific study of human social behaviour in Britain or, in other words, as an 'anthropology of ourselves', had been publicly announced in a letter printed in the *New Statesman* of 30 January 1937 and signed by the anthropologist Tom Harrisson, the documentary film-maker Humphrey Jennings, and the poet Charles Madge. Supported by figures including H. G. Wells, Olaf Stapledon and Julian Huxley, Mass Observation attracted the participation of members of the left-wing intelligentsia such as J. B. S. Haldane, Naomi Mitchison, William Empson, Frances Partridge, Jack Lindsay, Kathleen Raine, and David Gascoyne. While Harrisson headed-up a project to investigate the everyday lives of the industrial working class in Bolton ('Worktown'), Jennings and Madge ran a 'National Panel' of public volunteers – recruited through the pages of publications ranging from the *Daily Mirror* to *Left Review* – who were initially required to keep day-diaries for the twelfth of each month as well as answering 'directives' instructing them to describe aspects of their lives ranging from their smoking and reading habits to the contents of their mantelpieces. After the first year, the day-diaries gave way to more structured directives covering a number of different areas of enquiry for each month. At the outbreak of the war, Mass Observation asked its panellists to begin keeping day-to-day personal diaries for them. A number of these war diaries have since been published, including that of Nella Last, which was adapted into the 2006 television drama *Housewife, 49* starring Victoria Wood.

# REVIEW

One might expect Orwell to have disapproved of Mass Observation on principle precisely because so many of its key figures might be included amongst those he described in 'My Country Right or Left' (1940) as 'the boiled rabbits of the left' (*CWGO* 14: 272); incapable of connecting to the patriotism and military values he considered necessary to save Britain during the war. Indeed, in his March 1940 review for *Time and Tide* of Mass Observation's *War Begins At Home* (1940), he had criticised the organisation precisely for an inability to recognise the patriotism of the common people: 'If one may make a guess at the reason, it is that people capable of even imagining a thing like Mass Observation are necessarily exceptional people – exceptional enough not to share the rather unthinking patriotism of the ordinary man' (*CWGO* 12: 17). He also pointed out that a similar deficiency had characterised Mass Observation's first book, *May the Twelfth: Mass-Observation Day-Surveys 1937* (1937), which had provided 400 pages of analysis mostly concerning the coronation of King George VI without 'any indication that royalist sentiment is still a reality in England' (ibid). However, as the war progressed, Orwell's attitude to Mass Observation became more positive.

In his 'London Letter' to *Partisan Review* of 19 August 1942, Orwell cited Mass Observation as demonstrating that 'many factory workers are actually *afraid* of the war ending, because they foresee a prompt return to the old conditions, with three million unemployed, etc.' (*CWGO* 13: 521). He used this evidence to make the point that the masses had not yet caught up with the idea that laissez-faire capitalism was finished beyond a vague understanding that 'things will be different'. However, Orwell, himself was not sure why things would not return to normal after the war, as they had in 1919, apart from his belief that old-style capitalism was incapable of supporting a victory. It was only later that he really came to appreciate how government planning was essential to both complete a victory and to organise post-war society for the benefit of everyone. This change can be seen in his review of Mass Observation's book on demobilisation and post-war reconstruction, *The Journey Home* (1944). Here, he approvingly notes that Mass Observation's work from the beginning of the war onwards suggests 'that Britain suffers from too little government rather than too much' (*CWGO* 16: 248). The transformation of his attitude to the organisation was complete by 28 March 1947, when he devoted part of his regular 'As I Please' column to looking back at the 'hostility' with which Mass Observation had been greeted when it was founded ten years earlier: 'On the whole the opposition to this or any other kind of social survey comes from people of Conservative opinions, who often seem to be genuinely indignant at the idea of finding out what the big public is thinking' (*CWGO* 19: 91).

Viewed in this wider context, Orwell's review of *The Pub and the People* may be seen as one of a series of stages in the wider shift of his political outlook from that of pre-war English rebel to post-war British intellectual and supporter of the Attlee government; a process which saw him become friends with people such as Stephen Spender, whom he had previously scorned as one of the 'Nancy poets'. Therefore, it is significant that the principle author of *The Pub and the People* was the communist novelist, John Sommerfield, a former schoolboy contemporary of Spender, who had fought for the International Brigades in the defence of Madrid in late 1936 just before Orwell arrived in Spain. Sommerfield's memoir of his experiences in Spain, *Volunteer in Spain* (1937), which focused on his friend the poet John Cornford, who died in the fighting, was reviewed dismissively by Orwell shortly after his return from Spain. Understandably revolted by the communists for their behaviour in Catalonia, Orwell pulled no punches: 'Seeing that the International Brigade is in some sense fighting for all of us … it may seem ungracious to say that this book is a piece of sentimental tripe; but so it is' (*CWGO* 11: 52).

However, other critics, such as Cyril Connolly, praised Sommerfield's book and it still reads freshly today. Moreover, there are enough parallels – such as shared descriptions of the wealthy middle classes wearing boiler suits in revolutionary Barcelona (an image which subsequently informed *Nineteen Eighty-Four*) – between *Volunteer in Spain* and *Homage to Catalonia* (1938) to suggest that Orwell used the earlier book, and the example of Cornford (who first fought for the POUM and then transferred to the International Brigades as Orwell hoped to do), as a template for his own there-and-back-again story of a popular front intellectual going to fight in Spain. He certainly would go on to use the example of Cornford as the central argument of his wartime essay 'My Country Right or Left' that public school patriots could transfer their loyalties to socialism.

By the time Orwell's unfavourable review of *Volunteer in Spain* appeared, Sommerfield was in Bolton working for Harrisson as Director of Fieldwork for Mass-Observation's 'Worktown' project. This full-scale exercise in participant observation, which is the subject of David Hall's engaging new history, involved the Mass Observers living in a terraced house in the middle of Bolton and studying all facets of everyday life up to the outbreak of the war. The impulse behind this exercise had shared affinities with the wider documentary movement of the 1930s. Indeed, Madge and Harrisson had even made a veiled reference to Orwell's *The Road to Wigan Pier* (1937) in their pamphlet, *Mass-Observation* (London: Frederick Muller, 1937), setting out the approach to be taken by observers: 'His squalid boarding-house will become for the observer what the entrails of the dog-fish are to the zoologist' (ibid: 29). As Hall relates, 85 Davenport Street was certainly squalid as bodies, paperwork and the debris of fish suppers competed for the limited available space. Harrisson worked 18-hour days to the constant accompaniment of a wind-up gramophone, often dictating from the bath. Sommerfield, wisely, bagged a tiny attic bedroom for himself.

REVIEW

One of the reasons that Mass Observation and 'Worktown' are not as well-known as they should be (although this has changed over the last ten years or so) is that they failed to fulfil their ambitious publishing programme. Planned books on 'How Religion Works', 'Politics and the Non-Voter' and the leisure behaviour of Worktowners on their annual week's holiday in Blackpool never appeared despite receiving advances from Gollancz. This was because, as Hall explains, despite the popular misconception that Mass Observation entailed a voyeuristic relationship between middle-class intellectuals and the masses, Harrisson's key employees were working-class men, such as Walter Hood, an unemployed miner form the North East, and Joe Wilcock, from a weaving family in nearby Farnworth. The advantage of Hood and Wilcock, as well as locals employed on a part-time basis by the project, was that they could fit in to the predominantly working-class society of Bolton without arousing a distrust for outsiders. However, the downside was that they had no real writing experience and, therefore, struggled in the time available to write up their material to the standard required of a book-length publication. Furthermore, Harrisson was reluctant to cede any autonomy to his team and his insistence that everything come through him acted as a brake on productivity.

Therefore, it is not coincidental that Sommerfield's *The Pub and the People* was the only 'Worktown' book that did appear, albeit not until 1943. Sommerfield was an established author, who had already written four books, and was also a regular contributor to left-wing newspapers and periodicals such as the *Daily Worker* and *Left Review*. In terms of both intellect and personality, he was a match for Harrisson, who treated him as an equal. On the one hand, his status as a communist and Spanish veteran gained him the respect and acceptance of left-wing circles in Bolton. On the other hand, his capacity to get on with people and his experience of having left school at 16 to work variously as a carpenter and a seaman meant he could mingle comfortably in the public bars of working-class Bolton pubs. Although in later life he complained that the constant beer drinking had damaged his health, Sommerfield seems to have enjoyed spending pretty much every evening for a year observing, and participating, in Bolton's drinking culture. Hall describes a typical night's work for Sommerfield visiting five pubs over the course of three hours and making notes on aspects ranging from the presence of spittoons or sawdust, the nature of the graffiti in the lavatories, and how fast pints were drunk. In particular, however, he surreptitiously recorded dialogue verbatim. Hall notes that Sommerfield's innumerable pub reports benefit from his having 'an eye for character and an ear for dialogue' (p. 157) and draws generously on accounts such as the following:

> At ten to ten a brass bell was rung, warning people of closing time. At ten it was rung again; no one took much notice; the chucker out – a chap of about 45, rather miserable and inefficient looking, in a faded blue uniform and peaked cap, shouted 'time' but not very loudly. At five past the barmen began to shout; by ten past about half the people had left, a few still had drinks. The doors leading into the main road were locked. People went out by the side. A few hung around in groups, most went off quite briskly. Round the corner the big sergeant of police with his walking stick was lurking (p. 158).

Therefore, it is disappointing when Hall simply repeats, rather than examines, the criticisms of historians such as James Hinton and Peter Gurney that Sommerfield exemplified a masculine contempt for women that was widespread among Mass Observers. Hall cites the artist Graham Bell, who is also Hinton's main source, as to

Sommerfield's 'constant smutty talk about women' (p. 174) but fails to put this allegation in the context of Bell's virulent disdain for Mass Observation as a whole. Later in *Worktown*, Hall reveals that Bell was only in Bolton for three weeks, mostly devoted to writing long letters of complaint to his girlfriend about how awful he found not just Sommerfield but also Madge, Wilcock and Hood (pp 238-244). The class condescension in his characterisation of the latter is typical: 'We share the house with Walter, almost the ugliest man in history and a dreadful bore. He tells me every day several times that when he was 18 he was union secretary over 1,800 men' (p. 242).

However, the case against Sommerfield is reinforced by selective quotation of his writing, such as his tendency to acknowledge his own presence in the pub scenes he is describing by, for example, registering the fact that the woman he is sitting next to is stroking his thigh. This can be seen as a smug voyeuristic celebration of class and gender difference or as a more complex, but playful, recognition of the full range of intersubjective interaction in such social spaces. The debate surrounding these issues provides interesting parallels with the accusation made by critics of Orwell that parts of his work such as the opening chapter of *The Road to Wigan Pier* are condescending about the people that he describes. In this respect, Sommerfield and Orwell both pay the price for employing ironic literary modes of writing in non-fiction work and yet, surely, they should be celebrated for breaking down the barriers between social classes and revealing an otherwise hidden set of non-hierarchical relationships between people.

Arguably, it is the social nonconformity, creative self-reflexivity and openness to intersubjective experience of people like Sommerfield and Orwell which constitute the real enduring value of Mass Observation and the wider documentary movement around it, as much as the data that was collected at the time. In this respect, it is difficult not to agree with Hall's argument that Mass Observation played a ground-breaking role in the erosion of the class divide and helped pave the way for those like him 'from a Northern working-class background, who went to university in the 1960s' (p. 6). It is this sense of wider long-term social change which lends *Worktown* an engaging impetus and makes it a worthwhile read for those wishing to learn more about Mass Observation and the wider background to Orwell's work in the 1930s and 1940s.

Nick Hubble,
Brunel University London

**The Prose Factory: Literary Life in England Since 1918**
D. J. Taylor
Chatto & Windus, London, 2016, pp 501
ISBN 978 0 7011 8613 5 (hbk)

The phrase 'the prose factory' is one of countless curios that D. J. Taylor has diligently winkled from somewhere in the vast library of diaries, letters, periodicals and literary works that he has consulted for this compendious new history. His cheerful industry and unfailing fluency make it hard to resist noting that Taylor is something of a prose factory himself. He produces regular novels, a ceaseless flow of book reviews, and has also written a range of spry, engagingly written books about literary culture. Some, including *Orwell: A Life* (2003) and *Bright Young Things: The Rise and Fall of a Generation 1918-1940* (2007) have charted parts of the century-sized territory which here receives a full sweep, in a survey that is concerned as much with the jobbing reviewer as the great novelist, and with paying the bills as much as developments in style and subject matter.

In the opening pages Taylor throws out a volley of agenda-setting questions about literary taste, giving the impression that a firm analytical hand will have hold of the material, but the book is far more of a grand miscellany than this suggests. Each chapter bursts with detail, with arresting quotations, anecdotes, facts and figures, while portraits and perspectives that do not fit are included as additional sketches. Taylor also has the habit of smuggling in choice cuts from his back catalogue of journalism. Chapters proceed chronologically, from the Georgian poets through the Angry Young Men to *Granta*'s young novelists and beyond, but they head off in a variety of directions, charting the procession of generations but also dwelling on the tragi-comic exploits of the Arts Council, say, and the rise and fall of the 'light essay' (p. 86).

The book still proceeds at a rollicking pace, thanks in large part to its vivid descriptions of Taylor's rotating cast of characters. Perhaps its greatest contribution is its dusting down of the less familiar of these figures, including some like J. C. Squire and Hugh Walpole who were big beasts of their day. Taylor is a deft portraitist, and gives all kind of recondite writers and editors generous treatment, especially if he thinks that they really belonged to a 'bygone era', or were an 'anachronism' in their day. Taylor, of course, cuts a charmingly antiquated figure: he is a writer steeped in the romance of Grub Street and the mythos of the man of letters. While he does not include himself in the book's genealogy, we certainly encounter some oblique self-portrait. Plummeting rates for reviews are reported, with figures cited from Taylor's own paper. We are told that most 'non-university critics' today are scared off writing literary history by the specialists (p. 440). Not this one, of course.

What kind of broader things does this intrepid critic's history have to tell us? All kinds of fascinating data is assembled for instance, of how much writers earned for their reviews and books, and how much they paid in rent and child support, but what does this all add up to? Principally that throughout the period the majority of writers struggled along, usually with the sense that there wasn't enough money to go round, yet a proportion lived comfortably, and a lucky few made stratospheric amounts. This truism is well told, but anything more precise remains out of focus. Taylor may have all the figures at his fingertips, but he does not treat them systematically. Carefully evaluating changes in income distribution and the cost of living may have made for a less light-footed book, but it would have told us a bit more.

As it is we are never quite sure what changes the century brings for writers. The distinction between relative and actual decline is blurred, with Taylor telling us that 'the history of English literary culture in the period after 1918 is a chronicle of dissolution' (p. 6), yet not long after that the writing profession had 'expanded three of fourfold' (p. 20), and that 'a large-scale and essentially mainstream literary culture' (p. 83) had developed. Taylor has the unsettling habit of putting his own claims into doubt, even when ostensibly trying to do the opposite. An account of low-earnings in the 1950s includes a defence against a hypothetical 'book-trade sociologist', who 'would probably retort that a certain kind of literary life has always been like this'. But Taylor's comeback, that 'this, though, is to ignore the sheer proliferation of outlets' for journalism evident in Gissing's *New Grub Street* (1891), is hardly convincing (p. 248). Similarly he imagines 'the reader who knows his way around the late Victorian publishing scene' believing that contemporary conditions do 'not differ in any essential regard from the world of *New Grub Street* a century before', but his lacklustre response, that today 'Gissing's all-purpose hack journalist ... would have his work cut out' is unlikely to change this reader's mind (p. 430).

## REVIEW

A reluctance to draw firm conclusions persists throughout the book. In one clear-sighted chapter, Taylor writes that 'almost any statement made about' The Movement poets 'needs to be qualified almost out of existence' (p. 276), but this sense descends upon him on many other occasions (and note he uses the word 'almost' twice to make the point). There are frequent appearances of the phrase 'on the other hand' and the construction 'if ... then', rendering his account unsatisfyingly provisional: 'If it was the era of the blanket condemnation', he tells us in another chapter, 'then it was also the era of the bitter personal attack' (p. 95). A related tendency is to proceed by dismissing quoted or rhetorical claims, like those of the phantom sociologist, where something 'would be an overstatement' but perhaps a watered-down version may be true. Equivocation occasionally produces what looks like contradiction, as when he tells us that Orwell's novels of the 1930s 'offer a withering critique of the literary culture of the day' (p. 130), but a page later that 'the view he takes of the literary world and the uses he puts to it are by no means clear cut' (p. 131).

There is a habit, too, of relying on simplifications that he occasionally concedes are just that. One theme is the fragmentation of the reading public, specifically the contention that the century saw a public sphere of 'shared tastes and universal standards' (p. 184) give way to an irremediably fractured one. Certainly as the reading public grew it became increasingly variegated, but this notion can lead critics to simplify the past into a myth of prelapsarian unity (and to romanticise it, as if variety of taste was necessarily a bad thing). Taylor knows this and provides the occasional caveat, but continues to use the idea in its most simplified form. Within a few pages he tells us of the passing of a 'single, dominant taste' (p. xxii), questions if 'this desirable entity had ever really existed' (ibid), then reverts to talking about 'the old, collective taste' (p. xxiv). The same manoeuvre occurs with the idea of a general, average or common reader, which Taylor occasionally will quibble with, as if doing so simply gets him off the hook.

The chronology of this fragmentation is also a problem. 'By the 1920s' we learn, 'there is no such thing as old-style homogenous "taste"' (p. xxii), yet hundreds of pages later we are told that 'there was a suspicion, steadily increasing as the 1960s wore on, that the old cultural certainties about reading publics and shared values could no longer be taken for granted' (p. 314). Were these not extinct by the 1920s? And if further reconfiguration was occurring, surely this was distinct from what happened forty years before? Considering these generalisations, it is interesting to note that when Taylor sets out his criticisms of T. S. Eliot he writes that Eliot's work is full of 'painful distinctions' (p. 60) arrived at by 'long hours of agonised brooding', as he thought that 'intelligent judgements can only be reached at the end of a long and arduous reasoning process' (p. 61). This equation of serious thinking and pain recurs when he talks of Terry Eagleton's qualms about literary theory, which involve 'painful dissection' (p. 383). Perhaps a little more pain would have given Taylor's own generalisations sturdier foundation.

Further concerns are prompted by Taylor's choice of material. The opening questions about taste, what is it, how is it shaped and diffused, why do some works succeed and not others and certain critical opinions hold sway, are not really those that guide the book. Taylor actually tells us in the first chapter that 'taste' by the early years of the century had 'so many meanings that the word is probably best left out of literary criticism altogether' (p. 10). Not following his commitments to the letter would not be much of a problem if Taylor's account were less idiosyncratic. As it is though the reader is likely to be curious about guiding principles, particularly the criteria for selecting writers and works for inclusion. Why for instance are there several pages about the novels of Malcolm Bradbury when there are none about those of Virginia Woolf or D. H. Lawrence. Why are five books by J. L. Carr mentioned, but none by Muriel Spark, V. S. Naipaul or J. G. Ballard?

One would think that modernism would play a major part in the survey, but it is for the most part seen only at a distance, merely something to be grumbled about by Taylor's leading figures. Dozens of their criticisms are recounted – not a single person, it seems, has had anything nice to say about it. One produced an 'interesting critique' of Joyce (p. 89), another pronounced *Ulysses* a 'confused failure' (p. 182), a 'devastating reassessment' of Woolf is filed (p. 321) and so on and so on. It may be a surprise for some readers to learn that these works have somehow remained in print, while many of those commended by Taylor have not. When modernism fleetingly appears, it is the Sitwells, of all people, who are granted centre stage, and the only work discussed is by Ronald Firbank (The leftists of the 1930s get the Sitwell treatment a few chapters later, when Brian Howard is discussed instead of someone such as Christopher Caudwell). Quite what Taylor thinks characterises modernism is unclear: we hear that there were 'any number of popular novelists keen to advertise their conversion to the modernist line' yet none are named (p. 46), Alec Waugh's novel *The Loom of Youth* (1917) surprisingly crops up, and Taylor writes without explanation of Huxley's 'modernist high style' (p. 70).0 While Eliot is featured, he is given a sharp write up and unfavourably compared to Edgell Rickword.

The main reason for all of these unusual decisions is that Taylor, though an altogether genial guide to literary history, has dyed-in-the-wool convictions, and these give undisclosed shape to his survey, determining what is included, what is side-lined and what gets less than complimentary treatment. He is a self-styled defender of the 'ordinary reader' against the high-brow powers that be, an agenda most clearly discernible in his disdain for academia. His first and almost last approving reference to anything approaching academic criticism comes near the end of the first chapter, where he compliments a cluster of primers including Percy Lubbock's *The Craft of Fiction* (1921) for 'bringing questions of style, narrative structure and technique a great deal closer to the averagely intelligent reader'. Even these inoffensive volumes though only get off with a caution: 'There was a price to be paid for this absorption in the mechanics of writing, and it came in jargon' (p. 27).

Needless to say, when Taylor reaches the rise of theory it is not given a warm reception. His antipathy stops him from delving deeply: we learn little of post-structuralism beyond the fact that Derrida

**REVIEW**

believed there to be 'nothing outside the text' (p. 382). Sympathy is always with the generalist or the humble reviewer over the specialist, so undue attention is given to figures like Arthur Quiller-Couch. I. A. Richards and William Empson, meanwhile, apparently 'never managed to establish anything resembling a school of criticism' (p. 170). F. R. Leavis is given a predictable trouncing, treated as if he epitomised academia, while the bulk of ordinary scholarship is neglected along with any positives that growing numbers of people studying literature at university may have had. And is Taylor's contention that theory reduced the popular appeal of literary criticism entirely accurate? Theory was heard all round the world and its influence was felt in all kinds of disciplines, which is more than can be said for most belle-lettrist criticism.

Malcolm Bradbury and David Lodge receive praise, but for their satirical portraits of academic life rather than their day jobs. Lodge is complimented for wishing to bridge the gap between the academy and the 'ordinary reader', but this is in spite of him not being 'averse to dressing up in the glad rags of literary theory' (p. 379). The one academic close to Taylor's heart is the no-nonsense egalitarian and anti-academic's academic John Carey. The discussion of his polemic against the modernists, *The Intellectuals and the Masses* (1992), is a parody of feigned even-handedness: a cursory 'if we believe Professor Carey' included in his synopsis is cancelled out in the next sentence by a 'no doubt Carey is right' (pp 91-92). Carey is an important figure whose strident anti-elitism naturally appeals to Taylor, but it is odd to have quite so many references to his oeuvre – 19 in the index, some of which span multiple pages – when so many other important figures are overlooked, many of whom also produced literary journalism alongside their scholarship.

Taylor's preference is, in fact, not simply for journalism over scholarship, but a particular kind of journalism. *The London Review of Books* is excluded from discussion of post-war literary magazines, and James Wood receives a chilly appraisal. We are told of how Wood's 'exacting brand of Olympianism' and 'pageants of stately prose' make great demands on the reader (p. 409), hardly a fair description of the pieces he regularly writes for *The New Yorker*. When Taylor disapprovingly quotes a few aphoristic sentences, such as 'The novel is the virtuoso of exceptionalism: it always wriggles out of the rules around it' (p. 409), they do not sound self-evidently objectionable, especially since they have been shorn of context. Wood is one of many residents of Mount Olympus. This is Taylor's image for his elites: he writes of 'the view from Mount Olympus, as occupied by Eliot, Virginia Woolf and the Sitwells' (p. 286), of the 'vertiginous crag' from which Eliot dispensed opinion to 'the smaller fry writing their criticism and compiling their poems on the ground' (p. 62). Wood is the contemporary descendant of this disdained 'Olympian' tendency. Taylor by implication is the opposite, but is he really all that grounded?

*The Prose Factory* makes plenty of its own demands on the reader, expecting them to know about Imagism and Vorticism, about *The Yellow Book* and *The Great Tradition*. The *Lady Chatterley* trial (of 1960) is glossed over as if it were too familiar to mention. A revealing caveat is given about Gissing's *New Grub Street*, where Taylor writes of its 'fascination…at any rate to those professionally enmired in the world of literature' (p. 138). It's a sub clause that could be added to any number of sections of the book.

In spite of avowed support for the ordinary reader, *The Prose Factory* is also oddly not much concerned with popular fiction: best-sellers are rarely discussed, and genre fiction is conspicuous by its absence. Taylor's interest is, in fact, with what we might categorise as the upper middlebrow, particularly those working in his particular traditions: the short-form book reviewer, hence him singling out Desmond MacCarthy from the Bloomsbury group, and the social novelist, which explains why the novels that receive most coverage are *Angel's Pavement* and *London Belongs to Me*. Anything more elevated he perceives as haughty and abstruse, but anything below this is unworthy of extended consideration. Discussing a symposium on the state of fiction that ran in the *New Review* in 1978, Taylor quips that contributors only took interest in what they considered 'serious' writing ('no one, predictably, takes much interest in the non-serious kind'), but he too distinguishes between what he considers serious and non-serious, and largely sticks to the latter (p. 389).

# REVIEW

This is one of several questionable accusations of snobbery. Orwell is reprimanded for writing of the novelist Jack Hilton that 'in every industrial town, there are men by scores of thousands whose attitude to life, if only they could express it, would be very much what Mr. Hilton's is' (p. 106), but he meant if only they had the talent, which is not patronising at all. Taylor complains that Francis and Ralph Partridge do not consider that 'the ability of well-bred intellectual types to debate the circumstances in which they will or won't support military conflict depends on the possession of a private income' (p. 194), but who says that it does? Eliot is scolded for the elitism of the objective correlative, which Taylor believes is 'the suggestion that it could be possible, with the right training, for every serious reader to acquire the powers of judgement necessary for them to formulate the correct opinions about books' (p. xxiii), when it is nothing of the sort.

Taylor is keen to root out snobbery, but on occasion his position inadvertently patronises those he intends to support. A succinct example comes in a discussion about literary influence in popular music, where he writes about the 'brisk little nods' of The Beatles to Lewis Carroll and Edgar Allan Poe (p. 385). This is followed by disparaging noises about subsequent 'middle-class performers' and their 'intellectual interests', Joy Division apparently among them (p. 386). His view of culture does not seem to allow for a working class artist like Ian Curtis to find inspiration in Dostoevsky and Sartre.

The paradoxes of Taylor's outlook are most evident in his closing chapter. Having whisked us through a history peopled by writers prematurely lamenting decline, Taylor knows this is a perennial feature of literary life, yet he cannot quite shake the feeling that this time it's for real. He equivocates a little, but presents a gloomy report from the coalface. Given his alleged faith in the public, and disdain for Olympianism though, how can he complain of an alleged declining interest in literature? And isn't what he reports as the demotion of the professional tastemaker a democratisation that he should welcome, another hit against the elites?

'Fair play to the Amazon reviewers, you might say' (p. 443), he concedes half-heartedly. Having fought for ordinary readers through a century of literary history, Taylor by its end appears to find himself abandoned by them. As he writes so well of John Lehmann in an earlier chapter, Taylor 'strikes a note common to nearly every decade of recent English literary history: the lament of a cultivated literary gentleman who finds himself marooned on an inhospitable strand by the changing tides of public taste' (p. 223). The prose factory isn't shutting up shop just yet.

Simon Hammond,
University College London

### George Orwell: English Rebel
Robert Colls
Oxford University Press, Oxford, 2015, pp 330
ISBN 978 0 1996 8081 8 (hbk)

In 1940, George Orwell wrote: 'To this day it gives me a faint feeling of sacrilege not to stand to attention during "God save the King"' (p.143). He was a patriot. And yet he would in years to come describe a 'socialist United States of Europe' as 'the only worthwhile political objective' (p. 202). In the present climate this seems like a contradiction, yet Robert Colls's exhaustive inquiry into Orwell's Englishness suggests that it is, instead, indicative of a blend of nationalism and socialism that was not only considered, but central to Orwell's world view.

Colls's study is thus a timely critical intervention – raising obvious questions about whether Orwell's views on national identity and politics can offer insights into our present predicament.

*George Orwell: English Rebel* starts off with the slightly sheepish caveat that its author is 'not saying in this book that Englishness is the key to Orwell', but that it was instead 'something that he thought *with* as well as about' (p. 7). And yet Colls's account concludes with the bold claim that Orwell's 'belly-to-earth Englishness always insisted on the terrain first and the politics second' (p. 218).

Can Colls really be claiming that Orwell put England before politics? An author whose self-professed long-term aim was to make 'political writing into an art'? Who is by many considered to have been the scourge of the establishment and of Empire? And besides, didn't Orwell spend much of his life trying to escape England – be it to Burma, Paris, Morocco, Catalonia, or Jura? Nonetheless, the evidence is compelling.

Of course, before accepting this possibility it is necessary to acknowledge that Orwell's Englishness 'was not typical of the 1930s (no cricket, no foolishness about country cottages, definitely not quiescent)' (p. 207). Colls is keen to stress that 'sets of national characteristics' are 'a poor guide' to understanding Orwell's idiosyncratic brand of Englishness (p. 194). The same goes for 'party attachments', 'values' and even 'the past' (ibid). So in what sense, exactly, was Orwell to be considered someone who put his allegiance to England before all other things?

*English Rebel* takes the form of a loosely biographical journey through Orwell's writing career, demonstrating through a series of thoughtful critical assessments of the key works, diary entries, journalism and correspondence how Orwell came to develop a revolutionary patriotism with which to counter the authoritarian and jingoistic nationalism of Oswald Mosley and others on the right.

Colls starts by claiming that Orwell's four books published up to 1936 – *Down and Out in Paris and London, Burmese Days, A Clergyman's Daughter* and *Keep the Aspidistra Flying* – 'have no political point other than that England is wrong' (p. 39). He elaborates: 'Destitution is wrong. Poverty is wrong. Gentility is wrong. Empire is wrong. Racism is wrong. The Masses are wrong. The Elite is wrong. Capitalism is wrong (but you may have to go with it). Only *The People* unto whom wrongs are done are right' (p. 39). This is the key component of Orwell's nationalism, according to Colls: it was people-centred. Rather than being an ideology, it was a reflection of the collective will and of public interest.

Though finding evidence of this belief in 'the people' in the early works, Colls argues that it was not until Orwell's experiences in the north of England and in Spain that it really translated itself into a positive force for good. He writes that in Lancashire and Yorkshire Orwell 'believed he had found the real England in a class of people whose loyalty was not to something abstract', but was instead 'to each other, face to face, here and now' (p. 74). He goes on to argue that Orwell 'intuited the same instincts in the Spanish working class which he had found in the English' (p. 74).

Thereafter, Orwell's attitude towards the English is transformed. He no longer parodies and scorns them (as he does in *A Clergyman's Daughter* and *Keep the Aspidistra Flying*) but, instead, celebrates them as people who, though they may be 'gamblers, drunkards and exceptionally foul-mouthed', are nevertheless 'gentle and law-abiding' (p. 151). They are also – like George Bowling and Winston Smith – people who will not tolerate such things as hypocrisy or authoritarianism.

Colls's suggestion that Orwell's socialism was shaped by his encounters with and perceptions of the 'common people' is, perhaps, nothing new – echoing several critical commentaries on Orwell, for instance Stephen Ingle's description of Orwell's socialism as 'man-centred' in *The Social and Political Thought of George Orwell: A Reassessment* (2006: 65) and John Rodden's analysis of Orwell's 'Common Man Myth' in *George Orwell: The Politics of Literary Reputation* (1987: 178). But linking this to Orwell's patriotism adds an interesting twist, and goes some way towards explaining and bringing together disparate aspects of Orwell's work.

For instance, Orwell's antipathy towards leftist intellectuals can now be explained on the basis of their 'severance from the common culture of the country' (p. 44). In turn, it can be seen that the defining agenda of Orwell's mid-period was to place this very 'common culture' centre-stage by celebrating mainstream English literature and art – from essays on iconic English cultural figures such as Donald McGill, P. G. Wodehouse, Charles Dickens and Rudyard Kipling, to the state-of-the-nation novel *Coming Up for Air* and Orwell's most strongly polemic patriotic essay, *The Lion and the Unicorn*.

Colls argues that Orwell's progression from general cynicism to unshakable belief in the English people was a product of his learning to accept the English people 'as he found them – the good and the bad, the past and the present, the fat and the thin, the left and the right' (p. 128). It is on this basis that he argues Orwell can be seen to have put his country before his politics. He even goes so far as to suggest that Orwell 'showed no interest in imagining any life but the one people had now, only better' (p. 128).

This last suggestion starts to seem questionable when it is observed how conveniently Orwell's understanding of what the English people wanted aligns with what Orwell clearly wanted for them. In *The Lion and the Unicorn*, Orwell insisted, in a moment of characteristic wishful thinking: 'It is only by revolution that the native genius of the English people can be set free', and that 'by revolution we become more ourselves, not less' (p. 151). Orwell clearly wanted to have it both ways: he developed a politics that ostensibly foregrounded the will of the people, whilst at the same time casting this will as being fundamentally similar to his own – the people's socialist merely mirroring the people's socialism.

There are many questions worth asking. Who on earth did Orwell think he was, believing he could determine the will of the English people? Why did he feel the need to associate this notion of a collective will with a specific country? Do his crude and cliché-ridden characterisations of Englishness have any credibility? And how would Orwell have reacted if he had realised that his understanding of the collective will of the English people was inaccurate, and no longer in accordance with his own outlook?

Leaving these important concerns aside – it is still worth reflecting on the possible benefits of Orwell's patriotism, and on what a consideration of his writing on this subject says about the attitude of the left today. Reflecting on the financial crisis, cuts to benefits and nine years of Tory government, Colls remarks of the 1930s – the period during which Orwell established himself as a writer: 'Very rarely in the history of British politics had the politics of class, poverty, and nationhood come together so ominously' (p. 30). The same could very easily be said of the present. There are further parallels to be found in the fact that today, as then, right-wing populism monopolises patriotism. And, of course, in the fact that the left appear to be tragically out of touch with the lower case 'c' conservatism of the British people. In this context Orwell's patriotism starts to seem a little more defensible – as a pragmatic attempt to heal divisions between left and right, new and old.

Yet the lesson I'm suggesting might be learnt is not that we should all try to get our hands on an English flag. Instead, if Colls's reassessment of Orwell's work teaches us anything, it should be the importance of attending to, rather than dismissing, the different points of view held within any given nation – a lesson suggested just as much by Orwell's failure to do this adequately as it is by his advocacy of this position. I leave the reader to speculate on what that might mean in the context of the recent referendum...

Luke Davies,
University College London

## David Astor: A Life in Print
Jeremy Lewis
Jonathan Cape, London, 2016, pp 416
ISBN 978 0 2240 9090 2 (hbk)

David Astor was one of twentieth-century Britain's most high-minded and undogmatic upper-class radicals. Instinctively sympathetic to the underdog, he combined a suspicion of high theory with a respect for Britain's liberal traditions and a lively awareness of the centre-left's limitations. His supreme open-mindedness was one of the things which made him such a great editor of the *Observer* between 1948 and 1975. On Astor's watch the newspaper championed most of the great liberal causes of the day, lending its support to the construction of the welfare state, the decolonisation of Africa and the emergence of more relaxed attitudes towards personal morality. On the other hand, Astor never allowed it to become an uncritical mouthpiece for the verities of the Keynes-Beveridge consensus. Indeed, as befits a man whose opposition to Stalinism was one of the driving forces of his adult life, he was plagued by the anxiety that public ownership, punitive taxation and trade-union power were undermining Britain's immemorial traditions of tolerance and fair play. It is a testament to his extreme independence of mind that articles on these themes appeared in the *Observer* throughout the 1950s and 1960s. Whatever else he might have been, Astor was never a prisoner of the salon socialists with whom his paper was most closely associated.

In his Janus-faced efforts to advance the cause of the left while simultaneously exposing its weaknesses, Astor inevitably reminds one of his friend and mentor George Orwell. One of the great merits of Jeremy Lewis's compelling biography is that it throws the similarities between the two men into vivid relief. While never as unconventional as Orwell, Astor was just as much of a refugee from the genteel philistinism of bourgeois England. An early victim of his mother Nancy's famously overbearing personality, he was a profoundly shy man who lacked any semblance of clubbability. His lack of interest in the shallower aspects of upper-class culture was the making of him as a journalist and editor. Seeking to compensate for his awkwardness and lack of easy charm, he looked beyond the confines of the bourgeois drawing room to the teeming and turbulent world outside it. The result was a deep sense of empathy with the oppressed of all countries and continents. If Astor had been more successful on the upper-class social circuit – and if he had shied away from the company of bohemian misfits on the margins of English cultural life – he would never have become the wide-ranging commentator who did so much to bring the problems of postcolonial Africa or post-industrial Britain to the attention of his readers. The comparison with Orwell is an obvious one.

Orwell only makes infrequent appearances in Lewis's book, but his presence is a vividly contradictory one. His relationship with Astor clearly gave full scope for his trademark qualities of amiability and acerbity. As Lewis reminds us, Astor first encountered Orwell in 1942 when he asked Cyril Connolly to recommend new people to write about politics for the *Observer*. Having prepared himself for the meeting by reading *The Lion and the Unicorn*, he took Orwell to lunch at the Langham Hotel in London and immediately felt a shock of recognition: '[I] felt I had known him all my life: he was so straightforward' (p. 116). Nevertheless, Orwell's burgeoning friendship with Astor did nothing to guarantee smooth relations with the *Observer*'s editorial staff. When the notoriously dogmatic Ivor Brown rejected his tart review of C.S. Lewis's *Beyond Personality*, Orwell temporarily refused to accept further commissions on the grounds that 'I do not write for papers which do not allow at least a minimum of honesty' (p. 116). The fact that Astor was now a close personal friend was neither here nor there: personal loyalties were as nothing to Orwell if he believed that his literary integrity had been called into question.

## REVIEW

Although Lewis's book fails to dredge up any new facts about Orwell's relationship with Astor, it goes some way towards casting it in a fresh light. Lewis is especially good at showing how dependent Orwell became on Astor's thoughtfulness and largesse. When Orwell thought he would have to self-publish *Animal Farm* after its rejection by a series of publishers, Astor unhesitatingly agreed to stump up the cash. (It was only Fredric Warburg's last-minute offer to publish the book which saved him a substantial sum.) Anxious to realise his dream of getting away from London and starting life afresh on a Scottish island, Orwell relied on Astor to find him a suitably remote farmhouse on Jura. It was there that the bulk of *Nineteen Eighty-Four* was famously written. In a more melancholy key, Astor also arranged for a consignment of streptomycin to be imported into Britain when Orwell was being treated for tuberculosis in 1948. What Lewis omits from his account is the poignant upshot of this episode. Although Orwell initially responded well to the streptomycin, he subsequently endured such serious side effects that his treatment was discontinued. The remaining streptomycin was then administered to the other patients on his ward in Hairmyres Hospital, in Glasgow. All of them were cured.

Astor's services to Orwell did not cease when his friend died in 1950. Quite apart from coaxing the vicar at All Saints' Church in Sutton Courtenay into burying the irreligious Orwell in the churchyard, he also did a great deal to defend Orwell's posthumous reputation. As Lewis points out, he made an especially forceful intervention when Orwell was wrongly accused of collaborating with the British security services. In 1996, more than fifteen years after the information had first been divulged by Bernard Crick, an article in the *Guardian* revealed that Orwell had passed a list of 'crypto-communists' to the Information Research Department (IRD) in 1949. Although the IRD was primarily an anti-communist propaganda unit attached to the Foreign Office, Orwell's critics immediately claimed that he had endangered his fellow left-wingers by snitching on them to the 'secret state'. Of all the people who spoke up in Orwell's defence, Astor was one of the most impassioned. Pointing out that the IRD was never a branch of the security services – or at least that it had never been associated with espionage in Orwell's day – he argued that his friend's sole concern was to ensure that the production of anti-communist propaganda materials should not be entrusted to people of secret Stalinist sympathies: '[Orwell] was not giving them a blacklist. He was just telling the IRD whom not to employ' (p. 174). More broadly, he rejected the idea that Orwell's relationship with the IRD provided evidence of a cynical shift to the right. At a time when too many British socialists believed that there were no enemies on the left, Orwell – or so Astor's argument went – simply wanted to remind his fellow radicals that nothing posed a bigger threat to the prospect of human liberation than the totalitarian ambitions of their false Stalinist friends. Astor's pithy summary of Orwell's anti-communism could equally serve to encapsulate his own lifelong struggle to insulate the democratic left against the temptations of Stalinism: 'Orwell wasn't betraying the left – the pro-Communists were betraying us' (p. 174).

Philip Bounds,
Independent scholar

### Or Orwell: Writing and Democratic Socialism
Alex Woloch,
Massachusetts, London: Harvard University Press, 2016
ISBN 978 0 674 282483

Is it not intriguing to note how writers over the centuries have tended to look down on their literary journalism? Indeed, since their emergence in the early seventeenth century in Europe's cities, particularly London, the 'news media' (variously known as corantos, diurnals, gazettes, proceedings and mercuries) have been associated with scandal, gossip and 'low' culture. While the term journalist emerged in France in the 1830s to refer to writers on periodicals (distinguishing them from writers of literature), the identification of journalism largely with newspapers and mass culture has had a profound impact on the sensibilities of men and women of letters.

Typically George Orwell, considered by many as one of the greatest UK journalists of the last century, constantly looked down on his journalism as 'mere pamphleteering' and a lesser form of literature. On a basic level, journalism has provided writers with an income. Yet this very fact has reinforced journalism's position as a sub-literary genre. For while literature is often seen as the fruit of 'scholarship' and 'inspiration' – hence pure, disinterested and above market considerations – journalistic writing is viewed as distorted by the constraints of the market, tight deadlines or word limits.

Significantly, Orwell is best known as the author of *Animal Farm* (1945) and *Nineteen Eighty-Four* (1949) – and his journalism has been marginalised in the academy. But recently major studies by Paul Anderson (2006) and Peter Marks (2011) and the publication of Orwell's collected journalism (in *Seeing Things As They Are*, edited by Peter Davison, 2015) have helped place the spotlight on his 'pamphleteering'.

# REVIEW

This new, strangely titled, text by Alex Woloch, Professor of English at Stanford University, continues this trend – and comes lauded with high praise. According to Aidan Wasley, of the University of Georgia: 'This is a fascinating and important work, probably the best and most original book on Orwell I have read. It is the first book on Orwell that truly attends to the complexities of Orwell's language, composition technique and poetics.' While Jed Esty, of the University of Pennsylvania, comments: 'Woloch turns his considerable ingenuity and superb ear to the task of a slow, close investigation of Orwell's writing. ... An accomplished and subtle book.'

The first half examines the non-fiction prose, including 'A Hanging' (1931), *The Road to Wigan Pier* (1937) and the three essays, 'Charles Dickens', 'Boys' Weeklies' and 'Inside the Whale' which together made up the collection *Inside the Whale and Other Stories* (1940). The second half focuses entirely on the 80 'As I Please' columns Orwell contributed to the leftist journal, *Tribune*, between 1943 and 1947.

Woloch's writing style throughout is dense and extremely challenging for the reader. He is very slow getting into first gear: he begins with an 11-page Prologue, subtitled 'Reagan and Theory' and then moves on to an Introduction of 57 pages. Once he launches into the main body of his text ('The Paradoxes of the Plain Style: The 1930s') his writing appears to be bursting over with complexity – with one idea piling over another. It's almost as if the simple sentence cannot contain the intensity of his analytical project. So hardly a sentence goes by without its flow being broken by the inclusion of text inside a bracket. Let me provide just one example: on page 140, he writes:

While reflection takes place by 'stop[ping],' it also (perhaps *in* this very halt) creates a movement or 'ten[ency]' of its own. '[O]ne *tends to think* of explosions as the chief danger of mining' (passage 2, emphasis added).

Is it not significant that in the many Orwellian quotes dotted about the book there are hardly any brackets? Moreover, the text ends with 61 pages of Notes – another indication of the expansiveness of Woloch's style. And yet again is it not significant that Orwell hardly ever used a note in his writings – perhaps the result of having never enjoyed nor endured a university education.

Yet buried in the book are some wonderfully original insights. To take a few examples: Woloch argues (p. 9) that Orwell's plain style is political not merely because of how he communicates ('familiarly and, thus, democratically') but also 'because *what* Orwell aspires to communicate is explicitly a politics' (italics in the original). He is particularly concerned to highlight the many extraordinary complexities of the plain style: for instance, Orwell's constant focus in *Wigan Pier*, *Down and Out*, 'A Hanging' and in the 'As I Please' columns on what we are 'liable to miss', 'reveals a strange blankness, or emptiness, at the deliberate heart of Orwell's work' (p. 23). Later, he describes this 'withholding at the center of his style' as the 'poetics of exclusion' (p. 67).

He goes on to argue that the opening of 'A Hanging' crystallises the sense of a basic emptiness that lurks within any representation. 'The stated bareness of the cells functions, on this register, as an ironic imagining of the hollowness of linguistic representation. It is a projection, within the story-world itself, of our nagging awareness that even the most topically grounded or referentially charged language is nothing but a tissue of words, if not lies.' For Woloch, the amorphous status of the work between 'documentary', 'essay', 'sketch' and 'story' highlights its *generic* uncertainty (p. 73) and 'ontological instability' (p. 74).

In his detailed examination of *The Road to Wigan Pier*, Woloch argues that 'the conceptual framework of Orwell's democratic socialism helps motivate a specific articulation of literary irony' (p. 118). He notes how the book opens with Orwell highlighting the gap between the experience of the working class and the observations of a middle class writer. 'If this tension between observer and experience informs the opening paragraph – like a kind of warning at the entryway of the essay – it is most notably reflected in the structure of the work as a whole, which gets divided into two parts when Orwell changes topics, swerving away from the workers in northern England to write about how the class divide poses problems for Socialist intellectuals' (p. 122). Thus, 'empirically grounded observation gives way to self-reflection' (ibid).

On the five-page, eye-witness description of travelling through the tunnels to the coal face, Woloch argues that Orwell was making a 'theoretical' point: 'Attention to the difficult commute provides a brilliant image for a much more general process: the inevitable disjunction between a worker's experience of labor and the abstract definition of this labor under capitalism. The experience *of* work cannot be contained within the (wage) definition of this work by capital' (p. 130-131).

In his analysis of *Inside the Whale and Other Stories*, Woloch is fascinated by Orwell's use of the term 'semi-sociological' to describe it. The neologism 'hovers between technicality and familiarity, providing – if only by its alliterative, internally rhyming phonetic structure – a kind of bump in Orwell's famously plain style' (p. 145). Orwell concludes 'Inside the Whale' (the last essay in the collection) and his long evaluation of Henry Miller's *Tropic of Cancer* by stressing the 'impossibility' of writing in the contemporary world. Woloch continues:

> If *Inside the Whale* functions as such a pivot within Orwell's writing trajectory, it would suggest that a negativity inheres in the essay form itself, as Orwell conceives of it. The essay, as the most contingent form of writing, might always reflect its own transience – its own formal inadequacy – no matter how expressive, direct, or powerful its rhetorical and topical achievement (p. 147).

On the 'As I Please' weekly columns, Woloch suggests their enduring quality rests 'in the fragility of writing that these pieces – in their ephemeral topicality – both register and crystalliize' (p. 187). And he argues that they are 'paradoxically, a telling exploration of both freedom (most essentially in their heterogeneity) and the nature of thinking (most essentially as they interweave immediacy and reflection)' (p. 203).

The focus clearly in *Or Orwell* is on the text. Yet it is difficult to consider Orwell's journalism without reference to his audience – and this is missing here. In his 'As I Please' columns, for instance, Orwell used two strategies to promote his notion of 'the community of the left': firstly, through columns focusing on literary, social, cultural or political issues; and secondly, and most imaginatively, through developing a close relationship to his audience. This relationship was crucial to the flowing of Orwell's journalistic imagination. While he realised that mainstream journalism was essentially propaganda for dominant financial, political and cultural interests, at *Tribune* he was engaging in the crucial debates with engaged, activist, politically-aware people who mattered to him.

It is also a little surprising that Woloch does not engage with the leading theorists in the growing academic field of literary journalism – such as Applegate (1996), Bak and Reynolds (2011), Butler (1981), Campbell (1998), Gross (1969), Hartsock (2000), Italia (2005), Schudson (1978), Sims (1984), Treglown and Bennett (1998) and Wolfe (1973).

In his discussion of Orwell's essay 'Charles Dickens', Woloch notes how he imagines Dickens' face: 'It is the face of a man of about forty, with a small beard and a high colour. He is laughing, with a touch of anger in his laughter, but no triumph, no malignity' (p. 180). Cleverly, Woloch also highlights the similar way in which Raymond Williams, in his short text on Orwell, also comments on his face: 'The thing to do with his work, his history, is to read it, not imitate it. He is still there, tangibly, with the wound in his throat, the sad strong face, the plain words written in hardship and exposure' (p. 178).

Continuing the 'face' theme, whenever I read Orwell's journalism my face, I guess, will be constantly creased in smiles. I love Orwell's droll wit, the flow and clarity of his prose, the range of subject matter, the extraordinary flights of his imagination. In contrast, as I read *Or Orwell* there will be a constant frown on my face as I struggle with the complex prose. But given the range of Woloch's insights – it's a struggle (just about) worth the effort.

Richard Lance Keeble

**George Orwell Now!**
Richard Lance Keeble (ed.)
Peter Lang, New York, 2015, pp 235
ISBN 978 1 4331 2982 7 (pbk); 978 1 4331 2983 4 (hbk)

George Orwell died in 1950, yet it seems he is always with us. Orwell is for ever being quoted in the media in relation to contemporary political or other developments, and speculation about what his view would have been on a range of subjects is common. I have even found myself wondering recently, for example, how Orwell would have voted in the EU Referendum. Of course, we can't know the answer to questions such as this, but as the title of this very varied collection of essays proclaims, Orwell is still very much *now*. According to Peter Stansky in his Afterword: 'Orwell is more relevant today than he has ever been before' and his writings 'enable us to better understand our present situation'.

This collection of essays goes some way to helping us understand why Orwell, a self-styled political writer of the 1930s and 1940s, still resonates today. A clue may be found in the range of topics covered in this diverse collection of 13 essays, which includes: studies related to his great dystopian novel *Nineteen Eighty-Four*, linked with contemporary concerns about state surveillance; examinations of Orwell's literary canon and interpretations of his political standpoint; some international perspectives on Orwell; and a final section looking at Orwell as a journalist, with a focus on the influence of his work in radio and an examination of his stints as a war reporter.

Orwell's writing touched on so many areas of life, both political and social, that there is nearly always something of contemporary relevance to discover in the Orwell canon, no matter how obscure.

One of the essays in the collection illustrates this point very well, as Henk Vynckier introduces us to Orwell as a 'collector'. It is not a side of Orwell that perhaps many people have considered and, indeed, Vynckier suggests Orwell kept this aspect of his character low-key in the early stages of his writing career. By 1946, however, Orwell was writing essays about junk shops and a junk shop later played an important part in *Nineteen Eighty Four*. Orwell's collecting habits also informed other aspects of his literary output including his essay on seaside postcards ('The Art of Donald McGill') and his contribution to the book 'British Pamphleteers' (Orwell had an extensive pamphlet collection exceeding 2,000 items).

## REVIEW

Whilst Orwell remains most famous for his fiction, *George Orwell Now!* reminds us about his journalism. The journalism section includes a piece by Richard Lance Keeble contrasting Orwell's war reporting from the Spanish civil war, famously gathered together in *Homage to Catalonia*, with his time working for the *Observer* and *Manchester Evening News* in France and Germany in early 1945. Keeble contrasts the passion and assurance of Orwell's writing from the Spanish campaign with a less sure touch in 1945. Partly this might have been to do with Orwell's inability to find his voice as a 'mainstream' reporter in 1945, coupled with the death during this period of his wife Eileen. Keeble also rather intriguingly suggests that Orwell may have been distracted by being engaged in 'some kind of intelligence mission' at this time. It would be good to get more on this at some point in the future if documentation comes to light. Nevertheless, it is useful to be reminded about Orwell's time in continental Europe at the end of the war, as this is a period in his life which is not particularly well documented.

At the core of *George Orwell Now!* are two essays which paint differing pictures of Orwell's politics. An essay by Paul Anderson comes to the defence of Orwell's first full biographer Bernard Crick, who described Orwell as a 'pretty typical *Tribune* socialist'. This is a description which Anderson goes on to further justify in his wide-ranging piece. Later in the collection John Newsinger presents a different perspective in his essay 'Orwell's Socialism', in which he puts Orwell's socialism into a more radical context, and presents his *Tribune* involvement as merely offering 'him an opportunity to put his ideas and idiosyncrasies in front of a large section of the British left'.

Of course, as Paul Anderson rightly states, 'Orwell's politics have always been contentious'. In a sense, this is another reason why Orwell has lasted and is still relevant; he has not gone stale by being boxed into any narrow political tribe or position. Whilst without doubt a man of the left (there really is no convincing case otherwise), he was not prone to the inflexible thinking of much of the left, and this allows his political writing to cut through to the present day.

A good example of this phenomena, and how it resonates today, is highlighted in the essay by Philip Bounds focusing on the famous second half of Orwell's *The Road to Wigan Pier*. As he points out, recent attempts to revisit *Wigan Pier* have concentrated on the first half of the book, attempting to update the social conditions of the 1930s with a picture of conditions in austerity Britain. Bounds, though, is more interested in the second half, where Orwell famously took the left to task for its failure to connect with potential supporters despite the dreadful economic conditions that people were experiencing. Bounds looks at the left today in the context of some of the defects exposed by Orwell in *Wigan Pier*. What he finds is that eighty years later the left is making many of the same mistakes. For example, Bounds points out that the officiousness of the left is still prevalent, often taking the form of 'gross intolerance towards dedicated activists who refuse to accept every dot and comma of the party line'. It would be hard to find a better description of the current state of the Labour Party under the Corbyn personality cult! This thought-provoking essay contains other examples, identified by Orwell, of how the left continues to alienate many of those who should be its natural supporters.

Together this selection of essays contains something of interest for both the dedicated Orwell fan and the general reader. It is a valuable contribution to the field of Orwell studies, a field which stays fertile because the source material of Orwell's 'ideas and idiosyncrasies' still connects with us *now*.

Richard Young

SOUNDINGS

# The Mysteries Surrounding Andrew Gow

Writing in the *TLS* in February 2016, John Sutherland, Lord Northcliffe Professor Emeritus at University College London, focuses on the intriguing and arguably highly significant role Andrew Gow, Orwell's classics tutor at Eton (1917-1922), played in his life.

Sutherland suggests that Gow could not have been unaware of the homophobic sneers against him by 'manlier' boys at Eton. 'Orwell was not tolerant – at any period of his life – of "nancies". Blair penned a scurrilously homophobic poem printed in one of the school's papers. It opens: "Then up waddled Wog [Gow spelt backwards] and he squeaked in Greek / 'I've grown another hair on my cheek."'

After Blair came 137th out of 168 in the final school examinations, Gow told his father that it would be a 'disgrace to Eton' even to allow him to apply to Oxford or Cambridge. Sutherland ponders: 'It's preposterous on the face of it to have suggested that an Eton scholar, by no means at the bottom of the class, could not, with a month or two's cramming, have won an Oxbridge scholarship. Eric Blair was one of the cleverest boys in England. Why did Gow deliver the death sentence?'

Perhaps Gow did not want Blair around Cambridge where he, Gow, was determined to return out of pure malice: he had identified Blair as a 'nuisance'; or it could have been payback for the 'wog' doggerel.

After five years in the Burmese imperial police service, Blair returned to England. According to Sutherland, there then occurred 'a very strange event': 'Blair visited the man who had, effectively, dished his prospects at Eton, to get "advice" on what he should do next. And Gow was, apparently, pleased for Orwell to come and stay a day or two with him. After years of trying, the unhappy schoolmaster had finally got his Trinity job.' Gow remembers Orwell sat next to A. E. Housman at High Table.

Was Gow sizing up Orwell as a possible recruit as a spy? And for which side? Gow was a friend of fellow Trinity fellow Anthony Blunt, later infamous as the 'Fourth Man' in a team of Cambridge

Spies centred on Trinity College: Guy Burgess, Donald Maclean and Kim Philby were the first three to be exposed. Could Gow have been the 'Fifth Man'? Brian Sewell, in his memoir *The Outsider* (2012) certainly thought so.

Intriguingly, Gow visited Orwell in University College Hospital just days before his former pupil died. Orwell had just confided to Celia Kirwan, of the Information Research Department, his 'little list' of crypto communists. Sutherland continues:

> In his last days Orwell was visited in hospital by a selection of friends who were all involved in a covert CIA project: CCF, the Congress for Cultural Freedom. Its aim was to provide a counterweight to Marxist intellectual and cultural supremacy in Europe. The project, in which the IRD also played a part, would lead to the setting up of *Encounter* magazine and the CIA's acquisition of the film rights to Orwell's *Animal Farm*.

In 1950, the Cambridge Spies were very nervous men. A few months later Burgess and Maclean took flight to Moscow; Philby, although suspected, stayed until 1963. But in January 1950, Orwell dies alone. No one, apparently, witnessed the death or made any attempt to save him. 'Suffocation, the terse coroner's report said – caused by three years of tuberculosis. No suspicious circumstances. No autopsy necessary.' Sutherland ends enigmatically:

> One could make a cracking 'good-bad book' (to adapt Orwell's classification) out of this – a 'paranoid thriller'. The plotline writes itself. Down the gloomy corridors of University College Hospital comes a white-coated 'nurse', avoiding any eye-to-eye contact. He silently enters Orwell's private room and places a pillow over the face of the man in the bed – too weak, by now, to struggle. It's nonsense. But what one can conclude is that networks, some of them sinister, were being woven at Eton, and the college Etonians went to, which Eric Blair – thanks to Andrew Gow – did not.

- See George Orwell's master – and spymaster? by John Sutherland. Available online at http://www.the-tls.co.uk/tls/public/article1671159.ece

# Film of 'Shooting an Elephant'

A short film adaptation of Orwell's 1936 essay 'Shooting an Elephant' was released in April 2016 and shown to acclaim at the Tribeca Film Festival in the United States. Directed by Juan Pablo Rothie and with a screenplay by Alec Sokolov, it features Barry Sloane as Eric Blair and David Kaye as the Narrator. Full details at http://www.imdb.com/title/tt4026326/ and https://shootinganelephant.vhx.tv/packages/shooting-an-elephant-hd.

# Orwell Statue Finally Gets the Go-Ahead

Westminster City Council has given planning permission for a statue of George Orwell to be set up outside the BBC's headquarters in London. The figure – showing Orwell bending forward and holding a cigarette – is by Martin Jennings, a Fellow of the Royal British Society of Sculptors. The proposal for the statue was originally rejected by the BBC but was then revived after Lord Hall became director general in 2012. A trust was set up to raise funds by Ben Whitaker – and his widow, Janet, took up the project when he died in 2014.

The news prompted a fascinating letter to the *Daily Telegraph* from Orwellian expert Peter Davison. He wrote: 'I am delighted that a statue of George Orwell is to be erected outside Broadcasting House. However, the offices in which he worked were not in Broadcasting House. When Orwell joined the BBC he was temporarily located in Egton House, Langham Street. He then moved to 55 Portland Place. Early in June 1942, the department was moved to 200 Oxford Street and was nicknamed 'the Zoo' – c.f. *Animal Farm*. Room 101 in 55 Portland Place was where meetings of the Eastern Services Committee – which Orwell sometimes had to attend – were held. Perhaps the statue's plinth might have inscribed on it Orwell's assessment of the BBC: 'The thing that strikes one in the BBC ... is not so much the moral squalor and the ultimate futility of what we are doing, as the feeling of frustration, the impossibility of getting anything done.'

# George Orwell Studies

## Subscription information

Each volume contains two issues, published half-yearly.

### Annual Subscription (including postage)

*Personal Subscription*

| | |
|---|---|
| UK | £25 |
| Europe | £28 |
| RoW | £30 |

*Institutional Subscription*

| | |
|---|---|
| UK | £100 |
| Europe | £115 |
| RoW | £120 |

*Single Issue copies (subject to availability)*

| | |
|---|---|
| UK | £15 |
| Europe | £17 |
| RoW | £20 |

Enquiries regarding subscriptions and orders should be sent to:

Journals Fulfilment Department
Abramis Academic
ASK House
Northgate Avenue
Bury St Edmunds
Suffolk, IP32 6BB
UK

Tel: +44(0)1284 700321
Email: info@abramis.co.uk